LISTEN TO THE HERON'S WORDS

LISTEN TO THE HERON'S WORDS

Reimagining Gender and Kinship in North India

Gloria Goodwin Raheja
and
Ann Grodzins Gold

University of California Press
Berkeley • Los Angeles • London

University of California Press
Berkeley and Los Angeles, California

University of California Press, Ltd.
London, England

Library of Congress Cataloging-in-Publication Data

Raheja, Gloria Goodwin, 1950–
Listen to the heron's words: reimagining gender and kinship in North India / Gloria Goodwin Raheja and Ann Grodzins Gold.
p. cm.
Includes bibliographical references and index.
ISBN 0-520-08370-9 (alk. paper).—ISBN 0-520-08371-7 (pbk.: alk. paper)
1. Folk literature—India—Uttar Pradesh. 2. Folk literature—India—Rajasthan. 3. Women—India—Folklore. 4. Sex role—India. 5. Rajasthan (India)—Social life and customs. 6. Uttar Pradesh (India)—Social life and customs. I. Gold, Ann Grodzins, 1946– . II. Title.
GR305.5.U8R34 1994
398.2'0954'2—dc20 93-12586
CIP

Printed in the United States of America
9 8 7 6 5 4 3 2

The paper used in this publication meets the minimum requirements of American National Standard for Information Sciences—Permanence of Paper for Printed Library Materials, ANSI Z39.48-1984.

Contents

Illustrations

Figures

Plates

Note on Transcription and Transliteration

Our tape recordings of Hindi and Rajasthani songs and stories were transcribed by local literate scribes we employed. In Pahansu and Ghatiyali, these scribes were men, because there were no women who had received enough schooling to enable them to perform this task. Only in Hathchoya in 1990 was Gloria able to employ a young Brahman woman to work from her tapes.

These assistants were instructed to write down each sound as it was heard, and not to standardize spelling and grammar from the local dialects. There are therefore certain dialectal inconsistencies in spelling: the standard Hindi *strī* (woman), for example, appears variously as *triyā* and *tiriyā* in the Hindi proverbs and songs translated here, and in Rajasthani the spelling is *tariyā*. Distinctive local pronunciations—such as the standard Hindi syllable *ke* pronounced as *kai*—are generally preserved, though pronunciation differences within communities often produce spelling variations from one song to the next, and even within a particular song.

We have employed a standard system for transliterating Hindi and Rajasthani words. These are italicized and are given with diacritics whenever they occur. Proper nouns are reproduced in roman type without diacritics, and they sometimes appear as they are conventionally written, rather than as direct transliterations.

Note on Kinship Terms

In translating Hindi and Rajasthani kin terms, we have frequently employed the following standard anthropological abbreviations:

M mother

F father

Z sister

B brother

H husband

W wife

D daughter

S son

e elder

y younger

Thus, for example, the Hindi term meaning "mother's brother" is translated as MB, "husband's elder brother" as HeB, "father's sister's husband" as FZH, and "father's younger brother's wife" as FyBW.

Preface

Listening to Women in Rural North India

The heron is a bird of ambiguous moral significance in North Indian traditions. Graceful and white, circling herons guide the lost and thirsty to refreshing pools in popular stories and epics. But in hymns or *bhajans*, largely a male performance genre, in Sanskrit texts like the *Laws of Manu* and the *Panchatantra*, and in a number of Hindi proverbs, herons symbolize predatory hypocrisy. Appearing pure when really deceitful and corrupt, they seem to meditate as they stand perfectly still gazing into the water of a pond, when in fact they are looking for fish to eat. In women's songs, however, a heron's speech suggests a different moral configuration. Herons act as narrators, inviting listeners to consider tales of illicit encounters, resistance to dominating power, or both. Such accounts are resonant with genuine but commonly suppressed truths. One insult song begins: "On a banyan sat a heron, listen to the heron's words." The heron boldly tells of an adulterous liaison that results in a desired birth. A devotional song addressed to the lusty male deity, Bhairuji, opens: "A heron spoke on the water's edge." The song goes on to describe Bhairuji's attempt to enter a low-caste wine-seller woman's house in the night, the excuses she makes to keep her door shut, and the curses he showers upon her for this resistance.

The heron is not a female image; rather herons in women's songs are grammatically male. But in contrast to the massive body of male lore, where these birds signify a dichotomous split between purity and corruption or surface and core, in women's texts a heron's framing speech points to a potent shift in moral register. In inviting our readers to listen to the heron's words, we undertake to convey that shift and suggest that its spoken truths, if sometimes devalued in male-dominated expressive traditions, are compelling and consequential for the women we know in rural North India. The heron tells us of alternative moral perspectives on kinship, gender, and sexuality, ones that are shaped by women but are sometimes shared by men. This book describes such perspectives found in North Indian women's expressive traditions and begins to examine their consequences for the lives of these women in Uttar Pradesh and Rajasthan.

Neither Gloria Goodwin Raheja nor Ann Grodzins Gold went to India intending to study women, gender, or oral traditions. The existence of this volume bears testimony not only to the ways fieldwork has a mind of its own but to the strength of Indian women's voices and the complex, arresting beauties of their expressive genres. Gloria and Ann both attended graduate school in the seventies at the University of Chicago. There, although we learned a great deal about ways of understanding cultures, we received no education in women's studies or feminist theory. Though we had read much of the work on issues of gender in India, we first began to reflect seriously upon the implications of feminist anthropology after listening to women in rural India. Living in different villages in the adjacent but distinctive North Indian states of Uttar Pradesh and Rajasthan, we were persuaded by the power of women's voices to listen, pay attention, and attempt to comprehend their words. They spoke and sang of female lives—celebrating vitality, resisting devaluation, contesting subordination.

Although we studied with the same professors and read many of the same books, our intellectual inclinations and our writing styles are very different. Gloria began dissertation research in India when Ann was in her third year of course work, and was back in Chicago at the start of her "writing-up" phase around the time Ann was preparing to leave for her own fieldwork. Gloria is among perhaps a minority of scholars in our generation who took up the study of Indian culture for purely academic reasons (rather than because of previous links with India's traditions by way of gurus, the Peace Corps, childhood residence, or gypsy wanderings). Her marriage to Mahipal Tomar, an Indian man, has no doubt shaped her interpretations in ways, as she acknowledges, she may not yet fully understand. But her interest in Indian anthropology goes back to her undergraduate days, long before

Figure 1. Map of India

her marriage. Before entering graduate school, Ann was among those American youths who adventured through the subcontinent in the late sixties. Her dissertation research proposal was on the otherworldly aim of liberation and the romantic practice of pilgrimage. Gloria, by contrast, had planned to study kinship in relation to landholding and hierarchy, and eventually focused on caste, dominance, ritual, and exchange.

It strikes us as especially significant that, initially lacking a feminist perspective and with different approaches and different fieldwork goals, we reached similar conclusions concerning an apparently flawed representation of Indian women in much

Western scholarship. Both of us based our conclusions on the bearing, behavior, and words of the women with whom we lived. Independently we heard and wished to highlight in our writings the subversive and critically ironic refrains in North Indian women's oral traditions. We began this collaborative effort in 1988 shortly after Gloria returned from a second research period in India, when we first became aware of convergences in our thoughts and preliminary writings on North Indian women's oral traditions and lives.

We have learned from working together in the production of this volume that the ways we practice writing are as unlike as were our fieldwork goals. Both of us, alas, are slow, but for different reasons. Ann puts inchoate fragments down on paper and then revises them countless times until meaning and order emerge; thinking takes place as an integral part of the process of arranging words artistically. Gloria labors in her mind, synthesizing abstractions, until complicated thoughts emerge full-blown in sentence form. The resulting prose styles are dramatically different. Moreover, the performance traditions of Ghatiyali in Rajasthan, and Pahansu and Hathchoya in Uttar Pradesh—traditions that substantiate much of our argument in this book—are different too. As far as Gloria is aware, no insult songs in Pahansu are quite as sexually graphic as those performed in Ghatiyali. As far as Ann is aware, no dance songs in Ghatiyali recount long dramatic narratives like those Pahansu's women perform. Our translation styles are certainly unlike, but we are also translating unlike genres from unlike dialects. (An appendix provides transliterated texts for all songs.)

Foreigners with imperfect language skills, we are acutely aware of the multiple impositions and presumptions we make in attempting to convey the spirit and qualities of women whose lives we shared only partially and briefly. Teachers of courses on Indian culture, on folklore, and on gender, we are equally aware of a dominant mode in both academic and journalistic accounts depicting rural South Asian women as submissive if decorative, as kept in their subordinate place by a patriarchal economy and a religious tradition that devalues them, as ashamed of their bodies and their sexuality. Privileged white Americans commenting on relatively poor and often nonliterate Indian villagers, we recognize our attempt to interpret other lives as inherently compromised, but we feel strongly that it is worth the risk to add to the ethnographic record our impressions of North Indian women's identities as exuberant, resilient, and often refusing degradations imposed by male ideologies or structures of authority. It is striking to us and will be, we hope, to others that despite the ethnographic differences between our research areas and the differences in our own interests and intellectual styles, we find that the ways in which Rajasthani and Uttar Pradesh women redefine gender, kinship, and identity through song and story are fundamentally the same.

As a group, the women of rural North India impressed us overwhelmingly with their sense of their own power, dignity, and worth. This worth was not something nourished secretly in defiance of a degraded existence. Rather, it was integral to their daily lives, labors, relationships, and to the religious and cultural performances that imbued those lives with meaning. In the past decade, many Indian feminists have turned from a blanket rejection of Hindu traditions to reexamine them as possible sources of empowerment. We see such possibilities in the songs and stories we write about here.

We acknowledge from the start inevitable limitations and unhappy complicities that haunt any who set out from the "first world" to speak of "others." If we devote our efforts, as we do, to emphasizing positive aspects of rural South Asian women's imaginative lives, we might seem to lack appreciation for feminist initiatives that seek to make legal and social changes that will redress gender inequities and concretely better those lives. But it goes without saying that we wish only to support and not to undermine that work. We hope that recognition of rural women's poetic resistance to structures of power may help to ground feminist activities in local understandings of gender and power. If we recognize, as we do, that most rural South Asian women negotiate their existences from subordinate positions, we may seem to be insensitive outsiders judging Indian culture by standards alien to it. For us, there is no pure, uncompromised space from which to speak, and nothing but partial truths to tell.

While of course we possessed some kinds of power not given to the women we knew—the power, for example, to write of our lives and theirs and expect to see our words published and disseminated—we nevertheless wish to record that we were humbled and reminded of our dependence again and again by the persons on whose hospitality and goodwill we relied for our immediate creature comforts and future career success. The women we knew in Pahansu, Hathchoya, and Ghatiyali were proud of their work, of their children, of their appearance, of their knowledge and skill as singers, dancers, storytellers, ritual actors, and givers of gifts. They both pitied and berated us—although we were relatively wealthy, independent, and educated—for our lack of much that they most valued and for our incompetence at tasks they accomplished with skill and success. We ourselves felt our inferiority, because we so lamentably lacked those skills. And it was not infrequently that we felt that our insight into human relationships was meager in comparison to that of the women we knew.

We are both without brothers, and Indian women knew this to be a sorrowful condition without remedy. Neither of us ever learned how to clean or season vegetables properly; both of us, no matter how we tried to dress appropriately, were geese among the swans: clumsy and drab. Neither of us ever shed her own sense of embarrassment enough to sing and dance, and thus we were judged deficient in artistry and capacity for enjoyment. Both of us became subjects of stories and jokes that grew up around our mistakes and emotional weaknesses and were incorporated into the narrative repertoires of persons who knew us best.

We have each published monographs based on our first and longest research periods in the villages of Pahansu in Uttar Pradesh and Ghatiyali in Rajasthan. Our chapters in this volume grow out of the same sojourns in rural India, supplemented for Gloria by two subsequent stays in Uttar Pradesh and for Ann by one revisit. We choose not to summarize or repeat in this preface ethnographic details available elsewhere. Instead we recount, in personal voices, that background most immediately relevant to the theoretical introduction and the substantive chapters that follow: how we got to know Indian women and began to learn from them. Ann has previously described some of the ways she was taught to act, dress, and think about herself in the village of Ghatiyali; thus her account is somewhat briefer than Gloria's.

While we have discovered that many aspects of our experiences as female foreigners in Indian villages overlap and converge—hence this book's existence—some elements that significantly structured our lives "in the field" differed sharply. Most important, Gloria was "adopted" into a family and, from the moment of her arrival, was cast in the role of village daughter. Ann was never thus incorporated in clear-cut fashion, although many called her "aunt" and "sister." Because there was an American man, Joseph Miller, already working in Ghatiyali, Ann entered the village as his "father's brother's daughter"; perhaps as a result of this, her foreignness remained more palpable. We have tried in the descriptive accounts that follow to highlight some of the ways our experiences were different. At the same time, simple and similar revelations punctuate each of our separately composed narratives. These are mundane moments when our informal education in the meanings of village women's lives shattered preconceptions with what was, to us at least, revelatory impact.

GLORIA'S ACCOUNT

I went to India in 1977 planning to live in a village in western Uttar Pradesh and study the kinship practices of a dominant landholding caste. After spending several months visiting many villages in Muzaffarnagar and Saharanpur districts and trying to decide where to work, and doing some research in the National Archives, I visited Pahansu, a Gujar village in Saharanpur district. I stayed for a few days in the house of Amar Singh, spending most of my time with his brother's wife Shanti and his son's wife Omi. And I stayed briefly in the house next door to theirs, where a very large family of four married brothers, their mother, wives, and children lived. A week later, having decided on Pahansu as a research site and having returned to Delhi to pack my tape recorder and notebooks, I settled down in "banyan tree neighborhood" in the second house, the house of Telu Ram and Jabar Singh. I seemed to have been claimed by them; when I climbed down from the water-buffalo cart that had brought me there, my things were immediately taken into the house, before I could even sort out the difficulties in choosing between Amar Singh's house and Telu's. Nothing had been said to me about rent or the cost of my food. When I broached the topic after I had moved in, my question was greeted with shocked dismay. I was the sister of Telu Ram and Jabar Singh and the daughter of Asikaur, they said, and one never takes anything from a sister or daughter. It is acceptable, however, for a daughter or sister to give sets of cloth to her brothers' wives and to their children, and so I assuaged my conscience by bringing cloth and sweets and shawls anytime I made a trip outside the village and returned to Pahansu, which had become my *pīhar*, my natal village.

I suppose that I did not anticipate being anything other than anthropologist in the village, and I did not anticipate a need to transform myself in any way. But Telu's mother, Asikaur, did not like the saris I had been wearing. She considered this garment to be immodest, and advised me to wear *salvār-kamīz*, the long shirt and baggy pants worn by most women in Saharanpur and Muzaffarnagar villages. She found my appearance unsatisfactory on other counts too; a married woman, I was told, should wear glass bangles on her arms and toe rings on her feet, lest the absence of these tokens of *suhāg* (marital good fortune) cause harm to her husband. So I purchased these things and felt myself more and more understood as Gujar daughter and sister, and less and less as anthropologist. Throughout my stay in Pahansu, at each wedding I was urged to let the women beautify my palms with henna. Women could not understand my resistance to this. "Henna looks beautiful," they said. But the patterns traced in henna last a long time, I thought, and I felt that though I could put on the clothes and jewelry, I could not let my body itself be imprinted with this sign of an alien way of life, an alien way of being a woman. To be thus imprinted was too lasting a transformation. I did not want, then, to become too much like these women among whom I lived, and my resistance to the henna was, it seems to me now, a strategy for keeping some vestige of myself intact, away from them. I imagined, at that time, a great distance between myself and the women I knew there in Pahansu, a distance I attributed to the weight of a tradition that I couldn't, then, envision them resisting or subverting. Perhaps I had been persuaded to make this unthinking assumption then, in the 1970s, because so much of the colonial, anthropological, feminist, and journalistic writing on South Asian women stressed their submission to a monolithic "tradition," just as anthropological writing of the time so frequently assumed that Indian untouchables had fully internalized their own subordinate status and the morality of caste hierarchy.

My relationship as daughter and sister, though, extended to the *kamīns* (people of lower service castes attached to Gujar landholders in hereditary relationships) of the household as well as to the family itself. Just after I arrived in the village, I announced that I wanted to ride to Saharanpur on the next departing water-buffalo cart so that I could purchase a worktable. A week later, when I was becoming increasingly annoyed that no offer of a ride had been forthcoming, a very fine table appeared in my room. It had been made for me, I was told, by Chotu Barhai, the family's Carpenter, with wood supplied by Telu. I had at that point not even heard of Chotu Barhai, and I immediately wanted to be taken to him so that I could thank him and pay him for his work. Again, shocked dismay. Telu patiently explained to me that Chotu Barhai received a share of the harvest and additional compensation for such out-of-the-ordinary services he performed for their household, and besides, I was a "sister of the whole village" (*pūre gām kī bahan*), and no one there would take any money from me.

Though I may have been in some ways a "sister of the whole village," it soon became clear to me that I was considered to be "sister" more to some villagers than to others. First of all, I made no particular effort to hide the fact that my research focused on the Gujar farmers and landholders of the village; I came to know people of other castes very well, but my identification with the Gujars of the community was always taken for granted. I was not invited to and was not even made aware of some of the ritual activities of the untouchable Sweepers, for example, though I did visit frequently with Sweeper women in their homes. I was on fairly intimate terms with several Barber women and heard much about their rituals and their lives, but I always felt that I continued to be perceived as allied to the Gujar landholders for whom they worked. The fact that Asikaur continually admonished me not to accept any food from Brahman households (Gujars say they never take anything from Brahmans because Brahmans accept the dangerous ritual gifts called *dān*) was well known in the village. Just as Brahmans would never invite a Gujar to a meal in their house, I was never asked to eat in a Brahman household, though I was plied with many cups of tea in the Brahman neighborhood, and I established close relationships with several men and women there. (Asikaur was not altogether happy about even this tea drinking though.) Most of what I write about women's songs and women's lives, then, is grounded in my understanding of the words and experiences that Gujar women shared with me as I sat with them at their cooking hearths, watched them giving birth and caring for their children, traveled with them to their natal villages, and listened to them sing at births and weddings and festival days.

Not only was I seen as being particularly connected with the Gujars of the village, I was also identified with a particular *kunbā* (lineage) of Gujars, the *sādhu herā* lineage. This was the lineage of Telu's family, and I would hear people comment that I lived "among the *sādhu herā*." My ties throughout my stay in Pahansu were strongest with people of that lineage, and my presence in their houses was so much a part of the daily routine that people barely looked up from their work or their conversations when I entered a courtyard. My relationships with other families were generally a bit more formal: water would be set to boil for tea, work would be set aside, conversations dropped, and quarrels silenced when I paid visits to other households. But it was only in 1988, when several major disputes had broken out concerning the impending state-mandated land consolidation and redistribution, that I was asked by the women of Telu's house not to visit several other Gujar homes in the village, because tensions were running so high over land consolidation. I was the sister of Telu Ram and Jabar Singh, they said, and it would not do for me to sit with women in those courtyards. I did in fact visit with women I had been close to, in Rupram's house across the lane, and I was welcomed there, but there was nonetheless some tension in the air, so much was I perceived as part of Telu's family.

Though of course I could become a daughter of the village in only limited ways, and though I never did, at that time, have henna put on my palms, sometimes I did feel that I had internalized some of the expectations about women's behavior in Pahansu. While daughters never veil their faces in their natal village, they do keep their heads covered with their shawls; to go about with uncovered head or loosely flowing hair would be an open admission that one was *beśaram*, without modesty. I soon began to feel incompletely clothed if my head wasn't covered, and I often felt uncomfortable in the company of men who weren't known to me. And my own discomfort brought an understanding that just as I covered my head and avoided unwanted male gazes out of a sense of expediency and privacy, so too might other women in Pahansu veil not because they believe themselves to be inferior to men but because such a pose of deference and modesty is required if the honor of one's household is to be upheld.

The only village event that I was asked not to attend was a folk drama, a *sāng*, at the time of Holi, performed on the outskirts of the village by a troupe of traveling actors and musicians. Gujar women never attend these dramas, but I insisted that I should witness the event. It was with pained expressions that Telu and several other men of the family walked with me to the spot in the fields where the stage had been erected and sat with me through the first day's performance. And I too felt uncomfortable, because there were so many strangers there who had come only for the folk drama, and it happened that more eyes seemed to be focused on me, the very tall foreigner in the *salvār-kamīz*, than on the drama. When we returned home afterward, Telu again reminded me that Gujar wives and daughters never attend folk drama performances, and that it was a matter of the honor (*izzat*) of one's family that it should be so. I didn't go to the play the next day, thinking that the small increment of ethnographic knowledge that I would acquire was not adequate compensation for those pained expressions and my own unease.

I realized on the day I left Pahansu in 1979, at the conclusion of my dissertation research, just how hazardous to their honor it had seemed to Asikaur and her family to take me into their home for such a long time, as their daughter and sister. Just as I was leaving, with several of my Pahansu brothers who had decided to escort me to Delhi to catch the plane back to Chicago, Asikaur, with the relief evident in her voice, said, "Thank God nothing happened." I think she was expressing her relief that I had done nothing to disgrace them, and relief also that no one in Pahansu had insulted me or done me any harm, because in either case their *izzat*, their honor, would have been besmirched. And I realized, as I decided not to return to the *sāng* so many months before, that a woman might conform to certain cultural expectations not out of an inner conviction of her own inferiority but out of concern for the feelings and honor of others. It seems obvious that the North Indian women who behave as I did then, and who take to heart the common Hindi proverb "The woman who preserves the honor of her husband is the ornament of the house" (*tiriyā to hai śobhā ghar kī jo lāj rakhe apne nar kī*), are thereby complicit in the preservation of a system of inequality, since "honor" is so clearly part of an ideology that contributes to the power of men over women. But these same women may nonetheless be moved, as I also came to see, to resist this ideology in subtle ways.

Through my own limited participation, I began to recognize some of the complex ways in which women might mock conventions concerning modesty while adhering to them for the sake of honor. Gujar daughters, when they return from their husbands' villages for a visit, spend much time visiting neighbors and kin, gossiping, and going to various houses to "view the dowries" that are being given or received in the village and to pass judgment on whether the sets of cloth involved are *baṛhiyā* or *vaise-hī*, fine or not so fine, and whether sets of cloth have been given to all the right recipients. As this was pretty much how I spent my day, or at least how most people interpreted my activities, the role of daughter and sister that I fell into seemed appropriate. One major restriction that this role seemed to bring with it was that I should under no circumstances, even in jest, comport myself as a wife (*bahū*) of the village. Once when I had gone to a house on the other side of the village with the women of our house to look over dowries, I was joking about the necessity of veiling one's face as one walked through the streets. Asikaur and her daughters-in-law all appreciated my mocking jibes at the practice of *ghūṅghaṭ*, or veiling. Yet when I attempted to mimic the fairly complicated method of holding the shawl over the head that a wife employs when she walks veiled through the lanes of her husband's village, the mood of iconoclastic levity abruptly ended. The moment Asikaur saw me do this, she let loose the only torrent of reproach and anger that I ever received from her. What sort of shameless behavior was this? How could I, a daughter of the whole village, veil my face in my natal village? What would people say about my character and that of my family if I thus behaved as only a wife of the village should behave? To veil implied a sexuality that needed protection; in one's natal village no issues of sexuality ought to arise, for one is daughter and sister to all. Thus the same veiling that would signify modesty in a husband's village meant immoral wantonness in one's natal home. Asikaur's appreciation of the verbal mockery while angrily disapproving of my burlesque of the veiling made me see early on in my fieldwork that a woman may voice an ironic critique of a cultural practice while at the same time embracing that practice and much that it implies, to uphold her own honor and that of her family.

In other ways too I saw that women could subtly mock many conventions concerning kinship, gender, sexuality, and "modesty" (*śaram*). Babbli, the eldest of Jabar Singh's two daughters, was a lively and bright twelve year old when I left Pahansu in 1979. When I returned in 1988, she was married and pregnant with her first child. Though she was nearing the end of her pregnancy, she returned to Pahansu when she heard that I had arrived. As quick and animated now as I had remembered her, she seemed delighted to see me and to visit with her family, and she seemed rather to enjoy flaunting her disregard of the convention that women are too ashamed of their sexuality to visit their natal village when they are in an advanced stage of pregnancy. On the day of her arrival, Babbli sat in our courtyard companionably eating from the same plate as Kusum, her father's sister's daughter, who was also paying a visit to Pahansu. Just then one of the family's agricultural laborers came into the courtyard. He flashed a devilish smile at her and said, *kaṅghe te āyī,* "Where have you come from?" teasing the young bride who had returned from her husband's place. Babbli looked him straight in the eye, laughed conspiratorially and replied, *saṛak saṛakoṅ te,* "I've come by way of the roads." Far from exhibiting the modesty about referring to her husband's place that convention required, Babbli seemed to me to be satirizing that convention, by the mirth in her eyes and the jesting, mocking tone of her repartee. A few weeks later, when Babbli's husband came to fetch her back to her in-laws' home, she resumed before our eyes the posture of a shy and reticent wife.

It was from listening closely to Pahansu women that I first became vividly aware of how they reimagined gender and kinship and how those reimaginings subverted some of the generally more audible commonplaces of North Indian social life. One of the first things I did in Pahansu in 1977 was to take down genealogies, piecemeal, here and there, from both men and women. I was given, in answer to my questions, exactly what I expected: a web of kinship ties, among men, was traced out for me, and armed with this, I assumed that I would understand how everybody was related to everybody else in the village. I hadn't been in Pahansu for more than a few days, however, when I noticed that everything was not as neat and tidy as the genealogies seemed to suggest. Why was Omi not properly deferential to her husband's father's brother's wife? Why was Shanti not veiling before several of the men of her husband's *kunbā*? Why did Usha, Shanti's daughter-in-law, call two men of the lineage "brother" and joke with them, instead of silently veiling in their presence as a daughter-in-law should? I realized that women were constantly redefining patrilineal relationships in their husband's village, and gaining allies for themselves in the process, in the many cases in which genealogical ambiguity existed. By "accepting" even remote ties "from the direction of the natal village," when such ties could be traced, and disregarding the much more hierarchical (though genealogically much closer) relationship "from the direction of the husband's village," women were able to shift, if ever so slightly, the lines of authority and power in their conjugal village. These were subtle though important shifts, discernible only as I sat and listened to women's talk in their courtyards or listened to them tell tales of how they were able to depend on these natal ties in times of adversity. Yet these reimaginings of patrilineal kinship were never evident from interviews or in the genealogies; they emerged only in the particular contexts in which women invoked them. I don't think I would have become aware of their significance had I not sat companionably in so many courtyards for so many hours of the day.

It was from listening to and translating the words of women's songs that I began to realize that such negotiations of kinship relationships, and the defiance of authority in the husband's house that sometimes followed, were not viewed by women as deviations from a unitary set of norms but as positively valued and celebrated ways of constructing an alternative female identity in rural North India. In these songs, women's forthright speech was valued, and the complex visions of proper kinship behavior were articulated very differently from what I heard from men and from what I often heard from women too in abstract interview situations. What this meant to me was that the enormous gulf between us that I first imagined narrowed, when I saw that like me women in Pahansu and Hathchoya contested dominant gender ideologies and were not content to accept everything that male traditions said of them. I was able to feel that when I began to listen attentively to the songs.

When I had been in Pahansu in the 1970s, I had recorded some birth and marriage songs and rather desultorily translated a few of them. They seemed boring to me then—long, repetitive lists of kin; long, repetitive lists of ornaments demanded and ornaments received. I didn't really turn my attention seriously to women's expressive traditions until 1988. I had gone to Pahansu then with my six-year-old son and eighteen-month-old daughter. Lauren didn't take much to water-buffalo milk, and she compensated by demanding to breastfeed more frequently than usual. I found myself sitting in the courtyard with her in my lap for a good part of the day, and so I turned my attention to the tapes, old ones from my previous visit and new ones I was making then. While the men of our household could not understand why I would want to devote so much attention to something as insignificant as "women's songs," I was simply astonished at women's reaction to my new interest. I had only to take out my tape recorder, and I would be surrounded by women eager to "fill up" a tape with songs or to explicate the meaning of ones we listened to. I sometimes felt that my ability occasionally to grasp quickly the emotional nuances of a song gave them proof, finally, that I was a thinking and feeling human being. When women spoke with me about a song, they often spoke also about their own lives, about their relationships with brothers, husbands, mothers-in-law. I felt that through these songs I came to see a different side of the women I thought I had known so well. My most vivid memories of that 1988 trip to Pahansu are of Simla poignantly reminding me of the parallels between the words of a song and her own life, of young girls thinking of their own approaching marriages as they helped me translate a wedding song, of Rajavati mourning the loss of her brother many years before and thinking of her son's approaching marriage as she tried to explicate a song about a mother's brother's wedding gifts. I saw so clearly then that these songs question the dominant conventions concerning North Indian kinship and gender and reflect upon the ironies of women's lives in a patrilineal system. And this is why they are, to the women who sing them and to me, so emotionally compelling. The words of the songs, and women's commentaries on them, allowed me to hear, at last, that women were not the unquestioning bearers of "tradition" I had assumed them to be. They subtly but articulately challenged tradition at every turn. One need only listen to their words.

I spent the summer of 1990 in Hathchoya, doing almost nothing but tape-recording and translating women's songs. At the end of the summer, just before I left, I finally, after all those years, had henna applied to my palms. It looked beautiful. The distance I had originally sensed between myself and the women I knew there seemed to have diminished. Though of course I cannot claim to have abolished the postcolonial and academic legacies informing, ineluctably, my perceptions of those I tried to learn about, I had at least begun to see that critical reflection and resistance were as much characteristic of women's expressive genres there as I hope they are of mine.

ANN'S ACCOUNT

I went to India in 1979 intending to live in a village and study religious values, especially those associated with Hindu pilgrimage. I did not anticipate that these elusive values, or life in the "field," would be particularly affected by sexual difference. But to move from the United States of the seventies into a North Indian village is to move into a context where gender differences are much more blatantly highlighted and constitutive of behavior. Almost from the moment I set foot in the place called Ghatiyali, the women who lived there set about to teach me that any pretense of gender-free thought and behavior was folly.

Ghatiyali's women claimed me—with words and beckoning

gestures. Although I was a foreigner, and therefore visibly and verbally different from them, they told me that I was like them more than any man was. In the Rajasthani dialect they contrasted "women" (*lugāyā*) with "men" (*log*). Although in Hindi as I had learned it *log* meant "people" in the unmarked, ungendered, encompassing sense, in Ghatiyali women used *log* to mean the opposite of "people." Thus they might say about a place, "There's *nobody* to talk with over there, nothing but *log*," as if men were an alien species.

Groups of laughing women called to me, it seemed, from every housefront as I learned my way through the lanes of Ghatiyali. When I stopped to talk with them I was subjected to friendly interrogations that circled around family, clothing, and money. Once these points were established (I did have a husband and a son, my skirt was made of cloth from Jodhpur, the government paid me a stipend), talk often turned to food (What vegetable did you eat today?) or to the—for them—ever-fascinating topic of life in America (What's the price of wheat? Are small children and aging parents really abandoned into the care of strangers? Do you have the same moon?).

During my first months in Rajasthan I wearied of answering questions on the limited set of topics I had come to label "women's" interests. No longer flattered by their warm inclusion of me, anxious to get on with my serious quest for cultural values, I frequently preferred to shut myself up in rooms with educated men who could teach me the hidden meanings of esoteric hymns and who spoke clear Hindi and not the—to me—often murky Rajasthani.

Hierarchies of caste and gender manifest in control of language skills powerfully affected my early relationships in Ghatiyali. Because I knew Hindi and not the local dialect, the persons with whom I could have the most intelligent, wide-ranging, informative conversations were educated men. My own naïveté was such that it took me months to realize why women's conversations appeared so simpleminded and repetitive. They had readily perceived that I couldn't understand them when they said anything complex, and yet they were kindly determined to include me in the companionable sociability without which life was unthinkable. Therefore they repeated their elementary questions and no doubt felt bored themselves. (I know that they judged me fairly dull and obtuse, if comical enough to entertain.)

Although I never became perfectly fluent in Rajasthani, gradually my language skills improved enough that women could include me in discussions about their own world. I began to understand how much religious knowledge they possessed. For example, women were far better sources for the meanings of, and practices associated with, calendrical or life-cycle festivals than were men. If I asked a man what happens on such and such a day, the most common answer would be "We eat pudding" or some equivalent. It was women who readily explained what gods were worshiped, what stories were told, what results were expected—and they were the ones who knew the pudding recipe too. My respect for Ghatiyali's women increased vastly, and I began to relax in their company, no longer worried that I was "wasting time." But my research focus remained "religious values," not gender.

I had arrived in Rajasthan in 1979 with various preconceptions about Indian women, and most of them—drawn from gossip, fiction, films, and occasionally anthropology—were at least partially wrong. For example, I had been warned, seriously, by Indian men living in the United States not to tell the villagers that I was divorced, because they didn't have the concept of divorce and to them it could mean only that I was a "loose woman." I found, on the contrary, that they had a perfect understanding of divorce, although the term used to describe it meant "connection" and stressed not separation but union. Often women "ran off" and made new connections with men more desirable to them than the husbands with whom their parents had matched them in early childhood. But a second marriage could also be properly arranged. Excluding the Brahman, Rajput, and Baniya castes, the practice of making new connections was not infrequent.

I had been led to expect extreme reticence about sexual matters and about women's bodily processes. I found, to the contrary, that both marital sexuality and scandalous love affairs were subjects of frequent discussion, and often of jokes, playfulness, and occasional sentimentality—usually, it is true, only in unmixed company, although there were exceptions to this rule too. "Do you miss your husband?" village women whispered to me with both mischief and sympathy. "In which spot do you miss him?"

Even regarding menstruation—the ultimate polluting process that I had assumed would be taboo—I found Rajasthani women more frank and unabashed than I was. Once when I was sitting outside with a young woman she observed that I must have my period. Nervously, I replied, "What makes you say that?" and she responded that she knew because of the flies buzzing around my skirt. She and her friends, she continued, always guessed about and questioned one another in this way. To my professional discredit, rather than pursue this new avenue of ethnographic inquiry I covered up a sense of mortification by telling her rather brusquely that in *my* country it was not customary to talk about such things.

I was somewhat more prepared to see older women exercising considerable power in the domestic setting. But I was surprised by the ready acknowledgment given this power by mature men. My first and haughtiest male research assistant—a tall, handsome Brahman in his mid-thirties, with a wife, two children, and a reputation for womanizing—was the absolute dependent of his toothless, widowed mother (rather than vice versa, despite what is published on the lot of Hindu widows). This man was assisting Joe Miller and me in our attempt at a house-to-house census. Of course his own household was one of the first where he chose to try out our freshly printed census forms with their carefully constructed Hindi categories. One of these categories was *mukhya ādmī*, or chief man—intended to describe the head of household. At the end of the first day of census taking our assistant came to us and sheepishly explained his problem with this category. "In my house," he said, "the 'chief man' is a woman—my mother. What shall I do?" Obviously, we had erred in imposing male gender on the "head of household" category.

Ghatiyali was indeed a sexually segregated society, but I began to perceive that women felt comfortable among themselves partly because they had to assume postures of submission and modesty in the presence of men. Thus I began to understand, much as Gloria did through her everyday experiences in Pahansu and Hathchoya, that the gestures constituting purdah, or female seclusion, were recognized as poses—enforced by behavioral codes. Although the women of Ghatiyali certainly accepted these codes, covering their faces and lowering their voices accordingly, they were freer in thought, and their domestic influence more blatant than I had anticipated. They did not appear in the least to be fundamentally ashamed of female bodily processes.

It was performed stories and songs that persuasively turned my anthropological attention directly to the "female species" (*strī jāt*) in Ghatiyali. Initially, male power over language continued to impose a gulf between me and this material; for, as I rarely understood all the words of women's performances in action, I taped them, and they were then transcribed by one of several male research assistants jointly employed by Joe Miller and me. At that time, 1979–81, no woman in the village could write well enough to do transcription work, although Joe and I often employed one marginally literate woman to help our male assistants transcribe women's songs. Moreover, I used male assistants to explain Rajasthani song and story texts to me in Hindi, and thus male judgments affected my interpretations. Because men, like women, feel "shame" in discussing intimate matters with the opposite sex, most men would not work with me on genres of songs with sexual import.

Eventually a bold woman of an untouchable caste—my friend Lila, the drummer and dancer—was willing to sit with me and go over the words of *gālīs*, or insult songs. She helped me to master the vocabulary for bodily parts and sexual acts. Once I knew the words, it was not impossible to discuss these songs with some men. Here is what one of my research assistants wrote about this work, in an account of how foreigners had affected his life:

> At this time I was doing translations of Rajasthani folk songs with Ann. This was a completely new experience for me: [to note] the ways in which a woman, by means of a song, reveals her desires, and also reveals her happiness upon obtaining these desires. These songs express joy, grief, pleasure, and one's own needs, and they make some specific references too. I worked on translating all songs with Ann. Among them there were some songs that were so obscene I wouldn't be able to write them, but women easily sang them in the open bazaar.
>
> (Gujar and Gold 1992: 77)

In 1979–81 I almost never spoke with women about the texts of their performances. The questions I asked were usually about the meanings of ritual actions or about the myths surrounding holidays that songs accompanied. I did not ask women why they sang these songs or whether the songs expressed their inner feelings. But I did spend hours and hours in the company of singing, joking, dancing, laughing women, sharing with them the vital, emergent reality of performative situations. I was swept along within a closely packed group of energetic young women intensely hurling insults as they blocked a bridegroom's path; I relaxed in the peaceful, soothing companionship of middle-aged matrons melodically praising the goddesses and gods.

Most of my analytic thinking about women's oral traditions was done in the United States as I pondered transcribed texts several years after my return from Rajasthan. I was back in India in 1987–88—once again on a research project that had nothing to do with gender. Shobhag, heroine of chapter 6, drove with me and my family to the pilgrimage center of Pushkar, and on the way we happened to stop near a sugarcane stand. One of the engagingly ribald songs discussed in chapter 2 plays on an analogy between penises and sugarcane. Testing my grasp of the song's language, I recited two words only, in a kind of singsong: *sāṅṭo mīṭho* (Sugarcane is sweet). Although this might have made an ordinary descriptive statement, Shobhag dissolved into delighted laughter, and I glowed with happiness at the success of my small experiment. When she stopped laughing my companion muttered, half chiding, half informing, "Hey, that's the insult for *toraṇ mārnā*"—the striking by the groom of the wedding emblem before he enters his bride's door. She thus not only visibly enjoyed my having learned and spontaneously produced a bit of her cultural knowledge, but continued to educate me in the at least pro forma necessity for appropriate context. Even then, I refrained from asking more about sugarcane.

As I undertook to write about Rajasthani women I set out to educate myself in the current literature and found that much of it focused on sufferings, abuses, and discriminations to which women were subject. Moreover, there were chilling case studies and equally depressing statistics confirming cruel realities. It has always been difficult for me to reconcile these bleak images with my memories of Ghatiyali. I do vividly recall a funeral I witnessed in September 1979 of a small girl, a Barber's daughter. Her family was notoriously impoverished. When, beside the cremation fire,

Joe Miller asked her father, "Is there sorrow?" the man replied dully, "No, we hadn't married her yet."

A daughter's loss was grievous, we might conclude, only if one had already gone to the expense of performing her marriage. But many in the village shook their heads, clicked their tongues, and commented that this was a bleak house, a family with nothing. There seems to be a strong correlation in India between general poverty and increased female suffering. Confirming this, Indian feminist activists have observed that women from the comfortable peasant groups are less readily engaged in movements. In Ghatiyali in 1979–81 few lacked the physical necessities to live. Yet the women I know did, in their way, through artistic performances and sometimes through determined actions, resist male-authored gender inequities.

Most little girls in Ghatiyali were cherished, their spirits as buoyant as were their brothers', their giggles as loud, their behavior as gutsy. It was true that mothers and grandparents expressed special affection for their girl children by calling them "son," but this could be construed as negating gender difference as much as privileging males. (I think it is both.) I couldn't believe that girls were perceived or treated as second-rate human beings. Metaphorically, they were little birds destined to fly away —as one poignant wedding song puts it. But this departure is mourned rather than welcomed. Messages of love and yearning follow daughters when they go, and summon them home again. When Joe Miller and I undertook to do family portraits for every house in the village our systematic operation was infinitely hampered by the wish most parents had that we wait until daughters came home for a visit before taking a group photo. In-married wives might be present, but the family was not complete without the daughters born to the house.

That Ghatiyali's women had internalized neither submissiveness nor lack of worth was as evident in public oral performances as in private encounters. Women's rituals kept the world of domestic and community life orderly, auspicious, and productive. The stories they told and songs they sang as part of worship explicitly portrayed outspoken, beneficent, powerful women (and incidentally often featured passive, obedient, ineffectual, or blundering males). Women enjoyed and requested the presence of the tape recorder—calling it the "thing to be filled," offering to fill it with their words and melodies, and relishing hearing their voices emerge from it. Thus oral traditions reinforced the positive messages I received in daily interactions.

GLORIA AND ANN

One of the major arguments of this book is that the performances associated with Hindu festivals and the many rituals surrounding birth, children, and weddings are both expressions of and sources for women's positive self-images. The celebration of these festivals depends on surplus, and during the time we lived in Pahansu, Hathchoya, and Ghatiyali there was enough surplus to permit a rich ritual and festival life to flourish. But if the richness of cultural performances is dependent on the richness of performers, our conclusions may be partially undermined. Ann resided with well-off Rajputs, and Gloria with prosperous landowning Gujars. Certainly we moved, and carried our tape recorders with us, among many other groups. But neither of us spent a lot of time with women of the untouchable castes. We acknowledge the consequently partial nature of our conclusions, based largely on our experiences among women of relatively high caste. Yet Margaret Trawick's work among South Indian untouchable women suggests that reimaginings of the kind we heard among landowning farmer groups are voiced in song even by women in dire economic situations.

We are conscious of the documentable counterpoint realities to our portrayal of North Indian women as outspoken, free-minded, reveling in womanhood, and exercising genuine control over the terms of their lives. Did they possess land and livestock or decide on cash expenditures in ways comparable to men? Did they eat before or after men? Did they eat more or less than men? Did little girls receive more or less medicine than little boys? Why were so few females literate that no woman in Ghatiyali was able to act as research assistant? Would the songs and stories we write about here continue to be performed if the men of Pahansu, Hathchoya, or Ghatiyali decided that they posed an immediate threat to male authority? The unadorned answers to all these questions are the predictable ones, confirming female disadvantage in every case. What matter if women sing of the power of female sexuality and of their rethinking of patrilineal kinship if in real life their husbands beat them with community approval?

On the other hand, for those who will agree there is another hand, if we fail to hear Indian women's self-affirming voices or to appreciate their own sense of what constitutes a good life or to see how they skillfully negotiate their chance for such a life, we perpetuate the mistaken assumption that these women have completely internalized the dominant conventions of female subordination and fragmented identity. If we juxtapose the arenas of politics and economics to those of folklore and ritual without seeing the ways they meld and fluctuate in mutual regard, we perpetuate not only the old and false split between practice and ideology but the equally false notion that ideology is single and uncontested. This book argues not that one reality should obscure the other but rather that better pictures are to be had only by frequently shifting lenses.

A. K. Ramanujan's newly published collection of folktales from India contains this translation of an Urdu tale from the folk cycle about Akbar, the Moghul emperor, and his wise adviser Birbal:

Bring Me Four

One day Akbar said to Birbal, "Bring me four individuals: one, a modest person; two, a shameless person; three, a coward; four, a heroic person."

Next day Birbal brought a woman and had her stand before the emperor. Akbar said, "I asked for four people, and you have brought only one. Where are the others?"

Birbal said, "Refuge of the World, this one woman has the qualities of all four kinds of persons."

Akbar asked him, "How so?"

Birbal replied, "When she stays in her in-laws' house, out of modesty she doesn't even open her mouth. And when she sings obscene insult-songs at a marriage, her father and brothers and husband and in-laws and caste-people all sit and listen, but she's not ashamed. When she sits with her husband at night, she won't even go alone into the storeroom and she says, "I'm afraid to go." But then, if she takes a fancy to someone, she goes fearlessly to meet her lover at midnight, in the dark, all alone, with no weapon, and she is not at all afraid of robbers or evil spirits."

Hearing this, Akbar said, "You speak truly," and gave Birbal a reward.

(Ramanujan 1991b: 95)

This tale from male oral tradition expresses a stereotypical South Asian misogyny. Two men treat a voiceless female as an object. They see her as split between virtue and sexuality, weakness and strength, essentially duplicitous or hypocritical because of her multiplicity. But with a slight interpretive shift this same story could also point to aspects of infinite resourceful female power—fluid, shape-changing, boundless, formless—that are part of Hindu cosmology: *prakṛiti*, or the multiplicity of nature; *māyā*, or the goddess's art of illusion; *śakti*, or the fearless energy that activates everything in the universe.

In this book we wish to make that interpretive shift: to listen to the truth-speaking heron, to move from Akbar and Birbal's external and judgmental account of female multiplicity as duplicity to more interior, less fragmented views. Without denying the evident reality of male voices maligning a silent female figure and congratulating themselves, we argue that silence itself is a construct neither monolithic nor pervasive. We have seen the same women who veil with utmost modesty before in-laws boldly hurl obscene insult songs; we have seen that model wives sometimes do risk everything to seek enriched lives by meeting their lovers after dark or by defying husbands and in-laws to pursue religious goals; and we have seen the less dramatic ways, too, in which women may manipulate kinship ties to the advantage of themselves and the people they care most about. The object woman of the male tradition is a speaking, imagining, singing, acting person, whose multiplicity—both in artistic expressions and in everyday negotiations—makes her all the more whole and strong.

ACKNOWLEDGMENTS

Both Ann and Gloria wish to thank the institutions that have supported their work and the many people who have helped them in their research and in the writing of this book.

Gloria

My research in Pahansu was supported in 1977–79 by the Social Science Research Council/American Council of Learned Societies and by the American Institute of Indian Studies. Additional work there in 1988 was funded by the Wenner-Gren Foundation for

Anthropological Research. Fieldwork in the village of Hathchoya in 1990 was made possible by the McKnight Foundation, in the form of a McKnight-Land Grant Professorship from the University of Minnesota.

Portions of chapters 3 and 4 have been presented at seminars at Cornell University, the University of Rochester, the School of Oriental and African Studies at the University of London, the University of Virginia, and the Center for Advanced Feminist Studies at the University of Minnesota. Discussions generated at those presentations have enriched my analyses. I thank Jane Bestor, Carol Delaney, Richard Herrell, John Ingham, Patricia and Roger Jeffery, Frédérique Marglin, McKim Marriott, Mattison Mines, Cynthia Talbot, Mahipal Tomar, and especially Sylvia Vatuk for taking the time to comment extensively on these chapters. I also thank Ingrid Pars for help in preparing the final manuscript.

I must once again record my gratitude to Asikaur, Rajavati, Simla, Santroj, and Sarla for taking me into their home in Pahansu for eighteen months in the 1970s and for welcoming me and my children in 1988. Kevin and Lauren will not forget their *nānī* Asikaur, and I can never forget the generous hospitality always shown us in her house. Of the many women in Pahansu who instructed me and whose friendship sustained me, I wish especially to acknowledge Bugli, Atri, Kamala and Sansar, Omi and Shanti, and Sumitra Kaushik and Anguri.

My debts to my sisters-in-law Saroj and Prem are of a different sort; I cannot find words to express my affection and my admiration for them. I hope that this book is something Bugli Devi could have taken pride in had she lived to see its completion.

Ann

My research in India was supported by the American Institute of Indian Studies in 1979–81 and again in 1987–88 and by the Social Science Research Council in 1980–81. Chapters 2, 5, and 6 were originally composed between 1984 and 1988, have circulated widely, and formed the substance for numerous lectures and conference presentations. Along the way, more persons than I can name have helped to shape them. I must particularly thank Jane Atkinson, Wendy Doniger, Daniel Gold, Ruth Grodzins, Sudhir

Kakar, Jyotsna Kapur, Kath March, Frédérique Marglin, McKim Marriott, Gail Minault, Michael Moffatt, Kirin Narayan, Margaret Trawick, Anna Lowenhaupt Tsing, and Susan Wadley. Carol Delaney, Vijay Gambhir, and Mary Katzenstein responded most helpfully to my pleas for immediate feedback on the preface. My debt to Shobhag Kanvar and to Bhoju Ram Gujar, as ever, is of the kind unpayable in a single life.

Gloria and Ann

No institution or person named here is responsible for the final published form of these materials.

We dedicate this book to all the women who taught us to listen and to all the young girls now growing up in Pahansu, Hathchoya, and Ghatiyali (with a special cheer for Hemalata, Chinu, and Ghumar). May the births and lives of daughters be joyful.

1

Introduction: Gender Representation and the Problem of Language and Resistance in India

This book focuses on women's oral traditions and women's use of language in rural Uttar Pradesh and Rajasthan, northern India. We examine stories, ritual songs, personal narratives, and ordinary conversations from the villages of Pahansu, Hathchoya, and Ghatiyali and reflect on the ways in which these speech genres may be implicated in women's self-perceptions and self-fashioning, and the ways in which they may be understood as constituting a moral discourse in which gender and kinship identities are constructed, represented, negotiated, and contested in everyday life.

Several theoretical concerns inform our ethnographic analyses. At the most general level, we wish to position our arguments about gender in South Asia in such a way as to comment on current attempts to rethink the idea of culture in anthropology and in the social sciences, and attempts to understand the politics of representation in these disciplines. Second, we situate contemporary ethnography from western Uttar Pradesh and eastern Rajasthan in relation to the work of the *Subaltern Studies* historians, insofar as they are concerned with recovering the voices of those whose subjectivity and agency are generally obscured by most historical writing, and insofar as they offer theoretical perspectives on the interpretation of power and subaltern subjectivity. We share with those scholars an interest in what James Scott (1985) has called "everyday forms of resistance" to systems of ideological or material dominance. Our interests lie in exploring the "hidden transcripts" (Scott 1990) implicit in women's speech and song, the often veiled, but sometimes overt and public, words and actions through which women communicate their resistance to dominant

North Indian characterizations of "women's nature" (*triyā charitra*) and of kinship relationships. While our primary aim is to understand women's language—the words in which they construct and communicate alternative self-perceptions and alternative vantage points on their social world—we wish to comment also on the relationship between women's moral discourse and everyday resistance, on the one hand, and forms of power in North Indian social relationships, on the other. Third, we focus on the interrelationship between kinship and gender in northern India, specifically on the ways in which a consideration of women's voices and women's agency necessitates a rethinking of standard anthropological conceptualizations of marriage and patrilineality in South Asia. And finally, our consideration of women's speech genres speaks to broader issues of the relationship between language and gender, particularly those connected with the pragmatic aspects of language use, with speech play and verbal art as forms of discourse (Sherzer 1987a) and with women's communicative devices as loci of potentially subversive speech.

CULTURE AND THE POLITICS OF GENDER REPRESENTATION IN INDIA

The anthropological objectification of a social practice often takes the form of positioning that practice within a single determinate discourse, a single interpretive frame, which becomes, then, a token of a coherent and totalizing "culture." Within the terms of such a positioning, culture is envisioned either as a "mode of thought" that "incarcerates" the native in a fixed and definite "way of thinking" (Appadurai 1988: 37–38) or as a set of "laws" or "rules" that transforms social chaos into social order, with the result that all human behavior becomes either unambiguously "normative" or "non-normative" within a specific cultural system (Bourdieu 1977: 1–15; Das 1989a: 310; Rosaldo 1989: 102). The construction of such an understanding of a particular social practice has a number of further consequences. Any interpretive strategy that views culture as a completed process, a coherent, bounded, and internally homogeneous "whole," tends also to view experience as given directly in that coherent culture, and thus the necessity of examining experience, and the voices of particular thinking subjects, is rather dramatically obviated.[1] Second, attempts to understand a social practice as the typification of an ordered and knowable cultural totality focus attention almost exclusively on what Clifford Geertz referred to as "scope," the degree to which the determinate meaning of a particular pattern of thought or social practice does indeed resonate throughout a cultural whole (1968: 111–12). Geertz contrasts the scope of a cultural pattern with its force, "the thoroughness with which such a pattern is internalized in the personalities of the individuals who adopt it, its centrality or marginality in their lives." As Renato Rosaldo points out, in privileging the wholeness and coherence of culture while denying the import of particular positioned subjectivities, anthropologists have not generally attended to the "force" of a particular way of thinking or a particular social practice. If, however, we follow Rosaldo in recasting the notion of force to encompass an attention to the positioned subject (1989: 225–26 n.1), and if we begin to view culture not as a single totalizing discourse but as a universe of discourse and practice in which competing discourses may contend with and play off each other (Kelly 1988: 41), compose ironic commentaries on or subvert one another, or reflexively interrogate a given text or tradition or power relation (Das 1989a: 312; Ramanujan 1989b), we might then begin to interpret experience and subjectivity not in terms of a single, incarcerating mode of thought, but in terms of multiply voiced, contextually shifting, and often strategically deployed readings of the social practices we seek to explicate.

In speaking of gender and oral traditions in South Asia, we find that it is of critical importance to stress the multiplicity of discursive fields within which social relationships are constructed, defined, and commented upon.[2] The Indian woman has all too frequently been portrayed as a silent shadow, given in marriage

1. The limitations of this conception of stable and seamless cultural "wholes" have been explicitly discussed from a number of vantage points in contemporary anthropological writing. See, for example, Appadurai 1986, 1988; Clifford 1988:63–64.

2. For some of the many ethnographic examples of the interplay of multiple and sometimes competing discourses in South Asian social life, from a variety of theoretical perspectives, see Egnor 1986; Gold 1988a; Grima 1991; Holmberg 1989; March 1984; Oldenburg 1990; Prakash 1991; Raheja 1988b, 1993; Wadley n.d. (forthcoming).

by one patrilineal group to another, veiled and mute before affinal kinsmen, and unquestioningly accepting a single discourse that ratifies her own subordination and a negative view of femaleness and sexuality. Such a unitary representation of feminine passivity in India has a very long history. Colonial reports on the practice of *satī*, for example, often stress women's submissive, unquestioning obedience to the dictates of "religion," and their identity as passive bearers of a rigidly circumscribed "tradition" (Mani 1985, 1989). Such colonial documents also tend to infantilize women, in speaking of the widow as a "tender child," even though most *satīs* were undertaken by women over the age of forty (Mani 1989: 97–98; Yang 1989). These representations of female passivity played a double role in British efforts to construct a moral justification for colonial rule in India. As Partha Chatterjee has pointed out, the representation of Indian women as voiceless and oppressed provided a rationale for British colonial intervention:

> Apart from the characterization of the political condition of India preceding the British conquest as a state of anarchy, lawlessness and arbitrary despotism, a central element in the ideological justification of British colonial rule was the criticism of the "degenerate and barbaric" social customs of the Indian people, sanctioned, or so it was believed, by their religious tradition. Alongside the project of instituting orderly, lawful and rational procedures of governance, therefore, colonialism also saw itself as performing a "civilizing mission." In identifying this tradition as "degenerate and barbaric," colonialist critics invariably repeated a long list of atrocities perpetrated on Indian women, not so much by men or certain classes of men, but by an entire body of scriptural canons and ritual practices which, they said, by rationalizing such atrocities within a complete framework of religious doctrine, made them appear to perpetrators and sufferers alike as the necessary marks of right conduct. By assuming a position of sympathy with the unfree and oppressed womanhood of India, the colonial mind was able to transform this figure of the Indian woman into a sign of the inherently oppressive and unfree nature of the entire cultural tradition of a country.
> (Chatterjee 1989: 622)

The "protection" of weak and passive Hindu women became, then, a strategy of colonial domination, and gender characterizations became vehicles for moral claims on the part of colonial administrators, missionaries, and so forth (Mani 1989; O'Hanlon 1991).[3]

Apart from attempts to legitimate the colonial enterprise as a civilizing mission that would secure a greater degree of freedom for Indian womanhood, nineteenth-century British colonial authors also, as Ashis Nandy (1983) persuasively argues, attempted to differentiate themselves maximally from the colonized by articulating an ethic of "hyper-masculinity" (involving aggression, control, competition, power, and so on) for the West, and characterizing India as the feminine antithesis, as radically "other." Embodying colonially devalued "feminine" qualities, Indian society was seen as unfit to rule itself and as morally inferior to the masculine West. Representations of women's silent submission to the dictates of religious tradition became, then, politically strategic metonymic tropes for the passivity of India as a whole.

Chatterjee has written of the way in which late nineteenth- and early twentieth-century nationalism responded to the colonial critique by constructing yet another discourse about women and Indian society, in terms of a redefined "classical tradition":

> The social order . . . in which nationalists placed the new woman was contrasted not only with that of modern Western society; it was explicitly distinguished from the patriarchy of indigenous tradition, the same tradition that had been put on the dock by colonial interrogators. Sure enough, nationalism adopted several elements from tradition as marks of its native cultural identity, but this was now a "classicized" tradition—reformed, reconstructed, fortified against charges of barbarism and irrationality. . . . The new patriarchy was also sharply distinguished from the immediate social and cultural condition in which the majority of the people lived, for the "new" woman was quite the reverse of the "common" woman, who was coarse, vulgar, loud, quarrelsome, devoid of superior moral sense, sexually promiscuous, subjected to brutal physical oppression by males. It was precisely this degenerate condition of women which nationalism claimed it would reform.
>
> (Chatterjee 1989: 627)

Sumanta Banerjee (1989) has analyzed the profound effects of this nationalist redefinition of the ideal woman on women's ex-

3. See Suleri 1992:69–74 for an example of a similar portrayal of the pathos and vulnerability of Indian women, albeit with a different political agenda, in a play by Richard Sheridan first performed in England in 1799.

pressive traditions. In nineteenth-century Bengal, songs and other forms of women's popular culture were often critical of women's position in the society of the time. "Often stark and bitter in expressing the plight of women in a male-dominated society, the poems and songs popular among the lower social groups were, at the same time, tough, sensuous or bawdy, in an idiom specific to women" (Banerjee 1989: 131–32). From the mid-nineteenth century onward, Bengali men, influenced both by colonial education and by nationalist sentiment, attempted to arouse public opinion against these expressive genres, and there were concerted efforts to denigrate and suppress them as "corrupting," indecent, and unworthy of proper Hindu women.[4] In the early twentieth century, the singing of such songs was viewed as a serious feminine shortcoming, and women's lack of formal education was cited as the cause of such moral failings, in women's didactic literature of the time (Kumar 1991: 21).

As Chatterjee observed, Indian nationalism came to view women as the guardians and preservers of tradition.[5] Ketu Katrak (1992) has argued that Gandhi further essentialized "tradition" and female sexuality through his appeals, in the nationalist cause, to the "female" virtues of sacrifice, purity, humility, and silent suffering that could be deployed in the service of the independence movement. His evocation of the mythological figures of Sita, Draupadi, and Savitri as exemplars of noble forbearance and contained sexuality led him to ignore, Katrak suggests, the more defiant and less passively submissive women of Indian history and legend who could equally have served as models of female identity.[6]

The contours of a similar politically motivated deployment of a discourse concerning women, propriety, and "tradition" are evident in Julia Leslie's discussion (1989) of the Sanskrit text *Strīdharmapaddhati*. Written by Tryambakayajvan in an eighteenth-cen-

4. Tharu and Lalita (1991:187–90) provide translations of the songs of two female folksingers of this period.

5. This continues frequently to be the case in contemporary India. Dulali Nag (1990) has vividly drawn the contours of such a discourse on woman and "tradition" as it is deployed to market saris to middle- and upper-class Bengali women in advertisements in popular women's magazines.

6. The Gandhian legacy for women's movements in India is vastly more complex than this brief survey can comprise. The issue is further debated, as Katrak points out, in Jayawardana 1986 and Kishwar 1985.

tury Maratha court, the text outlines the duties and dispositions appropriate to the *pativratā*, the ideal wife who is devoted to and subordinate to her husband. Leslie suggests that the author's defense of an orthodox Hindu tradition concerning women represents a response to the challenges to that tradition posed by growing Muslim domination, by Christian missionary influence, and by the increasingly popular devotional movements (*bhakti*) that claimed, at least in their poetic traditions, that social distinctions between men and women were religiously insignificant (4). Leslie also points out that the polygamous milieu of the Maratha court presented certain political problems when queens and mistresses became involved in succession disputes and court intrigues. In such a milieu, she writes, "a work prescribing the proper behaviour of women might well have appeared to both kings and ministers to be a project of vital importance" (20). Thus, although the *Strīdharmapaddhati* presents itself as a treatise on the inherent nature of women grounded in the timelessness of the *dharmaśāstrik* texts, the internal and external political compulsions for its composition suggest to us some of the ways in which particular representations of gender are deployed for particular purposes in particular historical contexts (see Chakravarti 1991).

Further, the very existence of a text like the *Strīdharmapaddhati* indicates, perhaps, the existence of contrary discourses on gender and "women's nature." As Uma Chakravarti writes,

> A close look at the *Strīdharmapaddhati* indicates that the powerful model of the *pativratā* thus plays a crucial role in the "taming" of women. Once internalised by them it also makes them complicit in their own subordination. Ultimate social control is effectively and imperceptibly achieved when the subordinated not only accept their condition but consider it a mark of distinction. What the eighteenth century *Strīdharmapaddhati* also unwittingly indicates is that not all women at all times accepted their condition nor considered it a mark of distinction: Hence the need for repeated reiteration of the duties of women, including the exhortation to women to mount the husband's pyre. The *Strīdharmapaddhati* was a complete manual on the way women "ought" to behave, written in order to counteract the potential or actual "recalcitrance" of women.
>
> (Chakravarti 1991: 185)

Chakravarti's commentary here adumbrates an important aspect of the argument we attempt to make in these pages: that a discourse of gender and kinship found in certain admittedly authoritative texts and practices does not by any means exhaust or fully define women's subjectivities in South Asia. This seemingly obvious point has not often found its way into writing on the lives of ordinary women in South Asia.

May not other such discourses, whether indigenous or composed by outside observers, be strategically and politically motivated representations that grossly oversimplify and misinterpret women's consciousness? We do not wish in any way to minimize the difficulties and inequities experienced by women in northern India today and in the past; we wish only to highlight the fact that there are no women's voices in many of these representations (Spivak 1985a: 122), and the fact that, as Lata Mani has pointed out (1989: 90), these colonial, nationalist, and "traditional" discourses, and some similar contemporary Indian political discourses as well (Pathak and Rajan 1989), are not primarily about women; they are, rather, political commentaries on the authenticity and moral worth of a tradition.

Chandra Mohanty (1984) has written of the tendency, within Western feminist writing, to define women of the "third world" as victims of male control and of an unchanging "tradition," as unresisting objects in relation to ahistorical and uncontextualized images of "the veiled woman," "the obedient wife," and so forth. Such representations, she argues, define and maintain postcolonial relations between the first and third worlds by positing, implicitly or explicitly, the moral superiority of the West and the moral degradation of the "patriarchal" third world.[7]

We cannot of course claim to have extricated ourselves entirely from these colonial and postcolonial ways of thinking. We are painfully aware of the perils involved in presuming to speak with any authority about women whose lives are so different from our own. Edward Said (1979) exhibits a quote from Marx as an ani-

7. It is not only *representations* of gender that are implicated in postcolonialism; the often harsh realities of women's economic and political situations in India are of course produced in the context of postcolonial national politics and the global political economy. Mies (1982), for example, analyzes the location of Indian housewives' lace-making work within the contemporary global economy, and Spivak (1992) explicates Mahasweta Devi's short story "Douloti the Bountiful" as a critique of the production of women as bonded laborers and bonded prostitutes within the caste and class dominations of postcolonial Indian capitalism.

madversary epigraph to his *Orientalism*: "They cannot represent themselves; they must be represented."[8] It is precisely because of our conviction that Indian women can indeed represent themselves that we struggle to translate their words in these pages. Said explicitly castigates those totalizing and essentializing Orientalist discourses that privilege historically unchanging and univocal characterizations of social life in which human agency is radically deemphasized and a mute submission to "tradition" assumed. In attending to the multiple perspectives, shifting purposes, and reflexive and ironic commentaries evident in North Indian women's songs, stories, personal narratives, and everyday talk, it is our hope that the authority of such normalizing and essentialist discourses may begin to disintegrate as we come to understand both the heterogeneity and the resistance evident in women's speech. We do not intend, of course, to speak with any presumption of closure or totality with respect to the subjectivity of the North Indian women we know. When Indian women represent themselves in their own words, no single unitary voice is heard; we have only begun to listen to a few of these voices.

Trawick has recently commented that representations of Indian women as "repressed" and "submissive" are but half-truths (1990: 5). They are half-truths in the sense that they may not define the only discourse of selfhood and feminine identity available to women in India. Many such scholarly representations have involved assumptions concerning Indian women's "ideological self-abasement" (Spivak 1985a: 129), that is, the degree to which they have assimilated "traditional" devaluations of womanhood and female sexuality and values stressing women's submission to male kinsmen into their conceptions of selfhood. Thus Sudhir Kakar has argued that the identity and self-perceptions of Hindu women depend heavily on a set of male-authored mythic themes concerning the ideal woman condensed in the figure of Sita, the virtuous and faithful wife of Rama in the *Ramayana*. Kakar perceives a "formidable consensus" in India as a whole, rural and

8. For discussions of some of the specific guises Orientalist discourse assumes as it constructs its representations of Indian society, see Cohn 1968, 1984, 1985; Inden 1986a, 1986b, 1990; Mani 1985; Pinney 1989; Prakash 1990; Spivak 1985b; Suleri 1992.

urban, "traditional" and modern, in folklore and in myth, concerning the image of the ideal woman that Sita represents:

> The ideal of womanhood incorporated by Sita is one of chastity, purity, gentle tenderness and a singular faithfulness which cannot be destroyed or even disturbed by her husband's rejections, slights or thoughtlessness. . . . The moral is the familiar one: "Whether treated well or ill a wife should never indulge in ire."
>
> (Kakar 1978: 66)

Thus male psychological development, which is in fact Kakar's central focus, is profoundly affected by the mother's "aggressive, destructive impulses" or emotional claims directed toward her son as a result of her inability to challenge the ideals represented by Sita and to demand intimacy and a recognition of her worth as a woman from her husband (87–92). In Kakar's view, women either uphold a univocal normative order or deviate from it; there seems to be little recognition of a multiplicity of culturally valued strategies or perspectives for constructing selfhood and moral discourse.

A similar set of representations often defines the relationship between gender and sexuality in anthropological writing on South Asia, and a similar set of assumptions about women's subjectivity is often entailed. Both Sanskrit texts and vernacular oral traditions contain positive images of women as mother and as ritual partner and exhibit disdain and reproach for women as wives who are seen as sexually treacherous, sexually voracious, and polluting by virtue of their association with menstruation and childbearing (Bennett 1983; Kakar 1990: 17–20; Vatuk and Vatuk 1979b). These attitudes have undeniably serious implications both for women's self-perceptions and for the material and ideological relations of power in which they live their lives. But to assume that such characterizations define the limits of women's self-understandings and moral discourse is to ignore or silence meanings that are voiced in ritual songs and stories from Pahansu and Ghatiyali and in gestures and metamessages in ordinary language throughout northern India (Das 1988: 198), the existence of which indicates "the inadequacy of official kinship norms to give an exhaustive and definitive understanding of the sexuality of women" (202). If Indian women do unequivocally internalize certain admittedly prevalent South Asian views of female sexuality found both in texts and ordinary talk, as Patricia Jeffery, Roger Jeffery, and Andrew Lyon (1989) seem to assert, we would be justified in speaking of an ideological self-abasement. When, however, there are contextually shifting moral perspectives within a set of cultural traditions, the question of the relative force, the relative salience, and the relative persuasiveness of these discursive forms is of critical significance in the anthropological representation of the ideologies of gender and selfhood held by women and men. In the expressive traditions that we examine in chapters 2 and 4, women confront and voice their rejection of those devaluations of female sexuality, and they begin to comment critically on their implications for men's control over women's bodies and women's lives.

Characterizations of South Asian women as repressed and submissive are also half-truths in the sense that, at times, submission and silence may be conscious strategies of self-representation deployed when it is expedient to do so, before particular audiences and in particular contexts. There may often, in other words, be something of a discontinuity, a schism, between conventional representations and practices, on the one hand, and experience, on the other; certain discourses may be invoked and employed in particular circumstances, without exhausting the explanatory and evaluative possibilities within a given way of life (Jackson 1982: 30–31). But to say that a particular practice or a particular way of speaking is strategically deployed need not imply that it is motivated by individual sef-interest (de Certeau 1984: xi), that it is directed only toward political or economic ends, as Pierre Bourdieu's use of the term (1977) would suggest, or that it is disconnected from a set of culturally informed moral valuations. In his characterization of poetic discourse as "strategic," Kenneth Burke writes that literary texts may be thought of as adopting "various strategies for the encompassing of situations. These strategies size up the situations, name their structure and outstanding ingredients, and name them in a way that contains an attitude toward them" (1973: 1).[9] Burke suggests that the strategic aspects of poetic

9. My understanding of the relevance to anthropology of Burke's theoretical position owes much to conversations with Richard Herrell and to his work on gender identity in the United States (Herrell 1992).

discourse might be understood as exhibiting several of the properties of proverbs. A proverb takes its meaning not only from its overt imagery, its semantic content, the shared understandings it presupposes, but also from the context in which it is deployed, and the communicative functions it fulfills within a specific speech situation (Briggs 1985; Gossen 1973; Raheja 1993; Seitel 1977). Burke writes that "proverbs are *strategies* for dealing with *situations*" and that strategy here should be understood as an attitude, an evaluation, a perspective on a situation (1973: 296). Burke's critical writing continually stresses the multiplicity of strategies, of attitudes toward recurrent social situations that are created in literary discourse, paralleling the manner in which a proverbial utterance, in Hindi as in English, may be countered with another equally compelling proverb that evaluates the situation at hand in radically different moral terms. Like proverbs, the larger discursive forms we analyze here are invoked in particular circumstances and by particular positioned actors, as strategies in the construction of selfhood and relationship, gender and kinship, in Pahansu and Ghatiyali.[10]

In the preface to *Women, Androgynes, and Other Mythical Beasts* (1980), Wendy Doniger O'Flaherty writes that although her book is about images of women in the Hindu tradition, the relevant texts have all been composed by men. "If women composed their own mythologies," she goes on to say, "we do not have them." It is just this sort of image of the silent Indian woman that allows Kakar and Gayatri Chakravorty Spivak to see her as a passive assimilator of a one-dimensional and monologic set of cultural premises and moral perceptions.

In analyzing women's oral traditions and women's commentaries on them, it soon became apparent to us that women have in fact composed their own mythologies. Though they may not carry the authoritative weight of certain versions of the *Ramayana*,[11] women's songs and stories consistently compose ironic

10. De Certeau (1984:18–21) has also pointed out the analogies between proverbial enunciations and ways of using, manipulating, and recreating systems of meaning and valuation.

11. In fact, the many different *Ramayana* texts and oral renditions are not unanimous in depicting Sita as totally submissive to male authority. Variation on this point exists among the texts composed and performed by males (Lutgendorf 1991), and even more so in the *Ramayana* texts, in the form of song traditions,

and subversive commentaries on the representations of gender and kinship roles found in the epic texts, in male folklore genres, and in a good deal of everyday talk. This is not to suggest that women always and everywhere subvert North Indian kinship structures or discourses that place them in a subordinate position, or that they are equally inclined or empowered to do so. Rather, our work points to the polyvalent nature of women's discourse, and to the multiple moral perspectives encoded therein. When one listens to women in rural North India, Kakar's "formidable consensus" dissolves into a plurality of voices. In this book we attempt to discover how these varying interpretations of gender and kinship are situated in women's complexly figured identities, and how they shape the tenor of their everyday lives.

GENDER AND THE SUBALTERN VOICE: RESISTANCE, ACQUIESCENCE, AND WOMEN'S SUBJECTIVITY

The work of the *Subaltern Studies* historians has raised a series of critical questions concerning the existence of subtle modes of resistance to hegemonic forms of social and political hierarchy in South Asia. Their investigations focus on recovering the subaltern voice that has not generally been recognized or represented in historical writing. Although the six volumes of essays edited by Ranajit Guha and published under the title *Subaltern Studies* are concerned primarily with caste and class subalternity and resistance to colonial rule, several of the papers address the issue of gender and women's subjectivity from this historical perspective (e.g., Das 1989a; Guha 1987). These essays are subtle and provocative analyses. Yet several methodological and theoretical exigencies become apparent in these attempts to represent a gendered subaltern perspective.

The first is simply the inherent difficulty of retrieving the sub-

---

composed by women (Narayana Rao 1991). A sixteenth-century version of the epic composed in Telegu by the female poet Atukuri Molla also appears to speak of the vitality and strength of Sita more consistently than the male-authored renditions (Tharu and Lalita 1991:94–98). This heterogeneity of "tradition," and the alternative visions of female virtue to be found in these many *Ramayanas*, were ignored in the tremendously popular televised serial production of the *Ramayana* aired in India in 1987–88. Many Indian feminists have protested against the images of female subordination and female passivity depicted in the televised epic.

altern woman's voice from the South Asian historical archive, wherein there was little concern to preserve a record of such voices, the voices of ordinary and often illiterate women. Indeed, insofar as they did not speak in a voice agreeable to powerful males, women's voices were often quite literally *erased* from the historical record. In the early years of the twentieth century, Lt. Col. Charles Eckford Luard, an administrator serving in Central India, commissioned Indians serving under him to record women's songs "from the lips of the local people." In the margins of one of these handwritten records in the India Office Library, I found the following notation, made by an Indian serving under Luard: "This is quite obscene. I have therefore used pencil that this should be struck out if considered befitting" (Luard n.d.: 160). But, as we shall see in chapter 2, it is precisely through such supposedly "obscene" language that women voice potent critiques of prevailing gender ideologies. By shifting attention from the historical archive to ethnographic inquiry, then, we hope to reposition some of the theoretical and epistemological concerns of the *Subaltern Studies* scholars. We hope to grasp the relation between hegemonic discourses on kinship and gender, on the one hand, and women's subjectivity and agency, on the other, within the context of lives we have come to share, however marginally and intermittently, in Pahansu, Hathchoya, and Ghatiyali, and with reference to the language these particular women speak, a language we have struggled to recognize and translate in these pages, a language that is alive and not yet erased from all memory.

Such a repositioning is almost essential methodologically, given the limitations of the historical record, but it is also significant from a second, theoretical, standpoint. Spivak (1985c), Rosalind O'Hanlon (1988), and Veena Das (1989a) discuss a number of critical epistemological issues embedded in the subalternist project. Das, for example, points out that the term *subaltern* cannot refer to distinct and well-defined social groupings; rather, the term should be used with reference to certain kinds of perspectives on a cultural discourse or a set of social relationships (1989a: 324), perspectives that may employ reflexive devices to interrogate or subvert that dominant discourse (312) but that may not necessarily coalesce into a closed, unified, discrete, and knowable totality. In offering her critique of an essentialist view of subjectivity, Spivak has raised several caveats concerning the tendency of the *Subaltern Studies* scholars to posit a unified, consistent, and pristine subaltern consciousness, the tendency to create self-determination and continuity out of what may actually be heterogeneous determinations and discontinuous discourse (1985c: 10–15). Similarly, O'Hanlon suggests that the attempt to recover and represent the subjectivity of the subaltern and his resistance to hegemonic discourse has been predicated on an insufficiently problematized notion of "the self-originating, self-determining individual, who is at once a subject in his possession of a sovereign consciousness whose defining quality is reason, and an agent in his power of freedom" (1988: 191).[12] She argues that "the demand for a spectacular demonstration of the subaltern's independent will and self-determining power" has meant that the continuities between hegemonic discourse and subaltern culture have generally been ignored (213). She goes on to suggest that Guha (1983: 13), in speaking of the "sovereignty," "consistency," and "logic" of subaltern consciousness, has inadequately documented the limits of resistance, and the fact that the subaltern may at times speak from within the dominant discourse and at times stand outside and comment critically upon it (O'Hanlon 1988: 203, 219).[13]

12. These observations on the difficulties inherent in attempts to recover a subaltern subjectivity are analogous to those considered by de Lauretis (1984, 1986) with respect to the understanding of female subjectivity. The central problem is to articulate an understanding of subjectivity and experience that avoids, on the one hand, a totalizing and essentialist reading that sees subjectivity as *determined* by gender and, on the other hand, an overemphasis on free, rational intentionality. We share with de Lauretis a view of subjectivity as "a fluid interaction in constant motion and open to alteration by self-analyzing practice" (Alcoff 1988:425). The particular appropriateness of such a formulation for the understanding of South Asian selfhood and emotion is brilliantly illustrated by Trawick (1990).

13. But Guha has more recently, following Gramsci, written of the contradictory and fragmented nature of subaltern consciousness (Guha 1989). On this point, see also Arnold's discussion of the relevance of Gramsci's view of the contradictory nature of subaltern culture to peasant society in India (1984).

In a recent publication (1991), O'Hanlon has written explicitly of women's resistance to male-authored gender ideologies in nineteenth-century colonial India, and she has made the point that this resistance both critiques and perpetuates the dominant discourse. In the text she examines, a book written by Tarabai Shinde in 1882, she finds that this female author at times simply reverses essentializing male characterizations of female nature, instead of critiquing the very structure of patriarchy itself. I do not find this to be the case in the women's songs we consider in this volume. Rather, women contest the very notion of essential natures and the

Our ethnographic inquiries situate themselves within a similar set of epistemological concerns. We concur with Das's point that a subaltern perspective cannot be inextricably linked with concrete and invariable categories of persons, and with Spivak's and O'Hanlon's observations on the possible disunity and heterogeneity of subaltern subjectivity. The commentaries on kinship and gender evinced in women's oral traditions are dramatically different from the perspectives most frequently found in textual traditions and folklore genres performed by and for males. Yet, in everyday talk, women frequently speak from within the dominant discourse, and men may speak in terms set by the more muted discourse associated with women's speech genres.[14] It is precisely because men and women may shift from one perspective to another that we speak of strategic deployments of these varying discourses. Women may tend to use gender characterizations and valuations differently from men, but we do not find a unitary female voice opposed in all respects to a male discourse. Yet, in listening to women's voices in song, in story, and in ordinary talk, we become aware that there is a subversive discourse more likely to be invoked by women than by men. Our repositioning of the concerns of the *Subaltern Studies* scholars within an ethnographic inquiry permits us, then, not to "recover" a unitary subaltern voice unrecorded in the historical archive; it allows us, rather, to begin to recognize the discontinuity, the interpenetration of the hegemonic and the subversive, and their varied deployments, from moment to moment in everyday life. It permits us to ask questions concerning contextual shifts in meaning and value, sometimes indexed only by an ironic tone, a gesture, a pattern of rhyme in a wedding song. Sociality often finds its meaning in such evanescent subtlety, the embellishments and improvisations that provide the ground for creativity and resistance and

---

idea that domination arises from, say, the viciousness of male nature rather than from intricate structures of power that shape both male and female sensibilities. I have elsewhere made this argument explicitly and at greater length (Raheja 1991).

14. On the distinction between dominant and muted discourses and its relationship to issues of gender, see Ardener 1975. In these chapters, we use the word *muted* not to describe women's supposed silences but to allude to the fact that they may often be constrained from speaking overtly or publicly of their resistance to dominant ideologies.

that can only rarely be recovered from the historical archive. Ethnography is perhaps more likely than history to bear witness to such fluid and contextual creativity on the part of women who have all too often been denied the powers of literacy, and whose words have been erased from historical records when they proved unpalatable to those who did the writing. If in this book we direct our attention more to the resistance exhibited in expressive traditions than to the power relations that place women in subordinate positions, it is because we wish at first to counter colonial, and some anthropological and feminist, assumptions about the passivity of Indian women, just as the *Subaltern Studies* historians have generally had as their first priority the study of subaltern resistance, in order to question pervasive assumptions about peasant inertia, the internalization of structures of domination, and the "harmony" of Indian village society (Arnold 1984: 175).

KINSHIP AND GENDER

As anthropologists have come to reflect seriously on Levi-Strauss's observation, which he comes to only in the last paragraphs of *The Elementary Structures of Kinship*, that "woman could never become just a sign and nothing more, since even in a man's world she is still a person, and since insofar as she is defined as a sign she must be recognized as a generator of signs" (1969: 496),[15] we have become increasingly aware of the limitations of a perspective on kinship that attends only to the trails left by women as they move from natal home to conjugal home, weaving alliances between groups of male kinsmen (Das 1989b: 276; Kolenda 1984;

15. This isolated observation is of course at variance with Levi-Strauss's structural approach to the study of kinship systems, wherein systems of relationship are understood to construct themselves, as it were, behind the backs of actors, and wherein there is little concern with native experience and native theories of experience (Bourdieu 1977:4), multiple discursive possibilities, or individual intentions and strategies. Indeed, Spivak has rightly commented that if women had in fact been recognized as users of signs rather than as signs of a relationship between men, Levi-Strauss's theoretical edifice would have been seriously compromised (Spivak 1988:291n.45). With respect to South Asian anthropology, similar limitations characterize the work of Louis Dumont on caste (1980) and kinship (1957, 1966, 1986). For commentaries on such limitations insofar as the study of caste is concerned, see Raheja 1988a, 1988b, 1989; and with respect to kinship, see Trawick 1990:115–84.

March 1984; Meeker, Barlow, and Lipset 1986; Rubin 1975; Spivak 1985c: 356–60). We are reminded that as they are "given" or "exchanged" among kin groups, women seldom act or speak as if they were commodities, or signs rather than generators of signs (Holmberg 1989). They actively construct representations of marriage, gift giving, and kinship relationships, and these representations may often diverge dramatically from those generally invoked by men; and further, these alternative representations are frequently realized in particular kinship practices—marriage strategies, patterns of gift giving, terminological usages, deference behavior, and so forth—in which both men and women are involved. But in the totalizing projects of much ethnographic writing on kinship, these divergent discourses and divergent practices have often been ignored.

The Pahansu and Ghatiyali ethnography provides little evidence for unitary male or female perspectives on kinship relations (cf. Yanagisako and Collier 1987: 25–29). We find, rather, universes of discourse and universes of practice that tend to be drawn upon and used in different ways by men and women (Bourdieu 1977: 110, 122–23). Standard anthropological accounts of North Indian kinship speak in terms of a structured system of unequivocally defined relationships and an internally consistent and homogeneous cultural ideology stressing, first, the importance of patrilineally defined categories of kin (e.g., Mayer 1960; Parry 1979);[16] second, the hierarchical nature of the relationship between bride givers and bride receivers, its persistence through time to the following generation, and the importance of gift giving in relation to this enduring tie between groups of male agnates (Dumont 1966; Vatuk 1975); third, the idiom of marriage as *kanyādān* (the gift of a virgin), entailing the "complete dissimilation of the bride from her family of birth and her complete assimilation to that of her husband" (Trautmann 1981: 291; Inden and Nicholas 1977); and fourth, the necessary subordination of the bride to her husband and conjugal kin. In interview situations in

16. Vatuk, however, has presented exemplary ethnographic examples documenting the bilateral definitions of certain categories of kin in northern India (1975) and the uses of "matrilateral assymmetries" in urban North India (1971), and Jacobson (1977a) points out some of the ambiguities surrounding the rights of natal and conjugal kin with respect to a married woman. These studies provide important points of departure for the analyses of kinship set forth in these pages.

the villages in which we have worked, both men and women tend overwhelmingly to affirm the importance of these cultural constructions and in doing so seem to speak in a single voice. The ethnography from Uttar Pradesh and Rajasthan that we present in this study does not lead us to question the existence of such propositions in popular understanding; they are critical and pervasive aspects of local ideology and of power relations in vast regions of northern India, and they are embodied in many kinds of social practice.[17] If one fails to ask questions concerning the pragmatic deployment of such a discourse in everyday life, in ordinary speech, one might come to agree with Spivak's pronouncement that "the subaltern [as woman] cannot speak" in a language other than that of patriarchal authority (1985a: 130). Or one might with Spivak view North Indian women as having no identity apart from this dominant discourse:

> The figure of the woman, moving from clan to clan, and family to family as daughter/sister and wife/mother, syntaxes patriarchal authority even as she herself is drained of proper identity. In this particular area, the continuity of community or history, for subaltern and historian alike, is produced on (I intend the copulative metaphor—philosophically and sexually) the dissimulation of her discontinuity, on the repeated emptying of her meaning as instrument.
>
> (Spivak 1985c: 362)

In this book, we raise questions concerning the force, the persuasiveness, and the salience of dominant cultural propositions about patriliny, hierarchy, and women's subordination in everyday experience, and questions concerning the contexts in which they are likely to be invoked and who is likely to invoke them. We find that although neither men nor women would normally dispute these understandings of North Indian kinship relations in interview situations, they are clearly open to ironic, shifting, and ambiguous evaluations in the rhetoric and politics of everyday

17. For a discussion of some of the mechanisms through which these dominant propositions produce women as gendered subjects within the patrilineal and virilocal milieu of Indian society, see Dube 1988. But Dube also points out, at the end of her essay, that although the values and practices she considers are made to appear as part of a given and hence "natural" order of things, women are nonetheless able to question aspects of this order and their position within it.

language use, in strategies of marriage arrangement, and in certain genres of oral traditions, particularly those performed by women. Thus we must pay close attention to the contexts in which words are spoken. If we record only women's responses to our own questions, we may all too quickly come to the conclusion that they cannot speak subversively and critically, that their voices are muted by the weight of male dominance and their own acquiescence in the face of "tradition."

At least some of the speech genres used by women in Uttar Pradesh and Rajasthan tend more frequently than men's to stress the desirability of disrupting patrilineal unity in favor of a stress on conjugality; they speak of neutralizing hierarchical distinctions between bride givers and bride receivers, of the emotional significance to women of affinal prestations, of the enduring nature of a woman's ties to her natal kin and the shifting evaluations of marriage that this entails, and of the moral obligation to reject sometimes a subordinate role vis-à-vis one's conjugal kin. From the vantage point of such a discourse, patriliny, hierarchy, female subordination, and so on are seen not as aspects of a fixed and reified cultural system but as strategically invoked idioms in an ongoing negotiation of personhood and relationship that, like proverbial utterances, may often be countered with other contrasting idioms that evaluate the situation at hand in quite different moral terms. Indeed, as Rena Lederman points out, women's acts of resistance to men's definitions of social order "raise questions about the extent to which male ideology can be understood fully without appreciating how this ideology is an argument *against* women's ideas, rather than simply a positive, independent statement" (1980: 495–96).

While it will be obvious that the efficacious manipulation of these varying discourses in northern India depends to a great extent on one's position within a set of power relationships in which women may not inherit land, must move from natal village to conjugal village at marriage, and are generally expected to maintain a subordinate position relative to their husbands and conjugal kin, it is nonetheless apparent that women's self-perceptions are not reducible to the terms of the dominant discourse on kinship. And those self-perceptions, and the discourses in which they are constructed and negotiated, may subtly but distinctly alter the widely ramified networks of relationships in which both men and women live their lives.

LANGUAGE AND RESISTANCE: WHAT DO WOMEN DO WITH WORDS?

The shift in anthropology from a focus on culture as a fixed, internally homogeneous, and logically ordered totality to an emphasis on decentered, heterogeneous meanings negotiated and contested in social praxis is paralleled in linguistics by the shift away from a concern primarily with language as a formal abstract system, a structured grammar and semantic system (what de Saussure called *langue*) opposed to and distinct from speech (*parole*), the actualization of language in naturally occurring social and cultural contexts.[18] A "discourse-centered approach" to language and culture has been proposed as a perspective capable of encompassing attention to the agency of particularly positioned speakers and actors, to the relationship between culture as a system of shared meanings and culture as a set of contested and negotiated meanings, to the relationship of forms of discourse to the ongoing constitution of social life and social processes, and to the strategic use of forms of expression in everyday interactions. (See particularly Bauman 1986, Sherzer 1987a, and Urban 1991.) The linguistic significances of the term *discourse* relate in fact to a notion of praxis:

> Discourse is a level or component of language use, related to but distinct from grammar. It can be oral or written and can be approached in textual or sociocultural and social-interactional terms. . . . Discourse is an elusive area, an imprecise and constantly emerging and emergent interface between language and culture, created by actual instances of language in use and best defined specifically in terms of such instances. . . . Discourse includes and relates both textual patterning . . . and a situating of language in its natural contexts of use. Context is to be understood in two senses here: first, the social and cultural backdrop, the ground rules and assumptions of language usage; and second, the immediate, ongoing, and emerging actualities of speech events.
>
> (Sherzer 1987a: 296)

18. For an overview of the shift in anthropological theory, see Ortner 1984.

Attention to the emergent properties of praxis and discourse opens cultural and linguistic meanings to the circumstantiality of everyday life, the multiple interpretations, indeterminacies, and ambiguities therein, and the differing speech strategies of variously positioned speakers.

We wish here to begin to view North Indian women's relationship to language from such a perspective. We are less interested in the positivist enterprise of ascertaining the manner in which specific forms of speech behavior "reflect" gender differences than in the ways in which gender identities are created and negotiated in discourse.[19]

Joel Sherzer (1987a) suggests that it is in verbally artistic speech genres such as poetry, myth, magic, song, verbal dueling, and political rhetoric that the interface between language and culture is most salient and the creative possibilities of language most fully realized. He argues that to assume that features of social structure are somehow congealed into linguistic structures would in fact ignore the ways in which language use creates and recreates culture and the social parameters of everyday life. Sherzer in fact discusses several examples of such language use from northern India (drawing upon Tiwary 1968), pointing out that even in a society exhibiting overt and enduring social hierarchies verbal play may constitute a tactical negotiation of status and identity (Sherzer 1987a: 300–302). This discourse-centered approach, like praxis theory, views societies not primarily in terms of structural fixities but in terms of the processes through which relationships are constructed, negotiated, and contested.

How do these perspectives on the creativity of verbal play in everyday social life help us to understand women's relationship to language in northern India? Linguistic forms are strategic actions, and verbal interactions are often sites of struggle about gender, kinship, and power (Gal 1991: 176). In relation to questions of language and gender, Susan Gal has also pointed out that we need to focus not only on women's powerlessness and their "mutedness" but on the "processes by which women are ren-

19. For discussions of the limitations of the former approach to the study of language and gender, see Briggs 1992, Ochs 1992, and Sherzer 1987a, 1987b. Such an approach would, of course, be subject to the epistemological quandaries concerning the overdetermination of women's subjectivity discussed by de Lauretis (see n. 12 above).

dered 'mute' or manage to construct dissenting genres and resisting discourses" (190).

Roger Keesing (1985) provides an analysis of the micropolitics of women's speech about themselves and their society among the Kwaio of the Solomon Islands. He warns us that an anthropologist's failure to elicit from women reflective accounts of themselves and their place in a cultural tradition cannot be taken as evidence of their "muteness" or their uncritical acceptance of male ideology and male political hegemony. He argues that women's speech, like all speech, is produced in specific historical and micropolitical contexts, and that what women will say reflects the power relationships implicit in the elicitation situation, and their own perceptions of what their speech will accomplish. If we rely only on women's interview statements, or on our observations of women's public adherence to the norms of silence and submission, we run the risk of assuming that women are incapable of using verbal strategies to oppose that dominant ideology.

Precisely because the nature of power relations in northern India often prevents women from speaking in many political contexts and in the presence of senior male affines, women inevitably come to recognize that they must, as Das puts it, "learn to communicate . . . by non-verbal gestures, intonation of speech, and reading meta-messages in ordinary language" (1988: 198); and such communication often subverts the official language of the dominant discourse and subtly articulates a contrapuntal reading of gender and kinship relations.

Ordinary conversations in Pahansu and Ghatiyali are filled with such subversive communication. Women tend to deploy a distinctive set of proverbs, for example, as tokens of an alternative moral discourse (Raheja 1993). In the ethnographic descriptions contained in the following chapters, we are primarily interested, however, in certain relatively formal expressive genres performed by women in northern India. Ramanujan has written that the cultural traditions and verbal genres of South Asia are indissolubly plural and often contradictory, and that this plurality is organized both through context-sensitivity and through various forms of intertextuality (1989b: 189; see also 1986, 1989a). He goes on to suggest that a consideration of this context-sensitivity and reflexivity will enable us to go beyond grossly conceived frameworks (such as the distinction between a literate and written Great Tradition and an oral or folk Little Tradition) for the understanding of diversities, and to go beyond monolithic and totalizing conceptions, toward a comprehension of the points of closure and of openness in a textual or ethnographic domain (1989b: 191). Before his death, Ramanujan began to explore the reflexive worlds and the "counter-systems" he found in women's tales from South India (1991a). We find his observations to be a useful starting point for our own investigations of women's expressive traditions in North India.

While Ramanujan speaks of the plurality of verbal genres in South Asia, and Sherzer and Gal of the tactical uses of such discursive forms in the creation and negotiation of meaning in social life, it has also been suggested that the "muted" and often subversive social discourse of women is frequently embedded in such formal speech genres as songs, laments, jokes, poetry, and so forth (Warren and Bourque 1985; for some specific ethnographic examples, see Abu-Lughod 1986, Briggs 1992, Harrison 1989, Karp 1988, Narayan 1986, Seremetakis 1991, and Egnor 1986). Both T. O. Beidelman (1986) and Ramanujan (1986) stress the fact that such imaginative genres of folklore may enter into and transform the more dominant discursive frameworks of social life, and Margaret Trawick Egnor (1986) sets forth some provocative suggestions concerning the changes in cultural patterns that might potentially be instigated in songs sung by untouchable Paraiyar women of South India. Similarly, in emphasizing the interconnections between the social and the poetic, Richard Bauman (1986) attempts to understand verbal art as socially meaningful action.

We might contrast these positions and our perspective on the creative power of women's discourse in the negotiation of meaning with Stanley Tambiah's comment that critiques posed in North Indian women's songs might simply be "context-restricted 'rituals of rebellion' that leave the dominant male ideology more or less intact" (1989: 418). It was Max Gluckman (1963), of course, who argued that inversions of everyday behavior found in many "rituals of rebellion" has a socially cathartic significance, functioning to ensure that "conflicts" were enacted only in well-defined ritual contexts, allowing social unity and the dominant ideology otherwise to prevail in everyday life.

Guha has written at some length concerning ritual and linguistic inversions in India in *Elementary Aspects of Peasant Insurgency in Colonial India.* He shares Gluckman's perspective on these inversions and speaks of their predictability, conventionality, and recursivity as buttressing, rather than undermining, dominant patterns of traditional authority. "Ritual inversion," he writes, "stands for a continuity turned into sacred tradition by long recursive use under the aegis and inspiration of religion. As such, it represents the very antithesis of peasant insurgency. . . . For if the function of prescriptive reversal is to ensure the *continuity* of the political and moral order of society and *sacralize* it, that of peasant insurgency is to *disrupt* and *desecrate* it" (1983: 36). Guha goes on to speak of an "unquestioning obedience to authority" as characteristic of peasant "traditionalism" in India, and of outright rebellion as the only *real* semiotic break with the "traditional" codes governing relations of dominance and subordination. This sort of dichotomous thinking, which posits a rupture, an antithesis, between a fixed and invariant "tradition," on the one hand, and radical social transformation, on the other, essentializes and unifies what in fact seem to be polyphonic discursive formations within the "tradition" itself. The reflexivity and multiplicity of South Asian language, text, and ritual are thus elided, and the analysis does not capture the ways in which imaginative genres may provide alternative moral perspectives, serving as a ground for possible social transformation or for the contextual and strategic deployment of varying discourses by particularly positioned actors. Resistance and tradition may not inevitably be at odds with each other. Though the women we know in Uttar Pradesh and Rajasthan do in many ways assent to the dominant ideologies of gender and kinship, they also sing of their resistance to these ideologies, and we have tried to comprehend some of the ways in which they may come to insert this stance of resistance into their everyday lives.

In her discussion of ritual and festive sexual inversions in preindustrial Europe (1975), Natalie Zemon Davis has observed that while such reversals in some ways renewed and reinforced established hierarchies, there was at the same time some transformative spillover into everyday life. Comic inversions and play with gender imageries, she suggests, prompted new ways of reacting to systems of power and kept alive alternative ways of thinking about family structure. The women's expressive traditions we translate in the chapters that follow have similar overall functions; they may at some levels serve to perpetuate gender inequalities, but they also render conceivable and may indeed sanction women's active resistance. The "hidden transcript" found in women's speech genres can, we think, be viewed "as a condition of practical resistance rather than a substitute for it" (Scott 1990: 191). The active rebellion that may at one moment be impractical or impossible may at another moment become plausible precisely because the idea of social transformation has been nourished in proverbs, folk songs, jokes, rituals, legends, and language (Scott 1985: 37–41).

These perspectives on the multiplicity of cultural discourses, on the strategic uses to which they may be put, and on verbally artistic speech genres as potential loci of a language of resistance are critical vantage points for our interpretations of many aspects of women's language and women's oral traditions in rural North India. Far from speaking only in a language dominated by males, the women we have come to know imaginatively scrutinize and critique the social world they experience and give voice to that vision in a poetic language of song and story; as they do so those songs and stories may enter their lives and shift, however slightly or however consequentially, the terms in which their lives are led.

As we translated the stories and songs told and sung by the women we knew in Pahansu, Hathchoya, and Ghatiyali, we began to see that these expressive genres vividly and articulately depicted the most poignant experiences in women's lives—leaving one's natal home and going off to the unknown house of a new husband, the difficulties of submitting to the authority and domination of the husband's senior kin, the joys of intimacy and sexuality, giving birth, a husband's betrayal, the pleasures of adorning oneself with jewelry and fine cloth, and so forth. But we also began to see that despite this diversity of genre, region, language, and specific ritual or seasonal context in which a song is sung or a story told, these expressive genres converged in addressing several interrelated sets of contradictions within the dominant gender and kinship ideologies of northern India. The contradictions that women's speech genres especially comment upon are those that entail an implicit or explicit splitting of female identities, splittings that in every case work to the disadvantage of women. This book examines these various contradictions concerning women's identities, and the dissident, ironic, and resistant stances that women take up in relation to them.

Chapter 2 focuses on one of the most commonly postulated and widely ramified split images of women in Hindu South Asia: the deep and pervasive split between the destructive and threatening sexual potency of women as wives, on the one hand, and the beneficent, procreative, and positive capacities of women as mothers, on the other. Women as mothers contribute to the continuance of the male patriline, while women as sexual partners are seen to disrupt patrilineal solidarity among men. This ideological splitting has a number of practical and material consequences in women's lives. Because it is viewed as dangerous and volatile, female sexuality must be constantly controlled and brought under the surveillance of male kin; women must assume a posture of sexual reticence and shame and of withdrawal from any situations in which they might come into contact with men who are not close kin.

Several recent studies of women's lives in India assume that women have internalized this ideological split and are thus shameful of their bodies and their sexuality. Though women are certainly silent on the subject of sexuality and the pleasures of the body in many situations of everyday life and when the anthropologist elicits in an interview their views on these matters, the words of Rajasthani women's songs tell us, in genres created by women, of another perspective. In these songs there is evidence of an exuberant sexuality, a positive valuation of sexual pleasures, and a conjoining of eroticism and birth giving that undermine and resist that split between sexuality and fertility posited in the dominant ideology. In subverting such split images of female identity, women are at the same time questioning that authoritative discourse of male control over female sexuality and female lives.

A second contradiction within North Indian gender ideologies concerns women's transfer from natal home to conjugal home at marriage. In her natal home, a woman does not veil her face and remain silent in the presence of men, she need not show particular deference to senior kin, and she is not obliged to perform arduous domestic labor. This comparative freedom ends when she is married and moves to her *sasurāl,* her husband's home. Though she is expected to transfer her loyalties from natal home to conjugal home upon her marriage, she is nonetheless often viewed as an outsider there, one who has the capacity to alienate her husband from his natal kin, precisely because of her sexual powers. Thus attempts may be made to curb a too rapidly developing conjugal intimacy, in the interests of maintaining the solidarity of the husband's patrilineal kin. The abrupt ending of the pleasures of her life in her natal home, coupled with this devaluation of the conjugal bond, may place the young wife in a situation of emotional turmoil and powerlessness. No longer "one's own" to her natal kin nor yet "one's own" in her *sasurāl,* she may come to feel a profound sense of isolation. In talk about the gifts given to her by a woman's natal kin, in songs, and in women's readings of genealogically ambiguous kinship relations, the analyses in chapter 3 discern a critically ironic female commentary on the split in a woman's identities as daughter and sister, on the one hand, and as wife, on the other, and on the contradiction in a kinship ideology that makes her "foreign" (*parāyī*) to her natal kin and yet still alien to her husband's.

This ironic stance is one voiced specifically by women speaking as daughters and as sisters, though all women in a neighborhood or kin group sing the songs together. But there are other songs that give voice to the woman speaking specifically as wife. Chapter 4 examines such songs, which stress not the persistence of a woman's natal ties but the necessity of establishing intimate conjugal bonds even if this entails a deemphasis of patrilineal solidarities and a curtailment of the power of a husband's senior kin over the wife. These songs are more openly subversive than those translated in chapter 3; they also involve powerful critiques of the norm of wifely silence and submission that are found in so many other South Asian expressive traditions. Taken together, then, the songs presented in chapters 3 and 4 are seen as interrogations of that dominant discourse that severs the continuity between a woman's life as daughter and her life as wife and daughter-in-law and that renders her powerless in her *sasurāl.*

Chapter 5 is a study of a single Rajasthani oral narrative, the tale of the "jungli rani," which is related by women as part of worship activities. The tellers of this story are concerned with false assumptions about female nature, an externally imposed split between female virtuosity and female virtue that is grounded in the idea that independent and powerful women are intrinsically dangerous and destructive. The tale of the jungli rani challenges this supposition and rejects such dichotomizing of power and virtue, which all too frequently succeeds in silencing and disempowering women.

Chapter 6 tells the story of a storyteller. Shobhag Kanvar of Ghatiyali is a skilled teller of tales and a woman possessing knowledge of ritual and healing that rivals that of any man in her community. She is the narrator of the tale of the jungli rani translated in chapter 5, and just as that story reads as an oppositional commentary on a discourse that imposes untenable splits in female identity, so too does the story of Shobhag Kanvar's life read as a series of strategies that successfully negotiate the whirlpools and the shoals of this discourse. In rejecting the imposed dichotomization of female identity that says that a woman cannot simultaneously pursue her own aims as an independently acting religious adept and remain a virtuous woman, Shobhag Kanvar has challenged masculine authority along with the discourse that views female agency and female independence with suspicion and with fear. We see her and the other women whose strategies we have tried to explicate in these pages as inserting the resistance found in song and story into their everyday lives and practically (as well as poetically) challenging the cultural discourse encoding female subordination.

The words that we have attempted to translate and to understand are diverse and heterogeneous. There is no single South Asian female voice, no single female consciousness, that unequivocally rejects or accepts prevailing North Indian ideologies of gender and kinship. There are many voices, of women in varied kinship, class, and caste positionings. Yet the expressive genres from Uttar Pradesh and Rajasthan that we have tried to understand do converge in viewing the imposed splits between sexuality and virtue, between natal loyalties and conjugal ties, and between female power and female virtue as essentially contestable cultural forms.

2

Sexuality, Fertility, and Erotic Imagination in Rajasthani Women's Songs

Students of South Asian society, mythology, and psychology frequently portray the cultural image of Hindu women as ambivalently construed and inherently split.[1] Variously characterized, this split image is generally grounded in two linked perceptions. The first of these is that for Hindus there exists a deep disjunction between women's sexual potency and their procreative and nurturing capacities as respectively dangerous and essential to men. Contrasting forms of the great goddess reveal this split, writ large in terms of destructiveness and beneficence. The solitary and wild dance of blood-drinking, gruesome, disheveled Kali threatens the cosmos; but stately, beautiful, well-groomed Lakshmi —paired with and tamed by a divine mate—brings prosperity to the home.[2]

1. Some works that present various aspects of the split-image theory of South Asian females, highlighting different dimensions of its social and cultural sources and consequences, include Amore and Shinn 1981:26–27; Das 1976a; Druvaranjan 1989; Dumont 1975:213; Fruzzetti 1982:31; Hershman 1977; Jacobson 1977b, 1978; Vatuk 1982b; Vatuk and Vatuk 1979b; and Wadley 1977. Three such accounts to which I give particular attention here are Bennett 1983, Kakar 1978, and O'Flaherty 1980. Hansen (1988), Robinson (1985), and Sax (1991) attempt in diverse and illuminating ways to develop less dualistic configurations of South Asian females, drawing on various dimensions of popular culture.

2. For characterizations of these well-known Hindu goddesses, see Kinsley 1987:19–34, 116–31. For a discussion of a cross-culturally apparent split "at the level of myth, religion, and high literature" between "sex/sensuousness and maternity/motherliness" see Friedrich 1978. In India, however, even at the mythological level an analysis of these images in terms of opposition distorts their meaning. Kali is, after all, adored and worshiped: see the marvelously titled *Grace and Mercy in Her Wild Hair* (Sen 1982). See also Coburn 1982 and Hiltebeitel 1988 for divine female multiplicity not reducible to splits. See Erndl 1993 for a spirited argument against the use of dualisms (especially Babb 1970) to interpret Hindu goddesses. Any Rajasthani villager will readily pronounce all goddesses to be manifestations of one Goddess; Babb (1976) and Nicholas (1982) convey ways evident splits merge in popular Hinduism of other regions.

The second notable aspect of a split female image derives from women's several strongly contrasting domestic and ritual roles within the kinship system. Among these roles, those sets that differ most strikingly are daughters and sisters, on the one hand, and wives and sons' wives, on the other. The following two chapters discuss some ways that women consciously bridge and undermine such splits in manipulating kin relationships. According to pure split-image theories, wives are in a double bind: they should be fertile and thus must be sexually active; simultaneously they must be absolutely chaste, in terms not only of marital fidelity but of sexual reticence.[3] This problematic chastity of wives evokes anxieties recreating the conceptual split between sexuality and fertility at the human level.

Without denying the strong and pervasive foundations in South Asian culture for these contrasting dimensions of female nature, I seek here to contribute an alternative and complementary view. This view explicitly and happily links erotic union with procreation and birth. Concomitantly, I propose another, equally self-evident notion: although to be a daughter, sister, bride, daughter-in-law, and mother certainly demands varying behaviors, women playing their multiple parts as they pass through life stages and between natal and marital homes do not necessarily perceive them as ultimately conflicted. The material presented in this chapter most directly concerns the apparent conflict or opposition between women's sexuality and fertility, specifically in the context of rural, Hindu North India. But I shall also touch on women's kin roles, particularly to consider the presumed incongruence between active sexual interest and motherhood in a good wife.

My argument in this chapter draws solely on women's songs recorded in Ghatiyali, the Rajasthani village where I lived from September 1979 through March 1981 and to which I returned for a few weeks in the winter of 1987–88.[4] Although I was not there

3. Jacobson (1978) portrays one woman's life lived according to this ideal. Jacobson's "chaste wife" is not a particularly happy woman, but she is proud of herself and explicitly proud of the contrast between her own success at chastity and the majority of women's, including her own daughter's, deviations from such an ideal.

4. My colleague Joseph Miller settled in this village in January 1979; thus our joint coverage of village events spanned a continuous two years and three months. As a folklorist, Joe recorded and had transcribed what amounted to hundreds of women's songs, and I have benefited greatly from access to his collec-

to do research on women or folklore, the interpretations I offer here draw shape and substance from twenty-one months of fieldwork, and frequent participation in the performance contexts of the songs I examine. These oral traditions, although hardly oblivious to the splits imposed by women's several roles in society and men's attitudes toward them, strikingly show female self-images that are simultaneously sexy and motherly, that explicitly celebrate continuities between erotic playfulness and procreation. Sometimes this celebration remains clearly within the bounds of marriage; sometimes it bursts through to more free-floating, promiscuous modes. Even in the latter case, the songs and their contexts deliver a cheerful and creative, rather than angry and destructive, portrait of womankind.[5]

First I exemplify some manifestations of the split-image paradigm as variously rendered by three scholars with different disciplinary orientations. Then I describe the sources of my alternative view, exploring these materials in two segments. In the first, I describe the use of one image—that of the "wrap" (*oṛhnī*), a garment essential to all married and adult women—in several genres of women's songs. In the second I offer a more general discussion of birth, sexuality, and erotic sensibilities as interwoven themes in the same corpus of traditional lore. In conclusion I stress the performative, "emergent" character of female self-imagery vitally produced in folklore.[6]

SPLIT IMAGES

Not all who write dualistic descriptions of South Asian female nature perceive the split as falling along exactly the same lines. Here I will briefly sketch, and certainly oversimplify, the cases made by three writers: a psychoanalyst, a Sanskritist and historian of

---

tions, both in the field and since returning. Songs that Joe recorded are marked with an asterisk after the title; all translations are my own.

5. For the regenerative quality of women's sexuality and its relation to Rajasthani villagers' ideas about death see Gold 1988a. Marglin (1981, 1985a, 1985b) develops a powerful argument for the positive, vital, and creative aspects of female sexuality in Hindu thought. See also Blanchet 1984:43, 47 for positive associations of women with communal fertility in rural Bangladesh that emerge even in the negative context of the author's focus on the polluting aspects of female reproductive processes.

6. For innovative, subversive, and political qualities of artistic, oral performances see, for example, Basso 1985; Bauman 1977, 1986; Egnor 1986; Limon 1981.

religions, and an anthropologist. These offer three lucid representations of a dominant vision of South Asian femaleness—a vision to which the authors of this book pose certain challenges. I do not present these sketches in order to attack their authors' unquestionable scholarship and insight, only to test their totalizing impact.

By speaking of images and visions I perpetuate a visual discourse that seems, or I should say appears, intrinsic to my subject. Split images may indeed derive from watching, rather than listening to, women. They may be based on assumptions of female voicelessness that subject women readily to definitions by others. South Asian women are too often perceived as veiled figures acting out graceful pantomimes of submission and debasement. Later in this chapter my aim will be to hear in their unmuffled voices explicitly worded expressions of power and pleasure.

Sudhir Kakar, a psychoanalyst with an anthropological bent, has in his examination of Hindu mythology and culture highlighted a prominent disjunction between the images of a good mother and a bad mother—the former all-nourishing, the latter threatening (1978: 79–112).[7] Underlying Kakar's portrayal of the divided perception of females is an idealized purity and chastity set against a dread of "lustful and rampant" sexuality. The source of the bad mother's lust Kakar locates in a general cultural repression of female sexuality that then becomes displaced onto the fragile egos of male children. Thus develops a terror of the larger-than-life, sexually aggressive, potentially destructive goddess.

Kakar does not claim that women share the experiences that, for men, shape split female images. While he does give attention to the development of female as well as male psychological complexes, and in fact attempts to follow the life course of a girl through marriage and motherhood (71–79), his sources—beyond Sanskrit literature—are for the most part secondhand, largely male-authored ethnography.[8] In any case, Kakar culls his most vivid analytic imagery from Hindu myth.

Along with many others, Kakar finds Lord Rama's consort Sita

7. Kakar's first book (1978), the subject of my discussion here, has had considerable influence on subsequent scholarship, although it has not gone unchallenged; see Kondos 1986 for a vigorous refutation and Derne 1988 for a faithful defense of Kakar's viewpoint.

8. Roy (1979) offers a salubrious Jungian alternative to Kakar's Freudian imagery in her treatment of women's life stages.

of the pan-Indian epic *Ramayana* tradition to be the personification of ideal womanhood "for both men and women in Hindu society" (63). She is forgiven (for sins never committed) by Rama after he sees his sons for the first time—presumably transforming his view of her sexuality from dangerous to virtuous.[9] Tales of Devi, or Durga—another form of the mother goddess, less frightening in appearance than Kali but nevertheless uncontrolled by any male—demanding self-castration from Shiva as sacrificial food support the image of "maternal threat" (102).

Some of Kakar's more recent work, especially his volume on sexuality (1990), draws on a much wider range of sources, including life histories, cinema, and folklore. In these he finds much evidence that women desire intimacy, but concludes that males do not share this desire, and that women are inevitably disappointed. He has not revised his bleak view of South Asian female sexuality and its potential for fulfillment. He continues, moreover, to ground his analysis in the split-image mode, speaking of an "age-old yet still persisting cultural splitting of the wife into a mother and a whore," and claiming that although women may be honored as ritual partners and mothers, "as a female sexual being . . . the patriarchal culture's horror and scorn are heaped upon the hapless wife" (1990: 17).[10]

Wendy Doniger O'Flaherty (1980) depicts and explains opposing types of goddesses more fully than does Kakar. She traces from the Upanishads a split in Hindu myth between dominated "goddesses of the breast" and dominating "goddesses of the tooth," or genitals (90–91). This split she also formulates as the sacred cow and the profane mare (239–80) or the fertile mother and the erotic whore (247–49). She suggests that such a mythological split is reflected in behavior patterns that in turn resonate in later myths, thus proposing a more complex, dialectical inter-

9. The *Ramayana*'s popularity has recently been boosted by a television maxiseries that has drawn severe criticism from Indian feminist activists for its portrayal of female passivity.

10. I am very grateful to Sudhir Kakar for reading and commenting on an earlier draft of this chapter. He elegantly contrasted his "analytic eye" as more prone to see things negatively with the "anthropological eye (and heart) [that] dwells in a 'roseate light'" (personal communication 1990). I have amended some of my discussion of Kakar's work on the basis of his thoughtful comments, and I apologize to him for any remaining injustice done here to his very compelling writings.

relationship between the natures of deities and humans than psychological projection.

Cow worship O'Flaherty explains as the worship of a nonerotic, fertile, nourishing female, while self-sacrificial devotion to a nonfertile, erotic Tantric goddess (the mare transformed) offers risky access to power for a devotee adept. Note that the mother/whore or fertile/erotic split does not quite jibe with Kakar's good mother/bad mother paradigm, since presumably neither the erotic whore nor her Tantric transformation is a mother at all. O'Flaherty does state that Devi "in her full form embodies both aspects of female divinity" (91). But the goddess gets split by her worshipers. And there is a sense that most of these worshipers —certainly those who authored the Sanskrit texts that are O'Flaherty's staple sources—are male.[11]

In the case of Lynn Bennett's *Dangerous Wives and Sacred Sisters,* however, the informants are women. Bennett spent many years in Nepal and clearly has an open, warm, and sympathetic attitude toward the high-caste women with whom she lived and worked. Bennett attempts to show how social and symbolic splits in female roles and identities are mutually reinforcing. Although she notes these Nepali women's fondness for jokes about "the phallic nature" of bananas and cucumbers (1983: 258 n. 18), and although many of her informants are frankly earthy in their references to sexual activities and appetites, Bennett has chosen not to focus on these relaxed and humorous attitudes toward female sexuality.

Instead, she is primarily concerned with contrasting two opposing perceptions of women in kinship complexes, which she labels "patrifocal" and "filiafocal" and which pertain to the respective roles of wife and sister. Thus she contrasts the sexuality of wives in their husbands' homes, necessary to increase the patriline but requiring vigilant control, with the asexuality of married women in relation to their natal families (241). All over South Asia the new, young wife has little status and power in her mari-

11. O'Flaherty suggests, provocatively, that women may have made "an oral contribution to the tales that were ultimately written down by men" (1986:11). In a forthcoming book on "sexual masquerades" this author (now publishing under the name Doniger) plans to pursue across cultures and genders the linked themes of splitting, doubling, and trading identities; here her interest in the psychological dimensions of split and double identities in myth and literature takes precedence over any focus on South Asia or on women (personal communication 1989).

tal home and looks forward to the freedom and relief from housework drudgery that she experiences on visits to her parents. When she is around, a husband's sister may be at times a cruel taskmaster to her brother's bride. Bennett locates the source of this status difference squarely in the wife's acknowledged sexuality.

In her conclusion Bennett notes that, like the title of her book, the oppositions and mediations she proposes are "essentially the Hindu male's perspective on women." And she agrees that women "must somehow integrate and internalize two different roles and valuations of the self" (316). Why then does she draw her portrait so dualistically? Certainly the voices of her informants, whom she often allows to speak at length, do not always convince us of the stark contrasts drawn in the analysis.

Bennett's polarized view of female nature, I would suggest, derives not so directly from women themselves as from the oppositions she initially defines as central to South Asian culture. Her work begins with dualities: the world of flux (*samsāra*) versus liberation from birth and death (*mukti*), householder versus ascetic, and purity versus pollution are among what she calls central oppositions (34–51).[12] It is Bennett's concern to understand the ritual and social life of women in terms of these binary tensions that leads her then to focus on striking absolute splits in women's roles. By doing so she neglects investigating the many ways that women, playing their multiple, responsive roles, may also forge for themselves and voice a sense of unified identity.

One further point from Bennett helps to summarize the three distinct but parallel analytic views that I have sketched. Bennett observes that motherhood mediates between the two opposed identities of sister and wife. "Female sexuality is not denied in the mother as it is symbolically in the sister and the daughter" (255). Motherhood, then, purifies dangerous wives and makes their sexuality auspicious instead of dangerous. This echoes Kakar's observation that Rama accepts Sita as a mother. It also recalls O'Flaherty's dominating "goddess of the breast" (or docile cow) as an unambiguously beneficent form of female power.

12. Here of course she follows Dumont (1975), espousing his view of the structural oppositions that define social relations in Hindu culture.

Although Kakar, O'Flaherty, and Bennett do not formulate the split female image in exactly congruent terms, they all, in fact, describe similar profound disjunctions. These are related to discontinuities between female beings' (women's or goddesses') sexuality and their fertility, or among their various roles as erotic partners, wives, and mothers. All three arguments—even Bennett's, which is based on extensive fieldwork—draw heavily on mythic images of the feminine. And, for all three authors, woman as genetrix is a critical fulcrum. In Kakar's analysis, the mother image can swing either way, presenting protective and nourishing or destructive, devouring, and sexual aspects. O'Flaherty also contrasts milk-giving cow mothers with blood-eating types, connecting the latter with myths of the toothed vagina. Thus for both Kakar and O'Flaherty maternal sexuality tends to be associated not with woman's nourishing but rather with her terrifying aspects.

Bennett points to similar contrasts in analyzing goddess mythology (indeed she draws frequently on O'Flaherty's earlier work). She suggests, significantly, that women are less inclined than men to worship blood-eating goddesses, preferring to give their devotion to female deities with whom they share painful but ultimately positive life-cycle experiences (1983: 306). Bennett finds in the social universe of high-caste Nepalis that the mother is singularly beneficent, her sexuality transformed and acceptable. For mortals if not for goddesses, then, motherhood may offer a solution to women's ambiguous status, rather than further conflicts; here there is no bad mother.[13]

The split-image approach to South Asian women derives largely from the male point of view. Although Bennett at various illuminating moments does present a feminine perspective in fragments, none of these authors claim to give women's view of women. In particular, none deal directly with how women may be able to understand their own sexuality, not viewing themselves as lust-maddened demonesses but simply as participants in a society strongly oriented toward fertility.

13. See Erndl 1989:243 for the Hindu aphorism "A mother can never be a bad mother," which is significantly quoted by the lusty deity Bhairo in praise of the great goddess after she has decapitated him.

The perspective I shall offer here, drawing on Rajasthani women's oral traditions of celebration and worship, is arguably a women's perspective on women.[14] But it is also a nonliterate or folk perspective that contrasts with textual, Sanskritic traditions. As such, I believe it is shared by men.[15] Rural North India is by and large a highly sexually segregated society, but although sexual segregation sets the formal tone of social interaction, it does not preclude many forms of social intercourse. Women may not sing with men, but they often sing at them and very often in close proximity to them. I fully concur with Bennett's view that women's worlds and worldviews should not be treated as separately construed and separately analyzable from men's. Indeed, I would argue that those positive, unified constructions of female being and power available in women's oral performance traditions often complement—although they may also significantly subvert, as we see in chapter 3—the male-generated order of things.

Rajasthani folk culture, transmitted in women's songs and stories, supplies many images of females that are simultaneously seductive and fertile, erotic and domestic, and positive. In striking contrast to Kakar's bleak portrayal of repressed female sexuality, this lore gives an impression of women as sexually playful and exuberant, taking pleasure in their own bodies and celebrating their bodies' capacities both for erotic engagement and for painful but fruitful birth giving. It displays, moreover, an erotic imagination both poetic and humorous, ranging from mundane, earthy metaphors to pure fancy.

14. The introduction and essays—especially those by Daniel, Egnor, and Wadley—in Wadley 1980c are important contributions to providing a more multidimensional and female-generated view, but they treat only Tamil women. This is also the case with Egnor 1978 and McGilvray 1982. Wadley (1978) points to and demonstrates the uses of oral traditions for deriving women's self-perceptions in North India. Henry (1975) and Jacobson (1975, 1982) report on bawdy singing without extensive analysis. Jacobson (1978) and Roy (1975) present women's life histories, also important sources for their own perspective.

15. Interestingly, modern Indian literature, authored by males, sometimes presents a merged rather than split vision of woman's sexuality and fertility. In the short story "Married Women," for example, Rakesh (1975) describes a young wife living apart from her husband for the sake of a job, whose erotic reveries are entirely fused with her intense desire for a child. Murthy's novel *Samskara* contains this image of a desired woman: "Not utterly black, nor pale white—her body the colour of the earth, fertile, ready for seed, warmed by the early sun" (1976:36).

SOURCES: ROMANCE AND ABUSE IN CHORUSED CONVERSATIONS

One dark moon night in spring I joined a group of women, mostly of the Potter caste, in a house neighboring my own where they had gathered to sing worshipful songs in order to please the spirits of dead children (Gold 1988a: 72–65).[16] After they had sung the requisite five songs and thrown in a few praise songs of the goddess and other local deities for good measure, the women were in no hurry to disperse. Feeling expansive—plied by their wealthy hostess with milky tea and brown sugar and excited by the novel presence of me and my tape recorder—they offered to sing for my benefit some songs special to the season called *keśyā*.

The tunes they proceeded to perform sounded very different from the previous gentle lullabies for baby ghosts, and there was a lot of giggling and wisecracking, at my expense, in between songs. I wasn't able to follow the word-for-word meanings but easily perceived a drift toward bawdiness. When I inquired—with deliberately exaggerated naïvete—whether my male, Brahman research assistant would be able to explain these songs to me the serenaders answered with virtual gales of laughter. A woman eventually helped me translate that night's recording, and it was quite a revelation. Some songs abused husbands in very strong language, and others praised lovers for their sexual capacities.

The Potter women had sung more than the promised *keśyā*, a genre named after the opening word of each verse, meaning "illicit lover" or "red flower." These *keśyā* were among the milder verses I recorded that night:

1. *Keśyā*

Keśyā, I brought a skirt from Agra, Lover,
and a wrap from Sanganeer;
Lover, through the wrap the whole body shows,
through the veil the fair cheeks show.
Bite, bite the whole body,
Don't bite the cheeks or husband will beat you.[17]

16. The lunar calendar that structures ritual life in rural North India divides each month into bright and dark halves, with the new moon and the full moon often marked by particular observances. Ghost deities are traditionally worshiped on the new moon night.

17. The Appendix provides transliterations of all translated songs in the order in which they are cited. I have generally attempted to transmit evocative "flavor"

At this point the significance of the revealing wrap had not yet struck me, but I was generally shocked and almost dismayed by the shattering of my own preconceptions about Hindu women. Where were their famed modesty, shame, and sexual innocence? Although I had already heard rumors of errant wives during my stay in the village, I had no evidence of actual adulterous liaisons, nor had I noted any awareness of the pleasures that would make adultery attractive. Those who spoke of sex at all portrayed it as something accomplished as rapidly as possible during that rare moment of privacy that couples in a joint-family household must await.

But these women appeared to be singing about flirtation, enticement, erotic bites, exciting entanglements. They were also, as another verse performed that night demonstrates, imagining the pleasures of a less confined setting for their amours:

2. *Keśyā*
If you want to fuck, go up on the hill, Lover,
If you want to fuck, go up on the hill;
From up there you can see Delhi and Agra.

Actually when they sang this for me they thoughtfully inserted "North America," but I later heard it many times with these two glamorous North Indian cities named. The fact that sex up on the hill with a view—an experience remote from ordinary existence—was gleefully imagined by these stolid Potters' wives provoked a gradual rethinking of my understanding of female sexuality in Indian culture.

Almost all women's songs either directly address a specified listener, as the illicit lover in *keśyā*, or, still more commonly, represent verbal interactions among different persons that might be described as alternating voices. However, as the songs are generally performed, these separate voices are in no way highlighted or distinguished. Indeed, as long as my foreign ears were unable to take in the meaning of sung words, I had no idea that the chorused songs I heard and recorded were so often made up of

---

rather than to execute perfectly literal, word-for-word renderings of these poetic texts. Moreover, if I am translating blatantly blunt terms, I use English equivalents (e.g., *chodnā* means "to fuck," not "to have sex").

questions and responses, spirited arguments, or suggestive flirtations. Usually, the speakers' identities and the sequence of their exchange are simply understood—indeed obvious to the cultural insider—from the content of their respective statements. Sometimes the songs have a narrator's voice and employ dialogue markers.

On the same night that I first heard *keśyā*, addressing the lover without providing his response, I also recorded the following lines in the form of an insult for me (Ainn-bai, or "Timothy's wife," as I had given them my ex-husband's name):

3. *Gālī*
That lewd hussy Timothy's wife lifted a load, yes![18]
She climbed on his chest and pissed on his mustache.
Yes-oh-yes!
She climbed on his chest and pissed on his mustache.
Yes-oh-yes!
Get away wanton woman, what have you done?
Yes-oh-yes!
I'm afraid of the dark, old man.
Yes-oh-yes!
If I did not wake you, you would not take me to piss.
Yes-oh-yes!
If you did not wake me, I would not take you to piss.
Yes-oh-yes!
That hussy Ainn-bai is bad too!

This outrageous and seminonsensical ditty, like most *gālīs*, is sung by women about one another, with different husbands' names substituted. Belted out in chorus with comradery and hilarity, it includes an antagonistic interchange between spouses. One woman explained to me that the husband has awakened his wife for sex. She takes a tricky revenge upon him for disturb-

18. This was the final song of the evening and began slowly after much chatter and laughter. The beginning of the first line was sung slowly in solo, as if trying something out, but by the middle of the line several voices joined in, and it is difficult to be sure of the words. It was transcribed *dārī ra dārī ra ṭīmalṭī bāḷī lūṅṭī bhī ūṅchī haṅ*. I was advised that *lūṅṭī* should have been written *lūṅchī*—a term for "lewd woman" that appears frequently in folklore and here would be echoing and reinforcing *dārī*. However, *lūṅṭī* could be the feminine verb of *lūṅṭno*, meaning not only "to rob" but "to have sexual intercourse," according to the dictionary. In that case, the line could mean "She had sex and lifted a load"—the load perhaps being her husband's body, or her own. After this line the chorused enunciation is loud and clear.

ing her sleep by assuming a dominant position that could be a prelude to more sexual activity (which incidentally I often heard women euphemize as *bātchit*, or conversation)—and then performing a rude, childish, unlikely act. Grammatically this interpretation is difficult to construe because "If I did not wake you" has a feminine verb form, and "If you did not wake me" has a masculine one, implying that she has awakened him.[19] Either way, bantering antagonism and active sexuality combine here, and the foreign listener with her suspiciously absent spouse is included in the jolly circle of self-proclaimed "bad" (*khoṭī*) women.

Women's songs are filled with verbalized expressions of misunderstandings and debates, conflicts and confusions, of which the preceding example is perhaps a peculiar example. But there are no exceptions to the choral unity that overlies these. What is the meaning of this harmonized multivocality? One obvious point is that most sung conversations would not take place in real life. That is, the songs imagine rather than replicate human interactions, making speakers forthright in unlikely contexts, and at times making women articulate and assertive where they would more probably be tongue-tied or acquiescing. Another general characteristic of these conversations is that some kind of tension seems evident in all the situations they suppose. Both these factors are clear in the example just given, as well as many we encounter below—from the playfully opposed wills of the bride who wants a valuable gift and the husband who wants to retire pleasantly to bed ("Song of the Seven-colored Wrap") to the more subtle and painful three-part conversation between a devoted wife, lecherous father-in-law, and unpleasant sister-in-law ("Song of Pea Pods"). Thus the songs' words tend to express testy interpersonal situations, while the singing style in which they are presented smooths over any hint of histrionics.

Situations and relationships marked by self-imposed silence, restraint, lack of communication, or other kinds of stress appear frequently in women's songs. Through the songs' imagined conversations, these stressful situations and relationships are eased and opened up: grievances expressed, dominance defied, love de-

19. My research assistant, Bhoju Ram Gujar, suggested that the problem was the singers' attempt to use Hindi grammar on my behalf. But see Trawick 1988 on the deliberate confusion or merging of identities and voices in Tamil songs.

clared, contact established. At the same time, no risks are taken even on the level of imagined discourse, for the choral performance superimposes harmony over dissonance, and the unemotional delivery inherent in the tunes and singing styles masks emotional chords that may be struck by the words. Chorused conversations submerge discord between the sexes even while they suggest behavioral alternatives that may blatantly contravert dominant ideas about how women should act.

Rajasthani women's songs are embedded in situations; songs are evoked and typed largely by context. Personal repertoire and choice are certainly involved in determining which songs within a given category are performed at any given time, but the scope for choice is fairly circumscribed, at least conventionally. The Potter women consulted among themselves before performing *keśyā*, assuring one another that Phalgun, the month for *keśyā*, wasn't over yet. It was thus that they understood the switch from worship to play, rather than by reference to mood or persons. Songs' meanings then are understood as situationally appropriate—prescribed by season, event, activity, or the presence of certain relations. Songs' primary reference is essentially to groups or categories of persons, not individuals; the emotions to which they give vent are similarly patterned. At times, it is true, particular persons confided a particular song's strong resonance with their own state of mind or current social predicament, but such identification is incidental rather than integral to performance.[20] Central, rather, is a strong sense of appropriateness to time, place, and company.

At many life-cycle celebrations, annual festivals, and other events, Rajasthani village women sing, both metaphorically and explicitly, of sexual engagement with spouses and lovers. Songs sung at rites concerned with birth, child rearing, and many stages of weddings tend to hint, through oblique references and pretty metaphors, at wives' tender and exciting unions with their husbands. Insult songs hurled at specific junctures between marrying parties and *keśyā*—bawdy verses sung on and around certain

20. In this respect Rajasthani songs offer a strong contrast to the expressive singing reported by Abu-Lughod (1986) among the Bedouins. Their songs, although the words may be conventionalized, are deliberately sung to reveal intense personal emotions. This does not seem to be the case in Rajasthan.

holidays—include the equivalent of four-letter words for body parts and sexual intercourse; both these genres may speak of infidelity and promiscuity.

The women who enjoy singing such songs justly claim for themselves the same behavioral standards of modesty and shame required of the ideal Hindu wife as anthropological literature habitually depicts her. Yet clearly the songs express other powerful cultural motifs. For example, illicit liaisons evoked in wedding insult songs result, happily, in pregnancy. Singers themselves do not recognize a conflict between acting out the values of wifely devotion and lustily singing out such countervailing themes. They may describe the playful singing of such songs as making "jokes," but the humor is grounded in positive attitudes toward reproduction and pleasure that coexist with more austere Hindu precepts.

While the following chapters look specifically at subversion of domestic power hierarchies in certain narrative songs, my argument here is for coexistence, not inversion or subversion. The songs do not represent temporary reversals of a monolithic normative value system but powerfully express another, also valued worldview.[21] Certainly some festival events in the Hindu calendar—notably Holi—explicitly turn hierarchies and moral codes upside down for a limited period of carnivalesque revelries (Marriott 1966). But, at least where I lived in Rajasthan, female sexual exuberance appears in so many contexts and genres that it cannot be relegated to a seamy, repressed underside of a truly dominant ideology's structured universe. There are just too many of these songs and too many occasions for singing them to warrant this kind of interpretation. Nor can we conveniently file these materials under "low-caste" or "tribal." Women throughout the caste hierarchy indulge in this kind of musical play. In terms of public performances, Rajput wives are admittedly excluded, but the wildest, most explicitly sexual dances I have seen were in a cloistered Rajput courtyard.

I draw on a number of genres in this chapter. Indigenous clas-

21. Ramanujan (1986) offers a way of looking at alternative worldviews as contextually constituted "realms" of folklore. Daniel's elegant formulations of a "toolbox approach" to causality (1983), and of multiple models for marital relationships (1980), also suggest the pervasiveness of coexisting perspectives in South Asia.

sifications of Rajasthani songs are often finely drawn, but they may vary according to the classifier's involvement in performance. For example, what male scribes blanket-labeled "women's songs" (*auratoṅ ke gīt*) or "wedding songs" (*śādī ke gīt*) the singers themselves assign to many subcategories. Among wedding songs one class called *banā,* meaning "bridegroom-prince," will be of particular interest here. Caste sisters and neighbors gather to sing *banā* around a bride-to-be for days before her wedding, and women also perform these auspicious, happy songs at celebrations of the birth and early life-cycle rites of sons. *Banā* tend to the romantic vein but may contain "deep" or "hidden" sexual allusions. Other wedding songs and postpartum "songs of the new-mother queen" (*jachchā rānī ke gīt*) provide additional source material.

Of blatantly bawdy songs there are two basic categories: *gālī* and *keśyā.*[22] *Gālī* means "insult" and may refer to any verbal abuse. In this sense it is not limited to abuse incorporating sexual terms but also covers curses and milder exclamations—sometimes humorous—referred to as "small *gālī*s." Sung *gālī*s are always sexually oriented; they are appropriate to many occasions of encounter between relatives by marriage, although several moments in the protracted sequence of wedding events are prime opportunities for their performance. Essentially, *gālī*s are sung when a group of women encounter in a semiformal situation men who stand in the relation of bride givers or bride takers to them. As one person put it, "When a daughter's or son's connections by marriage are there, insults can be sung." The singers, usually a party of the same caste and lineage, would include in-married wives as well as the out-married daughters who happen to be present, as they often are for life-cycle events involving their brothers and nephews.

Hearing *gālī*s energetically sung at my village home when daughters' husbands' kin arrived, I at first assumed that this

22. *Gālī* and related genres have been reported and recorded from various parts of northern and central India. See Archer 1985:45, 107–10, Henry 1975:65–66, 76, 80–81, 85–87, and Jacobson 1975:48–54 for examples and discussions of such genres. Henry and Jacobson both give several examples of explicitly sexual *gālī*s performed at weddings in Uttar Pradesh and Madhya Pradesh that are quite similar in tone and import to those encountered in Rajasthan; see Lutgendorf 1991:251 for *gālī* singing at recreations of Lord Ram's wedding. See also Kolenda 1990:128–29 on wedding jokes.

choral impertinence was a way for the ever-subservient, ever-polite bride givers to get back at these demanding guests. However, the groom's female relatives sing *gālīs* at the bride's male kin, and therefore I had to conclude that the songs possess no particular function of hierarchy reversals between in-laws. Certainly, as Doranne Jacobson points out (1982: 100–101), such singing offers welcome relief from the formality that characterizes an often tense relationship.

The genre of songs called *keśyā* is sung in relation neither to life-cycle rites nor to marriage connections. Mixed-caste parties of women, rather than groups of female kin, perform *keśyā* during specific annual festivals. During the festive spring month of Phalgun (our March–April) and on into the hot-weather month of Chaitra (our April–May), *keśyā*'s characteristic rowdy tune resounds from time to time. This season opens with Holi, a two-day celebration given over to all kinds of play, and includes the day of Sitala Worship (rites for the goddess of smallpox) and Gangaur (a celebration of divine and human marriage).[23] In the last month of the rainy season (our early fall), women again perform *keśyā* with zest on Bach Bahras (Calf Twelfth).[24]

All the sources I draw on here are from women's performance traditions, and it is true that women sometimes enjoy their bawdiest fun when the courtyard doors are safely barred against male intruders. Nonetheless, on many occasions, women sing these

23. In 1993 (just as this book was going to press), back in Ghatiyali for a research project focusing on agricultural and seasonal rituals, I had a new interest in the festival of Holi because of its association with the grain harvest. On the full moon night of Holi, a dead tree or tree branch embodying the wicked aunt of the great devotee Prahlad is burned. Believing that my graying hair gave me license to violate gender norms (which I could not risk twelve years earlier), I attended the Gardener caste's Holi fire. There many men, a number of whom were drunk, were dancing with abandon and singing—*keśyā*. They used the same tune women use. I heard and understood several verses with words identical with those in women's versions. Because women sing *keśyā* on several occasions for extended periods of time, and men only sing it—I am assured by male and female villagers—during the limited time that the Holi fire burns, I am inclined to continue to consider *keśyā* a woman's genre. And Holi is indeed a festival of role reversal, as Marriott (1966) points out. But a fuller understanding of gender, genre, and sexually explicit songs awaits further research. For a description of Holi elsewhere in rural North India, see Marriott's essay. Studies of Sitala Mata, "Cool Mother," or the goddess of smallpox, are plentiful; see, for example, Dimock 1982, Kolenda 1982, Nicholas and Sarkar 1976, and Wadley 1980b. Erdman (1985) vividly depicts Gangaur in the city of Jaipur.

24. For the Rajasthani celebration of Calf Twelfth see Gold 1988a:123–31.

sexy songs in the presence of men. Indeed, the insult songs are hurled directly at men and could hardly fall on deaf ears. Testimony to male assimilation of this material is that several times male informants, when they were shy about explaining something sexual to me, cited a verse from a women's song that made the matter quite explicit. If largely voiced by women, then, these traditions are well known to both sexes.

ALLUREMENT UNDER WRAPS

Skirts and blouses, not saris, are customary apparel in rural Rajasthan. A third and separate piece of cloth that tucks into the waist, wraps around the hips, and is pulled up over the back, head, and at appropriate moments fully over the face (a gesture called *ghūṅghaṭ*) is the garment with which Rajasthani women observe the strictures of purdah and the niceties of modesty and affected "shame" (*śaram*).[25] While *oṛhnī*, which literally translates "wrap," is the pedestrian, generic term for this cloth, a profuse vocabulary (including *chīra, chūndaṛī, dhanakpurī, sāḷū,* and *syāḷūṛo*) denotes various styles, colors, and patterns of full coverings in speech and song. In considering wrap imagery, I have also used songs about half-coverings or "shawls." These include the *ḍapaṭo*, flung over the shoulders and used like other wraps to cover the head and face by women or girls in Muslim or Punjabi-style pants and long tops, and the *dusālo*, wrapped over other garments for warmth in the cold season.

Wraps and shawls appear in a broad array of women's songs: they are envied, borrowed, begged for, danced in, and offered to the goddess. In these songs it becomes clear that their wraps are for women polyvocal media of self-presentation.[26] Certainly, the wrap epitomizes female modesty, neutralizing women's sexuality. It thus serves a double function—protecting men from overexposure to women's power and protecting women from unwanted male attentions (Papanek and Minault 1982). But in many songs

25. As we see in the following chapters, the term *ghūṅghaṭ* refers to a woman covering her face with the appropriate part of whatever garment is worn, including her sari end or *ḍupaṭā*. The term is used throughout North and Central India (see, for example, Jacobson 1982).

26. Abu-Lughod (1986) offers among many other things a fine, multidimensional interpretation of the veiling of women in a Bedouin community, using oral traditions as a major source.

the wrap becomes primarily beautifying: it enhances and subtly reveals its wearer's charms, enticing rather than cutting off male gazes. Finally, in some abusive songs, wraps and shawls become backdrops for and witnesses to the very adultery they are supposed to prevent.

The following dance song was recorded among a group of Gujar (Cowherd) women during premarital celebrations for a young groom in their family. While one or two women, their faces completely draped, dance rhythmically and gracefully, others surrounding them sing; turns are taken at dancing. Men may be clustered nearby, paying no obvious attention to the presence or actions of the women, but the song suggests a keen mutual awareness. Despite or perhaps because of being under a wrap, the dancer consciously attracts the gaze of her beloved.

4. *Dance Song**

Your wrap sparkles and glitters,
sparkles and glitters.
Your body bows and bends,
Bends, your body bends.
Slowly dance, slowly dance, proud woman,
Your groom watches, your husband watches,
Slowly dance.

Your nose ring sparkles and glitters
Your bangles sparkle and glitter.
Your body bows and bends,
Bends, your body bends.
Slowly dance, slowly dance, proud woman,
Your groom watches, your husband watches,
Slowly dance.

[Repeats]
Slowly dance, slowly dance, proud woman,
Your white man prints, your white man sees,
Slowly dance.

Thus in a final chorus these women acknowledged the presence of my colleague Joseph Miller with his camera and recording equipment. By the words "Your white man prints," they referred, of course, to photographs. Ghatiyali's women were well aware of the potential pictures in the camera and loved to look at the printed results. It is perhaps relevant to note that village women tended to identify the anomalously unmarried male Miller's elaborate appliances with his sexuality. On other, rowdier occasions they explicitly joked about his microphone, calling it a penis.

When I read the transcription of this dance song I realized that veiled women were not only conscious of men's eyes upon them, but that they enjoyed and sought after such admiration. While it is the husband's gaze that is enticed in the previous song, the *keśyā* verses I heard from the Potter women celebrate an explicitly extramarital eroticism. With the Agra skirt and the Sanganeeri wrap the idea of clothes that hide the body is subordinated to an image of exotic apparel that seductively reveals it. The lines "Bite, bite the whole body,/Don't bite the cheeks or husband will beat you" imply that the husband would notice marks on the cheeks but fail to see those on the body—perhaps because in this context his vision is less lascivious than the lover's.[27] Although eating the body may serve as a metaphor for intercourse, actual biting is an acknowledged, exciting part of village love play.

Women, then, sing of their veiled bodies on different occasions as attracting the husband's eyes, the lover's teeth. The wrap becomes an agent not of modesty but of dalliance in these songs. A wedding *gālī* goes farther still, making a shawl the backdrop for illicit intercourse, no longer on but underneath the woman's body.

5. *Gālī of the Borrowed Shawl**

Oh my fine colored shawl,
Oh my fine colored shawl,
Hey, Ram Kishan's wife came and took it away!
Yes, Gopiji's wife came and took it away!
She wrapped it, then spread it, that wanton woman,
She wrapped it, then spread it, that wanton woman;
She got stains on my shawl,
Yes, she got stains on my shawl!
She became a laundress and washed it, that wanton woman;
She became a laundress and washed it, that wanton woman.
She went to the pond, then dried it,
Yes, she went to the pond, then dried it,
And she folded it neatly, that wanton woman,
And she folded it neatly, that wanton woman.

27. See Kakar 1986 for a vivid discussion of the erotic superiority of adultery to marriage in Hindu poetry from the male viewpoint. It is not surprising that women could imaginatively exalt the forbidden and clandestine in similar fashion.

Thousands come and thousands go, oh yes,
Thousands come and thousands go.

Oh my fine colored shawl,
Oh my fine colored shawl,
Hey, the Char co-wives came and took it away!
[Repeats]

Char is the lineage receiving insults on this occasion. The line "Thousands come and thousands go" is probably a hyperbolic reference to the Char women's lovers. The story here is clearly of a woman who borrows a shawl and then spreads it beneath herself and her lover during intercourse, after which she tries to wash out the telltale stains. It is hard to appraise how deliberate is the irony of portraying a garment normally used to preserve modesty and protect virtue as a setting for adultery. But the whole song is performed with a raucous, mocking tone.

Many other songs that are not generally of the bawdy sort include requests to husbands for especially beautiful wraps and shawls. One such popular song in the "bring me a wrap" mode has numerous variations and is performed at many calendrical and life-cycle festivals, sometimes to the accompaniment of drumbeats and spontaneous dancing. It takes the form of a husband-and-wife dialogue: the woman speaks her admiration and envy of a shawl possessed by her husband's brother's wife and begs her husband to bring her one like it from the city. He asks her to model it, and she refuses for various reasons, some having to do with modesty. Usually the husband acquiesces to his bride in the end, promising to go get her the coveted garment.[28]

In most of these songs the shawl motif is associated with a bride's innocence; she is acquisitive, but appropriate shyness constrains her. However, the continuum between delicately romantic and more obviously sexual banter becomes clear in a somewhat more risqué variant. In the following example (recorded at a wedding celebration for two grooms of the Mina—a settled tribal caste), the wife's craving for a gorgeous, luxurious wrap is juxtaposed to her cravings for food and her inability to sleep—both

28. Gold (1982:77–79) provides two examples of this genre—dialogues between a mortal wife and husband and between the divinities Parvati and Shiva.

equatable with sexual desire. Her final complaint—"I miss my little brother"—provokes her husband into offering her a ride home, and she in turn finally admits that she cares for her bridegroom too. The bride manipulates this dialogue in a teasing but purposeful fashion.

6. Song of the Seven-colored Wrap (Banā)

Bridegroom-prince, please go to Jaipur, from Jaipur bring me a seven-colored wrap.
Bridegroom-prince, please go to Jaipur, from Jaipur bring me a seven-colored wrap.
Bride-princess, try it on, show me, how it will suit you, the seven-colored wrap.
Bride-princess, try it on, show me, what kind of a seven-colored wrap shall I bring?
Bridegroom-prince, it has a green border, and the middle is printed with peacocks and peahens.
Bridegroom-prince, it has a green border, and the middle is printed with peacocks and peahens.
Bride-princess, try it on, show me please, how it will suit you, the seven-colored wrap.
Bride-princess, try it on, show me please, how it will suit you, the seven-colored wrap.
Bridegroom-prince, how can I wrap it? I'm shy of your little brother.
Bride-princess, come into the castle, we'll go there and lie down.
Bride-princess, come into the castle, we'll go there and lie down.
Bridegroom-prince, I'm not at all sleepy; I'm dying of hunger, my liver is throbbing.
Bridegroom-prince, I'm not at all sleepy; I'm dying of hunger, my liver is throbbing.
Bride-princess, I'll bring a good measure of sweets and together we two will feast.
Bride-princess, I'll bring a good measure of sweets and together we two will feast.
Bridegroom-prince, I don't care for sweets, I miss my little brother.
Bridegroom-prince, please go to Kota, from Kota bring me a seven-colored wrap.
Bridegroom-prince, please go to Kota, from Kota bring me a seven-colored wrap.

[Repeats from this point until these final lines, the groom's response to "I miss my little brother"]

Bride-princess, I'll harness the chariot and take you to your little brother's.

Bridegroom-prince, I shan't sit in the chariot, then I would miss you.
Bridegroom-prince, if I sat in the chariot, then I would miss you.

This song combines implications of a woman's sexual power over her man with her traditional yearning for a covering that she wants to enhance, not hide, her beauty. The new wife denies that she is sleepy, which both thwarts her husband's amorous move and implies her own potential passion. She declares her hunger but will not yield to the enticement of sweets. Despite her own desires, this bride will not give into her groom's blandishments until he acknowledges her emotional needs.

The bride in the "Song of the Seven-colored Wrap" refers to her "shyness" (*śaram*) in front of her husband's little brother—normally the one male kin in a woman's marital home before whom shyness is not prescribed. In other "bring me a wrap" songs, however, the beautiful, enviable covering explicitly belongs to the husband's elder brother's wife, and the bride expresses her culturally imposed modesty in relation to him. Here the profession of shyness before the husband's younger brother may indicate the new bride's ultrashyness. In either case such verses acknowledge just those sexual undercurrents in the household that women's prescribed modesty is supposed to restrain. At the same time, the bashful bride is not acting particularly bashful or tongue-tied with her husband, and that could be the real point.

Looking at, or through, wrap imagery in Rajasthani women's lore has revealed one aspect of an unsplit feminine image. Coverings are not opaque; wraps can also unwrap; from the women's perspective, poses of sexual modesty and reticence can readily flow into allurement, involvement, and manipulation. Studies of purdah have often stressed its functions of separation and limitation, at best protecting women but fundamentally restricting them. Here I have tried to indicate the permeability of purdah and some of the ways it can be, at least poetically, manipulated by its wearers. In considering these aspects of women's self-images, I have not yet touched on themes of procreation. In the next section, moving beyond such conjunctions of modesty and allurement, I explore through other songs a more explicitly erotic sexuality that is nonetheless frequently a fertile one, sometimes involving liaisons with the husband's elder brothers.

BIRTH, SEX, AND PLEASURE

After the birth of a child, and before the ceremony of Sun Worship—performed on the ninth day or sooner, when the new mother is bathed, and birth pollution is considerably mitigated—close female relations and neighbors gather nightly outside the room where mother and infant lie. They have come to sing "songs for the new-mother queen" (*jachchā rānī ke gīt*).[29] Praise songs for the deities, in thanks for the wonderful gift of a living child, are part of each night's performance. But there are other songs of the new-mother queen that evoke in human terms the mysteries, pains, and delights of conception and birth.[30] These portray quite poignantly the mingled intimacy and formality that characterize relations between young husbands and wives in rural India.

Imaginary dialogues between baffled new fathers and deeply embarrassed but proud young wives evoke this humorous situation.[31] In one conversation song of this genre, the husband asks questions such as "Why is there howling in your room?" and "Why is your floor wet?" and the shy wife is evasive: "Two cats are fighting; two water pots spilled; I know nothing at all." Another song has the young father question not only his wife but his mother, sister, brother's wife, and neighbor, finally receiving the good news from an unabashed servant girl: "On one bed two persons slept, producing a third jewel." This song has the semi-nonsensical refrain "Son, she craves green beans cooked in oil." A woman's passion for green pod vegetables (as will become clearer shortly) is interpretable as a desire for sexual intimacy with the husband and is also one of several cravings associated with early

29. See Bryce 1964, Tewari 1988, and Wadley 1980a:59–61 for examples from other areas of Rajasthan and other regions of India.

30. According to Jeffery, Jeffery, and Lyon, who studied childbirth in western Uttar Pradesh, the new mother cannot enhance her self-respect by capitalizing on the power of "childbirth pollution" (1989:124). They state unequivocally, "The *jachā*'s condition is a *sharm-kī-bāt*; her physiological processes are embarrassing, distasteful and striking evidence of her sexuality" (150). Among Ghatiyali's matrons, a sense of *śaram* was not absent in relation to the physiology of childbirth, but it was considerably mitigated by expressions not only of pride but of power and competence.

31. These songs assume the proximity of the father in the postpartum period. Although it is common in some parts of India for wives to return to their natal homes for confinement, especially with a first child, this was not the prevailing custom in the area where I worked.

pregnancy. The refrain thus subtly bridges the gap between a young couple's sexual union and its fruits in the form of a child.

One new-mother queen song, however, suggests the conceptual merging of erotic attraction and birth giving more explicitly. Here, as in the shawl dialogue, a transition between sweets and sex is readily made. Women are supposed to be fed extremely rich sweets, loaded with clarified butter, sugar, expensive nuts, and other strengthening substances, during their postpartum confinements. Husbands as well as other members of the household are often portrayed in folklore as jealous or covetous of this food, sometimes stealing it or begging it from the new mother.

7. Song of the New-Mother Queen

Let me taste one spoonful of that halva you're feasting on, let me have a spoonful, lady.
The drum plays on, sir, the drum plays on.

Crazy, foolish husband, the halva costs a price, the spoonful costs a price, sir.
The drum plays on.

You gave birth to a son, let me have a peek, let me have a peek, lady.
The drum plays on, sir, the drum plays on.

Crazy, foolish husband, the baby costs a price, the son will cost a price, sir.
The drum plays on.

Crazy, foolish husband, I suffered labor pains, I suffered labor pains, sir.
The drum plays on, sir, the drum plays on.

You sleep on the cot, but have me sleep at its foot, you have me sleep at its foot, lady.
The drum plays on.

Crazy, foolish husband, on one side sleeps the darling boy, on the other side your beloved.
On the pillow lacquer bangles, at the foot ankle bracelets chime, sir.
The drum plays on.

Everyone I questioned about this song affirmed that the jingling of bangles and anklets in the final verse implies that the couple is having intercourse. I was puzzled by the husband being in the middle, rather than the wife, who could then nurse the child. According to my research assistant, however, if the husband lies down with his wife on his left side and his child on his right it is an explicit indication of sexual intentions. Women with whom I consulted told me that the chorus "The drum plays on" was just for the sound and had no specific reference. One man suggested, however, that it evokes the celebration that will take place on the day of Sun Worship when the new mother is washed and adorned for the first time. This celebration involves a public confirmation of paternity, by men outside the house, and a courtyard celebration by women.

In either case, the situation portrayed in this song is out of kilter with village custom. If the imagined encounter takes place before Sun Worship, then the husband is violating taboos that prevent him even from seeing his wife during this period, and brashly ignoring all that anthropological literature on Hinduism tells us about birth pollution and the danger of female blood (e.g., Jeffery, Jeffery, and Lyon 1989: 126). If it takes place during the celebrations that follow Sun Worship, then the young couple are blatantly affirming their private marital intimacy at a moment when the family should be concerned with its public image. Only as background to their love banter, the ritual drum plays on.

Nevertheless, such is the native exegesis. Moreover, precipitate intercourse after childbirth, when the womb was "open," could well produce another pregnancy quickly—a possibility one woman vividly evoked for me as *phaṭaphaṭ vāpas* (instant return). Here, then, we have the new mother, with baby by her side, as a teasingly seductive, and potentially once again fertile, wife—the total collapse of the erotic whore/fertile mother kind of split image.

Festivals celebrating life-cycle rites of children are also occasions for sexual innuendos in songs that anticipate the development of a male child into a bridegroom, but are usually voiced from the bride's point of view. The following song, recorded at a birth celebration among a group of Brahman women in very high spirits, expresses the difficulties that may surround a young wife's management of her sexuality among husband's relatives:

8. Song of Pea Pods

My father-in-law said, "Son's wife likes pea pods."
My father-in-law said, "Son's wife likes pea pods."
"Please don't bring me any, sir, my husband-lord will bring them."
"Please don't bring me any, sir, my husband-lord will bring them."
No sooner did he hear that much than he gave her two kicks in the waist;
No sooner did he hear that much than he kicked her in the waist.
And husband's sister said, "How do you like pea pods?"
And husband's sister said, "How do you like pea pods?"
But he lovingly brought pea pods in his pocket;
He lovingly brought pea pods in his bag.

[The singers dissolve in laughter.]

The bride in this song is subjected to the taunts, and perhaps the improper advances, of her father-in-law. Talking back to that figure of patriarchal authority, she draws his wrath and the husband's sister's mockery upon herself. But she wins in the end the loving, private attentions of her man. The bride's taste for pea pods, like the new mother's craving for green beans, implies both a taste for sexual pleasure and the desires of early pregnancy. Not only do seedy pods index fertility, but green pods are numbered among the foods pregnant women crave (Samskarta 1968: 75). However, the in-laws here appear to be reacting to the woman's craving as a craving for intimacy with her husband, not as a sign of pregnancy—a status that would bring sympathy rather than cruelty to a son's wife. The result of the encounters here is to stress the husband's devotion—which may explain why the singers trail off into hilarity. Although this song recognizes a potential for abuse, it is doubly positive in celebrating not only verbal resistance on the part of the woman but support from her husband.[32]

Female relatives of a first-born son perform songs of the bridegroom-prince (*banā*) at the boy's ritual first haircut (*jharūḷā*), after singing worshipful odes to the protective deity responsible

32. Nanuram Samskarta discusses pregnancy craving songs in Rajasthan—a genre called *hūṅs* that I did not record in Ghatiyali. In these songs, according to Samskarta, the bride asks her in-laws for the desired food substances, but they all refuse her. Only her husband brings them. The foods listed by Samskarta are sweets, watermelon, "green pods" (*phalī*), and "sour berries" (*bor*) (1968:75–77). Ghatiyali's "Song of Pea Pods" may well be related to such craving songs.

for the child's birth. These verses—extracted from longer songs—speak from the point of view of the child's future bride. In the course of our translation work, my embarrassed male assistants glossed over the obvious sexual metaphors by sagely referring to them as "very deep."

9. *Song of the Bridegroom-Prince*
Build a silver railroad, and a golden engine, Bridegroom-Prince,
He drives the train in fine white sand.
You're the driver, I'm the engine, Bridegroom-Prince,
We'll drive the train in the color-palace.
You're the driver, I'm the engine, Bridegroom-Prince.

["Color-palace" refers to the bridal chamber.]

10. *Song of the Bridegroom-Prince*
Bridegroom-Prince, your fan from Alwar has a golden stick.
Bridegroom-Prince, in the middle of your cot the fan will spin.

In neither of these verses is a bride's sexual nature portrayed as anything but eager. The songs stress sexual sport, not procreation, but their performance by maternal kin at a child's first haircut indicates continuities between celebrations of birth and sexual union.

Sometimes proud female relatives of a young boy may anticipate his growth to manhood and marriage yet still think of him, tenderly, as small. Companions to a bride may also tease her with the image of a small husband, and singers of insult songs make a husband's size into a sexual joke. Nonetheless, the laughably diminutive bridegroom may yet succeed in giving his wife a desired child. The image of the small husband, then, can unite maternal tenderness with sexual humor and procreative hopes.[33] Among many middle and lower castes of the area where I

33. See Bryce 1964:179–80 for a small-husband song with very maternal imagery; see also Trawick 1988 for a most interesting discussion of "vari-directional discourse" in dialogue songs from Tamilnad suggesting mother-son incest. Vatuk and Vatuk's discussion (1979b) of the "lustful stepmother" theme in Hindi folk dramas points to some absolute moral distinctions made between the role of nourishing mother and that of sexual partner—and the two different kinds of love associated with them. Yet the number of dramatic tales such as that of the lustful stepmother and others reported by Vatuk and Vatuk that revolve around attempted conflations of these roles indicates that such conflations readily stir popular imagination.

worked, especially when sets of brothers are married to sets of sisters, weddings may well include at least one groom who is indeed a very small child. Thus the small bridegroom is also a reality; not so his articulate, mocking wife as protrayed in songs. A child groom nowadays will have a bride even younger than himself.

Bride takers (women of Ghatiyali) performed the following small-husband song during a *gālī*-singing session aimed at bride givers (who had arrived for some preliminary negotiations). It sounds like doggerel (I have attempted to give a hint of the original rhythm and rhyme) but is not without meaning: the song plays with the "miracle" of phallic growth, the "male wonder" that could allow even a smallish husband to produce a son, and his bride to enjoy it.

11. *Gālī of the Small Husband**

On the cross-path grow those plants whose poison leaves are
yellow.
Ram Kishan had a son, a floppy-eared fellow.
Take down my full water pot, small husband dear.
Small, small what's to be done?
See the male wonder:
In nine months I'll feed a son.
Daughter have a lot of fun!

Sexual meanings in *gālīs* need no longer be hidden or deep. In many such abusive songs, fertility is directly associated with infidelity. From women's point of view it may be better to deceive one's husband than to remain childless.[34]

12. *Gālī of the Barren Woman**

On a banyan sat a heron,[35]
On a banyan sat a heron,

34. See Das 1988:201–2 for similar attitudes in Punjab.

35. See Doniger 1991:92 for the classical "hypocrisy of the heron." Here, as we have argued in the preface, it is not the heron's voice but rather those patriarchal values that encourage women to seek fertility outside their marriage beds that are to be judged hypocritical. In another genre of songs, dedicated to the deity Bhairuji, the heron's voice again describes a situation characterized by ambivalent morality: Bhairuji's attempt to force his way into a woman's house. Like the birth of a desired son through illicit means, the entry of a male divinity into a female devotee's home suggests subversive access to power, perhaps through sexual encounter. At the same time, the woman inside's resistance suggests unwillingness to accept male aggression, whether divine or mortal. Bhairuji's power seems posed as an extension of all male power. Why doesn't she want to let him in?

Listen to the heron's words,
Yes, listen to the heron's words:
For twelve years Ram Kishan's wife remained,
For twelve years Ram Kishan's wife remained,
Useless and empty she remained,
Yes, useless and empty she remained.
One night with Bhuraji she remained,
One night with Ramji she remained,
At once a boy child she obtained,
Yes at once a boy child she obtained.
You did well, my stout in-law,
You did well, my handsome in-law,
You removed the stain of "barren woman,"
Yes, you relieved the barren woman with a birth.

There is of course an ironic tone in these congratulations to an adulterer, who would by village custom be culpable and punishable. But, given the agony of barren women (see Gold 1988a: 149–54), the "relief" (*sudhāryo*, a term for support that is used in prayer) received by the woman is genuine. The word for "barren woman," *bāṅjhaṛī*, is an insult and almost a curse. To remain "useless and empty"—by which I translate the scornful phrase *ṭhalaṛak ṭhālaṛ*—is to be pitied, possibly supplanted (for a man whose wife is barren has just cause to seek another), and at worst despised and feared (for it is barren women who most often gain the reputation of being witches). And men themselves so desperately desire progeny that, at least as some popular folk traditions along with rumors have it, they may allow themselves to be deceived if the result is the desired birth of a boy.[36]

In referring to the fertilizing adulterer as "relation by marriage" (*biyāī*), the insult singers imply that he too is of the bride-taking group. Sometimes the adulterous progenitor is specifically identified with the husband's brothers (*devar-jeṭh*), and thus the wife's infidelity serves the approved end of perpetuating the groom's patrilineage.

*13. Gālī of the Ribbon**
My splendid gorgeous ribbon was lying in the yard,
Up came Ram Kishan's wife and seized it between her thighs.
What happened to the ribbon?

36. In Gold 1988b I discuss this gullibility in the context of self-satire in a folk drama.

It's with the gaudy lady.
Ribbon, ribbon, what to do? It's like husband's brothers.
Ribbon, ribbon, what to do? It's like husband's brothers.
Poor husband's brother, what to do?
She's left with Bhuraji's belly!

My male research assistant patiently explained to me that the reference to "husband's brothers" here has more to do with a "husband's younger brother" (*devar*) being defined as someone with whom sexual joking is possible than with the song recommending adultery with a brother-in-law. In other words, the implication of the reference is not that one's lover is one's husband's brother; rather, by saying the word for "husband's younger brother" one may with a very slight degree of discretion allude to a lover. The word for "husband's elder brother" (*jeṭh*) is thrown in—to continue with a male exegesis of this song—for its felicitous rhyme with "belly" (*peṭ*). However, a husband's elder brother is not by any means an appropriate lover. I am tempted to depart one step from this male explanation (and I haven't discussed this particular point with women) and add that the song may deliberately mock the shame and reticence epitomized by a woman's behavior toward her *jeṭh*, or husband's elder brother.

Genuine *ghoṭā*, a decorative trimming traditionally made with threads of real gold or silver that is sewn onto the edges of wraps, is a rare commodity nowadays in Rajasthan. The woman in this song is attracted by a man just as she would be attracted by sparkling, precious ribbon (*ghoṭā*). Seizing him between her thighs, she is hardly a modest wife. The term *alabelaṛī*, which I have rendered "gaudy lady," my assistant explained as "someone who dresses beautifully and doesn't care what people think." The dictionary glosses its masculine form as "dandy."

Combining these elements, this song presents a kind of gross variation on the "bring me a wrap" theme, where the shy bride envies her husband's elder brother's wife's lovely *oṛhnī*. Here, attracted by her brother-in-law (or lover) just as she would be attracted by sparkling ribbon, she seizes not only the costly ornamentation but the man as well. She is not behaving with appropriate wifely modesty, yet her lust is fertile. The reference to the husband's brothers may also suggest that the fertility through adultery evoked here remains after all in an appropriate lineage.

The most blatant of the wedding insult songs are sung when the groom's party enters the house of the bride. At this moment the groom, often on horseback and flanked by numbers of his male kin and friends, strikes with a sword a wooden emblem placed for the occasion above the bride's door, and tosses it up onto the roof. He then dismounts and pushes his way into the house, his passage almost blocked by the bride's kinswomen and companions who are boisterously singing verses slandering his mother—particularly addressing her sexual capacities or lack thereof. Once the groom has broken through the throng of women the Sanskritic portion of the marriage rites, performed by a Brahman pandit and including oblations poured into a Vedic fire, takes place with some decorum.

There are two popular *gālīs* hurled at the moment of the groom's entry (recorded by both Joseph Miller and me at a number of middle-caste weddings). One of these accuses the groom's mother, in a rhymed nonsense couplet, of lacking genitals:

14. *Gālī of the Groom's Mother*
Black sheep's not woolly,
Bridegroom's mother's got no pussy!

The second, slightly longer *gālī* attributes to this same personage an excessive taste for genital enjoyment—equating her craving for sweet sugarcane with her desire to copulate, and using the crudest terms available.

15. *Gālī of the Groom's Mother*
Bridegroom's mother asked for a sugarcane stick.
Take this one, a piece of prick.
Oh, but it's sweet! I'll plant more quick,
In my cunt I'll plant that prick,
In my cunt I'll plant that prick.

The differing contents of these two basic insults of the groom's mother may be seen as complementary. General Hindu morality holds that parents of a married son who has brought home a daughter-in-law should themselves cease sexual activity (see Vatuk 1980, 1985). The two *gālīs* of the groom's mother, sung as they generally are in alternation, seem to say that only if she had no genitals—as natural to women as wool is to sheep—would she, with her taste for sweets, be able to give up sex. Her lasciviousness, unlike that attributed to the younger wives of the groom's party, appears to be purely for pleasure—that is, not procreative. However, her very character at this juncture is as "mother." Although she has a grown son, the sexuality of the groom's mother, in the view expressed by these songs, is far from neutralized, as Bennett would have it.[37]

Before departing for his bride's village, the groom publicly gives one ritual suck to his mother's breast.[38] He thus affirms the continuities between his identity as son and as husband and accepts his mother's continuing nourishing and formative role in his life. Shortly after having thus parted from his mother, the groom, standing in his bride's doorway at the moment of symbolic penetration, must listen to "insults of his mother's genitals." In general, whether they speak of wives seeking lovers in order to become mothers or of mothers seeking lovers out of sheer lust, *gālīs* seem to associate women's sexuality with their birth-giving capacities rather than divorce the two aspects of their natures.

Keśyā verses celebrate a bawdy sexuality that is clearly promiscuous and ranges well beyond a husband's brothers. Indeed these verses sometimes describe prostitutes, and a gaping sexual hunger. This hunger, however, does not overpower and drain males but matches masculine lust, sometimes combatively, sometimes delicately. The vagina is wide and playful; the penis is large and aggressive. Mixed-caste groups of village women, including all the clean castes except Rajput, join together to sing *keśyā* repetitively in sessions broken frequently by jokes, chatting, and "goat talk" (imitation, with great hilarity, of male goats' mating cries). In the context of Sitala Mother's worship, sequences of *keśyā* are interspersed with songs of the goddess. Sitala is best known as the deity who both inflicts and protects from smallpox. However, she is also associated not only with the well-being of small children (their safety from all rash and fever diseases) but

37. In Rajasthan and other parts of North and Central India the groom's natal kin hold a mock, obscene wedding right after their son's departure for his bride's village, a practice offering further confirmation of these observations (Carstairs 1975:233–35; Jacobson 1975:56).

38. This Rajasthani custom appears in other North Indian regions as well (Archer 1985:30).

also with the fertility of newlyweds.[39] Bawdy verses please Sitala, and her worship, complete with avid singing of *keśyā*, is performed both to ward off childhood diseases and to improve community fertility.

Some of these verses are quite crude, but others display a rather brilliantly whimsical erotic imagination.

16. Keśyā

Keśyā, your penis is a pipal tree's trunk,[40]
Lover, your penis is a pipal tree's trunk.
And a prostitute's[41] vagina is four acres wide.

Keśyā, the big drum sounds on the water hole's bank,
Lover, the big drum sounds on the water hole's bank,
The two-mouthed flute sounds in the fine sand.

Keśyā, place the vagina to watch over the chick-peas,
Lover, place the vagina to watch over the chick-peas.
The penis comes and uproots the young plants.

On the vagina plays a black snake,
Lover, on the vagina plays a black snake.
Lover, within the skirt's waist plays a brown monkey.

Tie little bells on the vagina,
Lover, tie little bells on the vagina,
Lover, tie a big broken bell to the penis.

The vagina left hungry[42] at night
Will fix sweets and fried bread the next day.
The penis left hungry at night
Will fix sweets and fried bread the next day.

In thus personifying the sexual organs—giving them a life of their own—*keśyā* differ from *gālīs*. *Gālīs* focus on people, but *keśyā*,

39. For the relation of Sitala to fertility, see Das 1976a:137 and Kolenda 1982.

40. I had originally translated the words *phīpalī ko pheṛ* as "pipal tree," but Bhoju, my assistant, insisted that it must be "pipal tree's trunk." Perhaps this is because of the sacred and female identity of the pipal tree. In Rajasthan a pipal tree may be married like a daughter to a male deity.

41. I was told that *bhagataṅ* meant "prostitute," but it does not appear in the Rajasthani-Hindi dictionary. I can speculate that it derives from *bhag*, for "vagina," or from the verb *bhugatṇo*, meaning "to experience."

42. Although the usual meaning of *bāsī* is "leftover, something stale," I was told that here it refers specifically to the way someone feels in the morning when they haven't eaten the night before. The implication seems to be that when someone has eaten nothing but cold leftovers the night before (had unsatisfying sex?), they want something especially good in the morning.

although they may also treat characteristics of persons, often—as in most of these examples—simply describe poetically the sexual act itself. The pipal tree-trunk penis and the four-acre vagina suggest a grandiose, ultrahuman scale for the sexual engagement evoked in these jolly, ribald moments. Another verse I've heard but failed to record offers an even more capacious image: "In the prostitute's vagina you can fit the whole *rāvalā*," or the Rajput neighborhood. Rajputs are hereditary rulers and warriors; thus the vagina imaged here contains the noblest houses as well as the most virile men.

While the penis uprooting chick-peas is perhaps a simple image of masculine aggression and domination, the playful black snake and brown monkey, the charming contrast of bells, and the somewhat obscure flute in the sand are more delicate conceits with implications of mutuality. The vagina as brown monkey is always ready to play. The image of fine sand as a good place to sport, for children as well as lovers, is a recurrent one in desert Rajasthan, and the two-mouthed flute is the traditional instrument of Bhil tribals, whose sexual morals are supposed less rigid than those attributed to caste Hindus.[43] Of course the idea of sexual hunger being transferred to food represents an insight of folk psychology probably close to many women's experience;[44] it also recalls the hungry bride who sustains arousal by refusing sweets in the "bring me a wrap" song. The mutuality of male and female desire is again implied by the attribution of similar cravings to both organs.

Still other *keśyā* verses consider how the environment may enhance or diminish sexual pleasures. Some, such as the one about hilltop fucking introduced above, express a yearning for open spaces and vistas, which is quite understandable given the cramped quarters in which marital sex is accomplished, and the even more furtive arrangements made by lovers. Another verse recognizes the discomfort of sexual engagement in the hot season:

43. Ethnic or communal associations frequently mingle with biological ones in *keśyā* (Gold 1988a:130).

44. See, for example, Wadley n.d. (forthcoming); Narayana Rao (1989) provides many charming examples of homologies between sex and food in Telugu literature.

17. Keśyā
Keśyā, if you want to play, then play before Holi,
Lover, if you want to play, then play before Holi;
Later the fierce sun beats down.

Finally, a number of *keśyā* propose that the community of women is sexually active and interested in amorous pleasures. Perhaps the most often repeated *keśyā* verse is the following:

18. Keśyā
Lover, if you want to play, play with so-and-so's wife;
Lover, if you want to play, play with so-and-so's wife.
Others will cost you 150 rupees.

Since this will be sung over and over again, eventually employing the names of all participants, it affirms a universal willingness to play among village women. Here is one of the most forthright *keśyā* verses:

19. Keśyā
On these women's housetops
they're drying greens for sauce,
they're drying greens for sauce.
All women say this:
"A long prick gives me bliss!
A long prick gives me bliss!"

Drying wild greens, to serve in the lean hot season as a supplementary vegetable, is a very prosaic, domestic task. Thus women's collective acknowledgment of sexual enjoyment in this verse is deliberately united with an image of their dull but important food-preparation work for the benefit of their families. Despite the free-floating nature of women's sexuality as expressed in *keśyā*, its manifestations do not appear to be conceived of as dangerous or destructive, by women or by men.[45]

In the context of the festival seasons when they are performed, and the particular worships with which they are associated, *keśyā* are part of a religious complex concerned not only with human

45. Men are afraid to come too close to women singing *keśyā*, but that is because the women would taunt and physically attack them, a threat they find both laughable and worth avoiding.

fertility but with life's prevailing over death and the general well-being of earth and community. The Calf Twelfth festival with its reproductive jokes and ribald dancing celebrates women's capacity to renew life. The worship of Sitala should produce as well as protect children. Holi is associated with agricultural plenty and the end of the cold season.

Songs of the new-mother queen portray women in confinement, allude to their continuing status as sexual partners, and even invite husbands to ignore pollution constraints and lie down beside them. Songs of the bridegroom-prince have virgin brides speak as bold and imaginative mistresses or anticipate their young husbands' transformation into sexually active and fertilizing men. In wedding *gālīs* men are taunted by verses accusing their wives of being adulteresses and their mothers of being horny. But these taunts can be read in a sense as affirming both the sexual prowess and ultimate fertility of the groom's lineage. They may also advise bride takers that for women the entwined goals of motherhood and sexual fulfillment can override the virtue of fidelity to one man—if the husband is inadequate, if the "male wonder" does not materialize.

This lore quite frankly acknowledges women's active, pleasure-taking sexuality. But it should not be interpreted as placing Rajasthani village women at the opposite pole from idealized female chastity—thus to be characterized as sexually insatiable creatures who will drain their partners of vitality and destroy the proper order of society and cosmos. G. Morris Carstairs (1975) reports fears of women as predators expressed by men in a Rajasthan village. I too heard, from men, that the health of puny men married to robust wives was likely to deteriorate—unless they supplemented their diet with plenty of butter and eggs. But such views were expressed less with terror than with an appreciation for the access to pleasures, progeny, and power that may well be available through union with strong women.

Folklore persuasively offers images of female nature that include a sexuality not rampantly destructive but seeking mutuality with males. The erotic imagination displayed in *keśyā* suggests a relish for sexual encounter on both sides that is more human than demonic. These are earthy hungers—cravings for sweets—and not the blood thirst of the castrating goddess. Many women's songs portray desire as inherently procreative; others are performed in ritual contexts stressing communal fertility. In either case the sexual and maternal aspects of female nature seem fused rather than split, and generative rather than destructive images of female power emerge.

GENDER PERFORMED

Using women's own performance traditions, I have attempted to amend split-image theories of South Asian females prevailing in literary, psychoanalytic, and cultural analyses. Such theories, I have argued, tend to accept or emphasize one dominant perspective—deriving from overlapping traditions that we may call high-caste male, Sanskritic, or literary. Folklore can offer a different story or, as this chapter has demonstrated, sing different songs. It is through listening to these songs—chorused by female voices in a regional vernacular—that I have been able to suggest an alternative portrait of South Asian womanhood.

I propose that Rajasthani village women's poetic use of words strongly contradicts the alien split images imposed on them—whether by literate males of their own community or by foreign scholars. That my sources are oral performance traditions rather than ordinary talk is no accident. The particular power of performance traditions to present creative viewpoints and to serve as reservoirs for cultural alternatives has been highlighted by folklorists and anthropologists working on varied materials in various cultural settings. David Parkin, writing on the "creativity of abuse" in Kenya, says of ritual insults that they "free speakers to experiment with alternative, normally hidden, views of personal worth and power relations" (1980: 62).[46]

The power of oral performances spills over into everyday identities, just as it certainly draws upon them—as I will show in chapter 5, where I explore one accomplished singer and storyteller's life history. Here I have chosen to highlight aspects of female identity that seem the loudest, boldest, and most contradictory to prevailing stereotypes. That these emerge from the study

46. See also Bauman 1986 on storytelling in Texas, Basso 1985 on South American Indian narratives, Karp 1988 on women's marriage rituals among the Iteso of Kenya, and Limon 1981 on Chicano lore.

of songs dealing with bodily processes—birth giving and sexual intercourse—is also not incidental.[47]

Both anthropologist Veena Das and historian Ranajit Guha have recently suggested that women may have a special knowledge and subsequent power over speech concerning their own bodies. Guha writes:

> This knowledge constitutes a challenge which is genuinely dreaded by male authority. For it operates in an area of liminality not strictly governed by the will of husbands and fathers—an area which appears to the latter as fraught with uncertainty and danger, since women speak here in a language not fully comprehensible to men and conduct themselves by rituals that defy male reasoning.
> (Guha 1987: 163)

Das somewhat more tentatively suggests that

> much of the communication between women on matters sexual is not accessible to men. As the lawful wives of men, women pay allegiance to the entire male discourse on female sexuality. However, burdened with the task of maintaining the orderly world of patriarchy represented by law, they are not always averse to maintaining appearances at the cost of individual transgressions.
> (Das 1988: 201)

The example Das gives is one in which "a woman who was not able to conceive was advised by her sister-in-law to exchange her quilt—a verbal pun by which she was being advised to become pregnant by another man, thus confirming that maintaining order sometimes involves individual transgression" (201–2). As we have seen, Rajasthani wedding insult songs give similar advice, observing that a lover is a boon to a barren woman.

For Das the order maintained by such transgression feeds ultimately into the interests of patriarchy. Certainly all the well-being ritually generated by women's singing about sexual play could be interpreted as co-opted by men—who, after all, appear to control village politics and economy. But I am not ready to jump to that metalevel of cultural criticism. My purpose here has been to let the sounds and meanings of women's voices contribute to our

47. See Bynum 1987 for an exploration of medieval Christian women's use of alternative religious imagery based on "ordinary biological and social experiences," including giving birth.

understandings of gender in the Hindu world. Rather than fractured wholes, these voices portray shifting, polychromatic self-images.[48]

Recent appreciations of the relevance and realms of Indian folklore and women's traditions offer a broader base for the limited examples and localized context I have explored in this chapter. Ramanujan (1986) describes two realms within the domain of folk performance in South India that are at least partially congruent with two categories of classical Tamil poetry—*akam* and *puram,* or interior and exterior. Although not frozen as female to male, these categories are strongly gendered. The interior is associated with women and families, domesticity and love; the exterior with men and heroes, statesmanship and war. But, if the inner realm is characterized by use of less formal language, less naming of places and persons, it is far from a silent realm, nor is its poetry inferior.

Working only from the written residue of women's oral performances in a very different place and time—nineteenth-century Bengal—Sumanta Banerjee richly documents and explores motifs and meanings very similar to those I have discussed here. He also describes the systematic repression, tantamount to obliteration, of such living traditions by the colluded forces of "Christian missionaries, English administrators and the Bengali bhadralok"—the English-educated, reform-minded urban elite. Banerjee, whose essay I read with mounting excitement in March 1990 after completing an earlier draft of this chapter, suggests that "ritualistic displays of defiance in the form of female ribaldry" might have afforded women a "dissenting space" in a society "that did not allow them formal means of protest" (1989: 140–41). The thrust of Banerjee's article is, however, that this form of protest has virtually disappeared, having surrendered to "a hostile male world." Perhaps bawdy wedding jokes "may . . . still be alive in rural

48. Rosalind O'Hanlon in a very complex critique of attempts to recreate "subalterns" as individual subjects of their own history concludes that "histories and identities are necessarily constructed and produced from many fragments." She goes on to assert, however, that "this does not cause the history of the subaltern to dissolve once more into invisibility" (1988:197). Switching from a visual to an aural sensorial mode, I may still follow O'Hanlon in suggesting that if village women's self-portrayals in song display an awareness of multiple identities, they need not dissolve into silence.

areas," he comments wistfully (160). I hope he will be heartened to learn that in Rajasthan, at least, these oral traditions are not only alive but integral to ritual life.[49]

Although she is not concerned with implications of social protest, Joyce Flueckiger's very interesting study (1989) of how the oral epic of Lorik-Candā has developed differently in Chhattisgarh and in Uttar Pradesh does reveal direct links between women's actual social status and female images in folklore. In Chhattisgarh, where women have greater economic independence and generally higher status than in Uttar Pradesh, female epic characters are initiators of action and of romance and use their ingenuity rather than the power of chastity to solve problems. Flueckiger's findings are important because they indicate that folkloric representations of women's power, rather than being hollow, wishful, or nostalgic, may relate to actual social standing and influence.

David Shulman has approached female power through South Indian folklore sources, describing it as raw force that must be contained, but that nevertheless spills out, and should—the motif of the goddess in the box. He states that the folkloric world is one in which "powerful forces are constantly breaking through the barriers erected against them." Moreover, this perpetual breakthrough is productive, not destructive (1986: 119). Frédérique Marglin's ethnographic and historical research on the *devadāsīs*, or temple dancers, of Orissa argues most persuasively for the positive force in women's sexuality. Particularly in their mythic and ritually enacted capacity to seduce ascetic men, the *devadāsīs* are the ones who bring rain and food (1981, 1985a, 1985b).

Scholars who have painted split female images, including Kakar, O'Flaherty, and Bennett, have tended to neglect folkloric realms and women's traditions—at least while in the split-image

49. The impulse among the literate elite to suppress, if not the performance, at least the public knowledge, of "bawdy wedding songs" exists in Rajasthan too, however. It is remarkable that in a generally excellent scholarly work on Rajasthani folk literature the author depicts the groom's entrance into the bride's house after *toraṇ marnā* (see above) as a moment when "the women of the maiden's side bring the groom into the house with great love" (*kanyā pakṣ kī striyāṅ baṛe sneh se var ko ghar meṅ le jātī haiṅ*). The same work does refer to *gālīs* sung at other moments in the wedding process, consistently calling them "sweet" (*madhur*) and "melodious" (*surīlī*) as if thus to deny any abrasive import (Samskarta 1968:87–88).

mode of analysis.[50] I have noted that their major sources are largely male-authored (in the case of texts) or from the male viewpoint (in the case of ethnography). By thus contrasting their sources (male) with mine (female), I have not posed a "his" and a "hers" theory of separate worlds and worldviews. Rather, both visions coexist and are available to both sexes. Men can and do partake at times of the kinds of female-generated visions explored here, even as women often articulate perfectly and subscribe behaviorally to the prevalent set of values I have heuristically described as having male orientations and origins.[51]

In sum, this chapter presents a construction of female gender in South Asia that is accessible to all, if performed by women. I have characterized this construction as more unified than split, more auspicious than dangerous, more creative than destructive. Rather than opposing murderous, sexual females to nurturing, protective mothers, as in Kakar's and O'Flaherty's schematizations, songs like the "*Gālī* of the Small Husband" reveal a merged anticipation of sexual pleasure and motherhood from the bride's viewpoint. Distinctions between fertile mother and erotic, nonfertile whore dissolve both in the seductive new mother of the childbirth songs and the fertile adulteress of the *gālī*s. If a hint of the mother's incestuous desire remains, it is tender rather than frightening. I have seen grandmothers gently play with a baby's penis while happily joking about the great works it will someday accomplish.

Nor do these songs sustain Bennett's opposition of sexual and by implication degraded wives to asexual, pure, and sacred

50. Kakar's most recent work does analyze some folktales in which he finds confirmation for his familiar dichotomies. However, he makes generalizations about Indian folk traditions that clearly do not take into account women's storytelling. For example, he writes that Indian folk traditions do not have the "animal groom tales" common in Western lore, where a "maiden's devotion to her animal-lover . . . disenchants him and gives him back his human form" (1990:59). On the contrary, in Ghatiyali alone I recorded several tales of women married to snakes and one of a sword-husband in all of which the happy transformation to a handsome lover comes about through the wife's devotion. Moreover, all of these tales stressed a wife enjoying great intimacy and pleasure with her spouse—a possibility alien to Kakar's views.

51. For a complex approach from Western feminist literary criticism, see Jardine, who writes that the assumption that "the two sexes and their imaginations can somehow be separated" is incompatible with "the major challenges of modernity's fictions. If we all remain divided between the two, it is because they cannot be separated in any culture" (1985:40–41).

sisters. The husband's sister makes a nasty sexual joke in the "Song of Pea Pods," and in the *banā,* or songs of the bridegroom-prince, the sexual eagerness of wives is evidently auspicious. Were it not, such songs would surely not be heard at celebrations of the birth and marriage of sons—events crucial to the male householder's all-consuming goal of continuing his line.

Rajasthani women celebrate, loudly and in chorused song and graceful dance, the positive energies inherent in female bodies and enhanced by their adornment. The veil attracts as much as it blockades the amorous eye; if only for a few stolen or borrowed moments, the wrap is eminently unwrappable; a husband's elder brother, to whom one turns one's back in acute shame, is a potential lover and impregnator. The image of adulterous love play on the hilltop pleases a goddess protective of children and fertility. Rather than perilous to persons and society, women's emerging beauty and vital sexual engagement bring pleasure and new life to family and community.

3

On the Uses of Irony and Ambiguity: Shifting Perspectives on Patriliny and Women's Ties to Natal Kin

In rural Rajasthan and Uttar Pradesh, ideas about sexuality are linked in important ways to kinship ideologies and relations of power within the family. Women's sexuality may be viewed as dangerous and destructive in male expressive traditions and in many ordinary conversations partly because of the perceived threat that sexual bonds between men and women pose to the solidarity of males within the patrilineal household. Throughout her life in her husband's home, a woman may continue to be viewed as an outsider who poses a potent threat to the unity of that household. The same devaluations of female sexuality that are found in so many textual traditions may be used, in everyday speech, to limit the effects that strong conjugal bonds would have on the power of senior over junior men, the power of men over women, and the power of older women over younger brides. As women sing, as they do both in Rajasthan and in Uttar Pradesh, of the powers and pleasures of sexuality, and of a felicitous merging of eroticism and fertility, they are at least implicitly challenging those lines of power within North Indian kinship.

Powerful sexual and conjugal bonds may be viewed as dangerous, and wives may be seen as potentially disruptive of male solidarity, yet women are also said to become irrevocably "other" and "alien" (*parāyī*) to their natal kin as they marry and move, often at a great distance, to the villages of their husbands. The words of women's songs frequently reflect on this fact, that there may be no place that women may truly call "one's own home" (*apnā ghar*). But as they speak of this conundrum, they do so not in a unified, monolithic, or homogeneous female voice, but from the varied positionings of sister, daughter, and wife. Women speaking as sisters and daughters construct the relationship between natal place and conjugal place very differently from women speaking as wives, yet both perspectives are compelling and critical commentaries on some of the dominant conventions of the North Indian patrilineal discourse on marriage, gender, and authority.

This chapter focuses primarily on women's ties to their natal kin and on women's perspectives as daughters and sisters; the words of women speaking as wives and as daughters-in-law will be heard in chapter 4. I present here ethnographic observations on three interrelated sets of phenomena. First, I discuss gift giving between a woman and her natal kin, and the varying ways in which gifts and intentions are read by the recipients and the donors (a woman's brothers and her parents), and by women as sisters and women as wives. Second, I examine the ways in which several genres of women's ritual songs constitute a reflexive and often ironic commentary on pervasive cultural assumptions about a woman's natal ties, and the contradictory perspectives on natal ties voiced by daughters and sisters, on the one hand, and wives, on the other. I suggest that these songs constitute a powerful example of what Hayden White might call a "metatropological" form in which we find self-conscious and reflexive attempts to evaluate the experiential adequacy of a set of cultural tropes, of cultural frames of reference for interpreting social relationships, specifically, here, women's ties to their natal kin. Third, I discuss a number of cases of "double relationships," in which ties within a village can be traced in more than one way, through alternate genealogical links, and I examine the uses women make of the ambiguities embedded in the variant readings of these relationships, and the strategies through which a woman is able to use these genealogical ambiguities to redefine her position in her conjugal village, her *sasurāl*.

DAUGHTERS AS "OTHER," DAUGHTERS AS "ONE'S OWN": ON THE AMBIGUITIES OF THE GIFT

Throughout northern India, marriage is spoken of as a *kanyā dān* (gift of a virgin), the unreciprocated gifting away of a daughter along with lavish gifts for herself and for the people of her *sasurāl*, her husband's house. She is given away in the course of a complex set of ritual actions that are in part designed to effect her transformation from "one's own" (*apnī*) to her natal kin to "other" (*dūsrī*) and "alien" (*parāyī*) to them. The woman is often said to undergo a transformation at the wedding, in which she becomes the "half-body" of her husband, of one substance with him. His kinsmen become her own kinsmen, and her ties with her own natal kin are transformed as well; people in Pahansu say that unmarried girls share a "bodily connection" (*śarīr kā sambandh*) with their natal kin, but that after marriage there is only a "relationship" (*riśtā*).[1] Thomas Trautmann has summarized this aspect of the North Indian ideology of marriage:

> *Kanyādāna* entails several consequences. . . . The bride is . . . by gift marriage conceptually assimilated to her husband, constituting his other half (*aparārdha*) and so rendering him complete and capable of rendering sacrifice. From her natal kinsmen's point of view she is given away (*prattā*). The conception is inextricably patrilineal; all junior female kin may be classed either as born in the lineage (*gotrajā, kulajā*), subclassified into those who have or have not yet been given away in marriage (*prattā/aprattā*), or as in-marrying "brides of the lineage" (*kulavadhū*). The bride acquires the *gotra* of her husband upon marriage, and upon death is offered the *piṇḍa* by his kinsmen. The idiom of *kanyādāna* is the patrilineal idiom of complete dissimilation of the bride from her family of birth and her complete assimilation to that of her husband.
>
> (Trautmann 1981: 291)

This particular set of cultural propositions about patriliny, gift giving, and marriage has played a critical role in anthropological understandings of kinship and social life in South Asia. Ronald Inden and Ralph Nicholas (1977), for example, write that the bodily transformation of the Bengali wife is such that the people with whom her husband has a "shared body" relationship (*jnāti*) become her *jnāti*, and the people with whom her husband has a relationship defined by the gifting appropriate to relatives through marriage (his *kuṭumba* relations) become her *kuṭumba* relatives. This includes her own natal family; after her marriage, she is said to have only a "residual *jnāti*" or a *kuṭumba* relationship

1. This term *riśtā*, "relationship," is not used in connection with relationships within a "lineage" (*kunbā*); it is used to characterize only relationships through marriage. Thus a woman's relationship with her own natal kin is characterized, from this perspective, in the same way as a relationship through marriage.

with them, just as in Pahansu a woman's natal kin may say that they have only a *riśtā* connection with a married daughter or sister.

The analyses set forth by Trautmann, Inden and Nicholas, and others (e.g., Gough 1956: 841–42; Madan 1962) concerning the transfer of a woman from one kin group to another are seemingly predicated upon an understanding of culture as univocally rather than multiply voiced. Discerning a discourse concerned with women's transformed identities, they proceed with their analyses as though this discourse exhausts North Indian representational possibilities concerning kinship, marriage, and exchange, and as though the perspectives of both men and women may be interpreted in terms of this single set of cultural propositions.

The arguments of Trautmann and Inden and Nicholas are grounded largely in textual analyses, yet ideas about the alienation of the bride from her natal kin are not confined to Sanskrit texts or esoteric ritual. In their study based on fieldwork in rural Bijnor district in Uttar Pradesh, Jeffery, Jeffery, and Lyon stress the importance of a woman's continuing ties to natal kin in her resistance to the authority of her husband's kin, and the ways in which the ideology of a bride's necessary alienation from her brothers and parents and her incorporation into her husband's kin group may be invoked in order to limit her contacts with natal kin and to curtail such resistance (1989: 31–36). Men in Bijnor say, for example, that there will be too much "interference" if a woman visits her natal village too frequently or if marriages are arranged at too close a distance in the first place. The ideology of alienation from natal kin thus moves from the realm of a purely textual discourse to the realm of power relations in the conjugal village. Similarly, in the Uttarakhand region of northern India, men are apt to reject the idea of a woman's continuing relationship with natal kin because to acknowledge it would be to weaken their own power over their wives (Sax 1991: 77–78). And so, women's ironic commentaries on this discourse of alienation, voiced in song, are also commentaries on the power relations that frame their lives.

The discussion in this chapter builds on the observations of Jacobson (1977a), Sylvia Vatuk (1975), and Leela Dube (1988) on women's ties to natal kin and follows their analyses of the limits of "partiliny" in rural North India.[2] Jacobson argues that structural analyses of the patrilineal and patrilocal aspects of North Indian kinship, and interpretations that stress the completeness of the transfer of a woman from natal to conjugal kin, overlook the complexity of a woman's kinship relations. Though, she maintains, much of the ritual and ideology of rural North India does indeed stress patrilineality and the priority of a woman's ties to her husband's kin, many less formalized though no less important ideas and practices, such as extended visiting at the natal village, demonstrate the permanence of a woman's ties to parents and brothers. Vatuk's explicit critique of the emphasis on the lineal, corporate nature of North Indian kinship includes the argument that the "unbreakable bond" between a woman and her natal kin is related to the latter's obligation to supply her with gifts that ensure her security in her husband's home. Dube, in her discussion of the production of women as gendered subjects in the Indian patrilineal milieu, points out that certain contradictions within the kinship system produce an ambiguity surrounding women's transferal from natal home to conjugal home. While the lifelong tie between brothers and sisters is emphasized in ritual and everyday talk, young girls are nonetheless prepared for life in the husband's home by being told that a woman should be like water, which, having no shape of its own, can take the shape of the vessel into which it is poured, or that she should be like soft and malleable clay, which has no form until it is worked into shape by the potter. Thus, on the one hand, ritual perpetuates ties with natal kin, while, on the other, women are in some ways expected, as Dube notes, to discard their loyalties to natal kin, to be formed and shaped anew in the husband's family. It is women's experience of just this sort of ambiguity, their own reconstructions of it, and the uses to which these are put in women's everyday lives that is the focus of the present chapter.[3]

2. Jack Goody (1990:222–28) has also cautioned against the assumption that a woman's ties to her natal kin in North India are eclipsed by her being "gifted" to her husband and his kin group, citing as evidence the importance of ritual celebrations of the brother-sister tie, and Maharashtrian marriage songs published by Karve (1965). He also discusses the dowry as a female endowment of parental property. I do not follow him, however, in viewing the dowry as primarily a "gift to her [the bride], to the conjugal estate and to its heirs" (see Raheja n.d. [forthcoming]).

3. Sax (1991) has recently examined the way in which women's ties to their

Much of this ambiguity is lodged in concerns about the gifts given by natal kin to daughters and sisters. A woman's life, beginning with her birth, is permeated by concerns about this gift giving and the valuation of kinship ties that is communicated therein. When a son is born in rural North India, for six consecutive nights women gather in the courtyard of the house in which the birth has taken place to sing *byāī gīt,* songs celebrating the auspicious birth of a son and the happiness of the new mother. When a daughter is born, the courtyards are dark and silent at night, and when they learn of the birth of a girl, women inevitably murmur sorrowfully that "it is a matter of fate," or they signal their acceptance of the fortune that has been meted out by saying simply, "Whatever God has given has been given."

There are many reasons why sons are desired in North India, reasons connected with both land inheritance and soteriological goals. But the chief reason that the birth of a daughter brings sorrow to a house, and the reason why, according to village women, songs are not sung at the birth of a daughter, is the anticipation that "it will be necessary to give much in dowry." Such apprehension is voiced in a number of Hindi proverbs. When, for example, a family is straining its resources or perhaps going into debt to provide an adequate dowry, a neighbor or kinsman may comment, "Without a daughter, without a daughter's husband, one enjoys what one earns" (*dhī na dhiyānā āp hī kamānā āp hī khānā*). Yet, at the same time, *kanyā dān,* the unreciprocated gifting away of a daughter along with substantial amounts of jewelry, cloth, brass cooking vessels, cash, and other items, has such significant ritual and social consequences that most people say it is important that each married couple have at least one daughter to be given in marriage. And though there may be little joy at the

---

natal villages are represented in a major Himalayan pilgrimage. He persuasively argues that the rituals associated with the pilgrimage to Nandadevi affirm, for women at least, the persistence of their links to their natal place. Yet he concludes that "by participating in the rituals of Nandadevi, women in Uttarakhand help to reproduce the system of social relations that keep them in a subordinate position. They do so because the rituals offer something to them, a partial remedy for their frustration at being forcibly separated from, and public affirmation of their enduring links to, their natal places" (206). Sax sees in ritual and song women's complicity, and little possibility of actual resistance to structures of power in North Indian kinship relations.

birth of a daughter, there is also a recognition of the irony that though a daughter's birth may bring sorrow, her departure from her parent's home when she marries is equally sorrowful. This double-edged grief and its ironies are expressed in another Hindi proverb: "One has to fulfill one's responsibilities toward a valued daughter; there is sorrow at her birth and sorrow when she goes away" (*beṭī kā dhan nibhānā hai āte bhī rulāye jāte bhī rulāye*). Women's concerns about gift giving frequently center on their experiences of these seemingly contradictory perspectives on marriage prestations, and on their experiences of the shifting emotional valences of ties with daughters and sisters, to whom gifts must be given. In addition, because married women assume the gift-giving obligations of their husbands, and because they almost always arrange for the gift giving to their husbands' sisters, their concerns center also on women's experiences as givers, as well as recipients, of such gifts. I will suggest that women's understandings of the persistence of natal ties are multiple and shifting, and that their polyphonic discourse on relations to natal kin and conjugal kin are voiced largely in talk about giving and receiving, from their double positioning as both sisters and wives.

Though there are numerous ritually prescribed occasions on which gifts to daughters and sisters must be given, and numerous culturally elaborated rights and obligations implicated in acts of giving and receiving, the pattern of exchange in rural North India is not understandable simply as the rule-governed unfolding of a systematic code or the enactment of unambiguous cultural premises. Each potential act of giving is always subject to multiple strategic possibilities concerning, for example, the quality and quantity of items to be given, whether the gift is presented through an intermediary or by the donor himself, whether the donor gives freely or only after much expedient calculation of his own interests and prerogatives, and the relationship of the gift in question to the whole history of gift giving engaged in by the parties to the exchange.

As daughters and sisters, women are the primary recipients of many kinds of prestations, and they are the conduits of prestations flowing between affinally related households. Preparations for this gift giving begin long before the search for a groom is even thought of, as mothers begin to purchase cloth that will be given in their daughter's dowry, as girls begin to sew quilts and items of clothing they will take with them to their conjugal village, and as fathers begin to amass the cash and jewelry that must accompany the bride when she is given in *kanyā dān*. The Hindi term *dahej*, meaning "dowry," refers not just to the gifts given at the marriage ritual but also to the many prestations that are given to the bride and her husband's kin for many years thereafter. Apart from these ritually significant gifts, daughters also have the "right" (*hak*), throughout their lives, to expect numerous other prestations whenever they visit their natal village or whenever a brother or other man from their natal village visits their conjugal village, and it is often in terms of the quantity and quality of these latter gifts that daughters and sisters gauge the degree of love, affection, and "unity" (*mel*) with which they are regarded by their natal kin. Because kinship relations in northern India are so frequently defined in terms of the kind of giving and receiving appropriate to them (Eglar 1960; Inden and Nicholas 1977; Raheja 1988b), and because all of these gifts are subject to strategic manipulation and multiple interpretation as to purpose and motive, women see their relationships with their natal kin as always shifting and fluid, and they are poignantly aware that the tie they regard as being closer than any other may at times represent, for the brother, only one among many onerous obligations.

Many of the gifts given to daughters and sisters at marriage and on other ritual occasions are referred to as *dān*. This term is used to refer to prestations given to many kinds of recipients and in many different ritual contexts. Such gifts are given, villagers say, "to move away inauspiciousness" (*nāśubh haṭāne ke lie*) from the donor and transfer it to the recipient, who is thought of as a "receptacle" (*pātra*) for the inauspiciousness contained within the gift.[4] *Nāśubh* is the most inclusive term used in Pahansu to refer to a range of negative qualities and substances that may take the form of "hindrances" (*bādhā*), "faults" (*doṣ*), "afflictions" (*kaṣṭ*), "disease" (*rog*), "danger" (*saṅkaṭ*), or "evil" (*pāp*). Such inauspi-

4. Gujars in Pahansu, concerned as they are with their image of themselves as givers of *dān* and as guardians of the well-being of the village, frequently said to me that "all *dān*" is given to remove inauspiciousness, as if to assert that they were unconcerned with issues of prestige that are connected with such gift giving. They do concede, however, that some *dān*, like that given to the local Gujar college or to religious institutions, does not have this ritual function.

ciousness may afflict persons, houses, and villages at many times in the yearly cycle and at many times in the course of one's life, and each time it must be "moved away" by being gifted to an appropriate recipient if well-being is to be achieved. The recipient of such gifts is said to "take the afflictions" (*kaṣṭ lenā*) of the donor upon himself. If the gift is given to an appropriate recipient in the course of proper ritual actions, the inauspiciousness will be "digested" (*pachnā*) by the recipient, with the consequence that his *tej*, his internal "fiery energy," will be diminished. But if it is not properly digested, more overtly deleterious consequences will follow: disease will afflict him, he may become "mad" (*pāgal*), his family and lineage will decline, his intellect will be ruined, and "sin" and "evil" (*pāp*) will beset him.

The acceptance of such gifts is obviously dangerous and problematic. Why then would anyone be willing to accept a role as "receptacle" for such inauspiciousness? While one may in fact occasionally encounter cases in which a potential recipient refuses to be involved in such a perilous undertaking , a person is usually able to refuse to accept only if he is prepared to disavow other aspects of giving and receiving in village life and is prepared to isolate himself from his kinsmen or his fellow villagers. It is said to be the "right" (*hak*) of the donor to give, and the "appropriate obligation" (*pharmāyā*) of the recipient to accept *dān* and the inauspiciousness it contains; because such obligations are part of the very fabric of village ritual and social life, they cannot be circumvented without unraveling other aspects of kinship and intercaste relationships that involve not "obligations" but rights to receive, and rights to give in turn to yet other recipients. In addition, because *dān* prestations generally consist of cloth, foodstuffs, jewelry, or quantities of agricultural produce of considerable value, it is also often economically difficult to refuse to accept. Finally, while the greatest "prestige" (*izzat*) accrues to one who gives munificently, one's prestige is also augmented when the items received in *dān* are of such quantity and quality that they elicit favorable comment from one's kinsmen and neighbors.

The giving of *kanyā dān*, then, removes "evil" (*pāp*) and "danger" (*saṅkaṭ*) from the family of the donor. It brings the greatest danger, villagers say, if a daughter remains in her father's house after she attains marriageable age. She must be given in *dān* because to allow her to remain in her natal home would generate inauspiciousness and misfortune, and of course because of the ever-present fear of sexual transgressions that would adversely affect the *izzat* (honor) of her natal family. Inauspiciousness is transferred to the groom and his family through their acceptance of the *kanyā dān* and the many prestations that follow. This idea appears to have a very long history in Indic texts. In a hymn from the Rig Veda describing the marriage of Surya, the daughter of the sun, and Soma (verses of which are used in marriage rituals even today), there is a similar inauspiciousness attached to the blood of defloration. The marriage gown on which the stain of blood appears causes the bride's own family to prosper, but her husband's family is "bound in the bonds," and her husband himself may become "ugly and sinisterly pale" if he comes into contact with it. "It [the blood] burns, it bites, it has claws, as dangerous as poison is to eat." Some of the inauspiciousness involved in the acceptance of the *kanyā dān* is, in Pahansu, passed on to the groom's family Brahman priest, and this is the case in the Vedic hymn as well: "Throw away the gown, and distribute wealth to the priests. It becomes a magic spirit walking on feet, and like the wife it draws near the husband. . . . Only the priest who knows the Surya hymn is able to receive the marriage gown."[5]

This notion that the acceptance of a bride involves the acceptance of evil as well is unambiguously articulated in the Sanskrit verses that are recited at every wedding ritual, and much of the ritual is, in Pahansu, structured around this central concern. The first ritual act in the long sequence of marriage rites, for example, is the *sagāī*, the betrothal ceremony at which a "letter" (*chiṭṭhī*) formally opening the sequence of *dān* prestations and formally announcing the astrologically auspicious date for the *kanyā dān* is given by the bride's family to the groom. This *chiṭṭhī* embodies both the auspicious and life-affirming aspects of the marriage gifts as well as the inauspiciousness that is transferred to the groom. The letter, which has been prepared by the Brahman priest who serves the bride's family, and which may be opened only by the groom's priest, is daubed with auspicious turmeric and rice, and it is marked with other auspicious signs. But it also

5. These quotations from the Rig Veda are from the translation by O'Flaherty (1981).

contains 1¼ rupees, a ritually significant sum that is often utilized in transferals of inauspiciousness. Before the groom may safely accept this initial gift, he must be seated just outside his house upon a ritual design called *ṭakkarpūrat* (protection from harm), which absorbs some of the inauspiciousness and transfers it onward to the family Barber who accepts the flour from which the design was made as *dān*. The Barber also receives coins that are circled over the groom's head by the men of his family, and these coins too remove some of the harmful qualities that accompany the *chiṭṭhī*. But still the letter may not be opened. The Barber's wife has meanwhile drawn another *ṭakkarpūrat* design in the courtyard of the groom's house. Carrying the letter in the end of his shawl, the groom stands over this design while the women of his house and his neighborhood circle dishes of grain over his head. This grain, along with the flour from this second *ṭakkarpūrat*, is then given to the Barber's wife as *dān*, again for the protection of the groom. It is only after these two sets of protective actions have been performed that the letter may be opened. The 1¼ rupees are taken out of the letter and kept in the groom's house. Because of the inauspiciousness that it contains, the money may not be spent or otherwise used by the family. It is kept in a large clay pot for four or five years, after which it is usually given again in the *chiṭṭhī* of a sister of the groom, or if it is a silver rupee, it may be melted down and fashioned into an ornament to be given in *dān* at the time of her wedding. Inauspiciousness is thus dislodged from the house in which the silver had been kept, and "given onward" (*āge denā*) to the people who in turn receive a bride.

This theme of the dangers inherent in the acceptance of *dan* from the bride's natal family recurs throughout the course of the many rituals connected with marriage and a woman's first years in her conjugal home. The most important rite in this protracted series of performances and giftings is the *pherā*, the "circling" of the fire by the bride and groom that definitively transfers the bride from natal to conjugal kin. The *pherā* takes place in the courtyard of the bride's house. The priests of the bride's family and of the groom's, men from both sides, and the groom himself are seated around the place where the sacrificial fire will be lit. After some preliminary worship of the deities established at the site, and the ceremonial welcome of the groom by the bride's father, *dān* is offered to the groom: a small sum of money that in fact signifies all of the gifts that will later be bestowed upon him is given as *gau dān* (the gift of a cow). Immediately upon receiving this gift from the bride's father, the groom gives a portion of this money onward as *dān* to his own Brahman *purohit* (family priest). The Sanskrit verse spoken by the groom at this time indicates that this *dān* is given to the priest "to remove the faults caused by the acceptance of a cow" (*gau pratigraha doṣa nivāraṇārtham*). The sacrificial fire is then lit, and the bride's mother's brother leads the bride herself, very heavily veiled, into the courtyard and seats her at the side of the groom. The bride's father or the oldest man of her family recites the Sanskrit "resolution" (*saṅkalp*) for the giving of *kanyā dañ*. In this resolution the groom is addressed as *śarmanne var* (protecting groom) because of his role as recipient of *dān* from the bride's family. The groom pronounces that the gift has been received, and he says to the bride's father, in Hindi, "May auspiciousness be yours" (*tumhārā kalyāṇ ho*), thus indicating that the giving of *kanyā dān* assures the well-being of the donor. Immediately following his acceptance of the *kanyā dān*, the groom himself makes a resolution for the giving of a *gau dān* to his Brahman *purohit*. The resolution pronounces that this *dān* is given "to remove the faults caused by the acceptance of a wife" (*bhāryyā pratigraha doṣa nivāraṇārtham*). A sum of money is given as *dān* to the priest, and he is said to be one who "protects" the groom from some of the dangers involved, just as the priest in the Rig Vedic hymn receives the bloodstained bridal gown in order to protect the husband from its evil.

The *pherā* rite not only confers this *dān* upon the groom; in the course of the ritual the bride's relationship with her natal kin is also transformed. Before she is gifted away, she is "one's own" (*apnī*) to her natal kin, and she has a "bodily connection" (*śarīr kā sambandh*) with them. Just after the groom accepts the *kanyā dān*, the bride's mother's brother provides a piece of white cloth called a *kaṅjol*, measuring 1¼ *gaj*. The end of the bride's shawl is tied to the clothes of the groom with this cloth, and small stalks of grass, a few grains of rice, and a coin are tied in the knot of the *kaṅjol*. This cloth remains tied to the bride's clothing for several days. It may not be kept in the house after that, because of the inauspiciousness it contains; it is given to the *purohit* of the groom's family, in order to transfer the danger to him. The Sanskrit verses recited by the bride's family priest as the *kaṅjol* is tied affirm that this action is done "to protect the two masters" (i.e., the bride and the groom) from any inauspiciousness that would affect their future offspring, their wealth, or longevity, inauspiciousness that is generated because of the joining together of the bride and the groom. The tying of the *kaṅjol* both unites them and contains the negative qualities thereby set loose. After this tying together of the bride and the groom, and the circling of the sacrificial fire that follows, the bride is no longer "one's own" to her natal kin. People say that she is now "alien" (*parāyī*) to them and "of another house" (*begāne ghar kī*), and though she will always have a "relationship" (*riśtā*), she no longer shares a "bodily connection" with them.

Because she is "alien" to her natal kin, the bride is now deemed to be an appropriate recipient herself of *dān* prestations from them, for only one who "goes away to another house" can take away the inauspiciousness conveyed in the gift. She will return frequently to her *pīhar*, her natal village, throughout the course of her life, and on many of these occasions, she will be the "appropriate recipient" of prestations that ensure the well-being and auspiciousness of her brothers and their children. It will be her "obligation" to accept these gifts when sons are born to her brother, when his sons marry, and at certain times in her own life when inauspiciousness may afflict her brother (such as the death of her husband or when the first tooth of one of her own children appears in the upper rather than the lower jaw), and at a number of calendrical rituals observed by married women for the protection of their brothers.[6]

Such then are the meanings of *dān* as they are inscribed in the marriage ritual itself. This set of meanings enters explicitly into actors' intentionality as gifts are given to married daughters and sisters and their husbands; when they are asked why they give *dān*, people inevitably reply that it is given "for one's own well-being achieved through gift giving" (*apne khair-khairāt ke māro*) or

6. See Raheja 1988b:176–78, Peterson 1988, and Reynolds 1988 for descriptions of these rituals for brothers. Raheja (1988, 1989) provides detailed analyses of many kinds of *dān* prestations in Pahansu.

"to move away inauspiciousness" (*nāśubh haṭāne ke lie*). In such contexts, villagers always point out that it is the "right" of the donor to give *dān*, and the "obligation" of the recipient to accept. When speaking of these gifts, they frequently comment on the aptness of the proverb "Daughter, daughter's husband, and daughter's son, these three are not one's own" (*dhī jamāī bhānjā ye tīnoṅ nahīṅ apnā*); only one who is not "one's own" is a fit recipient of *dān* and the inauspiciousness it conveys.

The "obligation" of the recipient to accept *dān* is sometimes represented as begging, because it is said that those who accept *dān* must take whatever is offered, and this dependency is viewed in the same light as beggary. When the groom is given the cash, jewelry, brass vessels, bedding, and other items of the *dahej*, he must accept them in the *pallā*, the end of his shawl. When he spreads it out to receive *dān*, this gesture is called "spreading out the begging bag" (*jholī pasārnā*). People in Pahansu often comment that it is for this reason too that though they may want to receive the many items given in the dowry, there is nonetheless a certain hesitancy, a certain ambivalence, about its acceptance; "*Dān* should go from the house," they say.

Giving generously without regard to what one receives is also crucial in maintaining and augmenting one's *izzat* (prestige) in the village and among one's kinsmen.[7] Several days before a wedding or other gift-giving occasion, the items to be given (especially the pieces of cloth) are laid out on cots in the courtyard of the donor so that kinswomen and neighbors may inspect and evaluate them. The donor's prestige is enhanced if the quality and the quantity of the cloth to be given are viewed favorably. The procedure is repeated in the village of the recipient. When a married woman returns to her conjugal village after a trip to her natal village, the sets of cloth she has brought will be examined and appraised by the women of the village, and criticism and abuse will not be spared if the gifts are judged inferior.

Reluctance to give and niggardliness in giving open one to serious moral reproach. When I went to Pahansu for my second period of field research, accompanied by my two children, a number of women proposed with mock seriousness to find a potential

7. For an extensive discussion of *izzat* and gift giving in a South Asian Muslim community, much of which is relevant to Hindu practice, see Eglar 1960.

groom for my eighteen-month-old daughter among their own relations. In one such situation, I took up their bantering tone and replied that I would certainly avoid such a marriage in India, in order to circumvent the necessity of providing the large dowry that would be expected. At this remark, the whole tenor of our conversation changed abruptly. The levity and merriment subsided immediately, and I was severely chastised for exhibiting such a disinclination to give to my own daughter and her future husband. One woman said to me in all seriousness, with horrified bewilderment in her voice, that she hadn't known before that I was so greedy for money. My protestation that I was "only joking" was not, I'm afraid, terribly persuasive in the face of my overtly mercenary and grudging asseveration.

Though it provokes gossip and moral censure, there are nonetheless instances in which reluctance to give or begrudging calculations are evident in a person's attitudes and behavior. And though one gives for one's own well-being and auspiciousness, though unstinting and munificent giving enhances one's *izzat* and social position in the village, men and women may sometimes judge carefully and weigh the *izzat* to be gained against the costs of giving. Late one morning I was squatting at the threshold of her house with Asikaur, a village woman of a prominent and prosperous family, scrutinizing the wares of an itinerant cloth seller as she prepared to purchase cloth that would be given in *dān* prestations to two of her married daughters, Premo and Santosh. Asikaur finally made her purchases and took the cloth into the courtyard of the house, where her son Jabar Singh was eating his lunch. An argument instantly broke out between them and lasted nearly an hour. Jabar Singh was shouting that all of this giving and receiving was a custom of the "old times" and should be curtailed. Just as vehemently, Asikaur declared that "there are four brothers and four sisters [Asi had eight children, by then all married], and so there is the right to take and give" (*chār bhāī haiṅ aur chār bahaneṅ to lene dene kā hak hai*), and that one "must maintain one's prestige" (*izzat rākhnā paṛegā*) by giving to one's daughters and sisters and to their children. At that, Jabar Singh stood up, threw the remains of his lunch on the floor, and with all the magisterial authority of a man pronouncing a hoary and apodictic proverb composed the following utterance:

> If it weren't for daughters, you would enjoy your life;
> if it weren't for us [the four brothers], you would be destroyed.
>
> *beṭiyāṅ nahīṅ hotīṅ to terā mauj;*
> *ham nahīṅ hote to terā nāś.*

With that he stormed out of the courtyard. Premo, one of the sisters to whom the cloth in question was to be given, was visiting Pahansu, and she was sitting in the courtyard in tears as Jabar Singh and his mother wrangled over the prerogatives and responsibilities of brothers and sisters. Asikaur too was visibly shaken at the harsh words spoken by Jabar Singh concerning the gifts to be given to his sisters. But eight days later, Asikaur's younger son delivered five sets of cloth to Santosh in her conjugal village; and two months later, returning to her husband's house, Premo took twenty sets of cloth, including those purchased from the cloth seller that day.[8]

Premo is not a woman given easily to tears, but her distress at hearing her brother's words was intense. While men most often invoke issues of *izzat*, the dependency of recipients and the economic responsibilities of donors, and the ritual efficacies of giving *dān*, women, speaking as sisters, tend more frequently to speak of ritual efficacies, on the one hand, and of the "love" (*mohabbat*), "affection" (*māmtā*), and unity or "mixture" (*mel*) between brother and sister, on the other, as the primary considerations in gift giving. Thus, while Jabar Singh spoke of the money that he saw as being squandered on cloth that was destined, in all likelihood, to be "given onward" in further cycles of gift giving, from Premo's perspective his outburst represented a repudiation of the emotional tie with his sisters, a tie that sisters often value above all others.

The overwhelming significance of a woman's ties to her brothers is evident in numerous ways in North India. In contrast to the image of alienation from brothers entailed in the notion

8. I have recounted this anecdote elsewhere (Raheja 1988b:238–39), in a discussion of the connection between concerns about *izzat* and the giving and receiving of gifts. At the time that account was written, I was little concerned with women's reimaginings of kinship relations, and so I wrote nothing there of how women might respond critically to the sort of denial of the importance of women's continuing ties to their natal kin that Jabar Singh so eloquently made. The sets of cloth that Premo and Santosh took with them included both *dān* prestations and those given in *vādā*, to be described below.

that married women do not share a "bodily connection" with their natal kin, married women frequently bear tattoos of their brothers' names upon their arms. Those names are thus irrevocably inscribed upon their bodies, though the substances of those bodies, from one perspective, are said to intermingle no longer with those of the brothers and other natal kin.

The importance of ties to brothers is also evident in the blessing recited by senior women of the conjugal village when junior daughters-in-law of the village perform the deferential act of massaging the senior women's legs. The senior women murmur, "May your husband live long, may your brother live long, and may God give you a son" (*sāī jīte raho bhāī jīte raho beṭā de bhagvān*). The importance of all three of these relationships—with the husband, with the brother, with the son—is thus voiced in that blessing.

Women are generally inconsolable upon the death of a brother, and I have observed cases in which women took off all emblems of their marital auspiciousness—their glass bangles, toe rings, and so forth—in token of their extreme sorrow. The removal of these emblems and embodiments of *suhāg*, good fortune, is prescribed only upon the death of a husband. When these women "take off good fortune" upon the death of a brother, they perhaps are indicating in a subtly ironic and indeed subversive fashion that they consider the tie with the brother as important as that with the husband, insofar as their well-being, auspiciousness, and security are concerned. It is particularly significant that sorrow at the death of a brother is here semiotically conjoined with sorrow at the death of a husband; though the relationship with the brother is defined, in terms of the overt structure of North Indian kinship and its dominant discourse, as dramatically different from and less enduring than the relationship with the husband, in their actions these women comment on and interrogate the dominant discourse that represents them as "other" to their natal kin.

The link between gift giving and the emotional attachment of brothers and sisters is less overtly evident in *dān* prestations than in gifts of another sort that explicitly point up not the "otherness" of married daughters and sisters but their enduring ties with their natal kin. One such prestation is *milāī*. Translated literally, this term means "meeting," "joining," or "mixing," and *milāī* is given, people say, "to increase unity" (*mel baṛhāne ke lie*) between brothers and sisters. The most common situation in which *milāī* is given is when a brother visits the conjugal village of one of his "sisters" (his own sister, a woman of his own clan, or a woman from his own village). He is then expected to visit her home and give her a small gift, usually one or two rupees. Sisters, however distantly they may in fact be related, complain bitterly if a brother fails to pay such a visit and thus fails to exhibit in her conjugal village the degree to which he holds his sister in regard. When he does give *milāī*, every possible degree of intimacy and affection is carefully considered. Did the brother give the *milāī* and then leave hastily, or did he drink a cup of tea and talk with his sister? Did he stay for a meal in his sister's house? Did he make the appropriate inquiries about her welfare and that of her children? If he had other affairs to attend to in the village, did he visit his sister first and stay longest in her courtyard, or did his actions imply that his other concerns there took precedence? Thus, while a brother might be in compliance with the "rule" that *milāī* should be given to one's sister, it is altogether possible that the style in which it is given might partly subvert, in the eyes of his sister, the formal meaning of the gift. In any event, the sister experiences the event not simply as the fulfillment of a cultural expectation that the brother is obliged to give *milāī*; she experiences it largely in terms of the strategies and improvisations that contextualize the act and reveal the intentionality of the donor, her brother.

A prestation that evokes a similar set of considerations is that given to a woman by her mother, her brothers, and their wives as she is about to return to her conjugal home after visiting her natal village. When *dān* is given, there is very often a fixed number of sets of cloth or a fixed quantity of grain or a certain number of brass vessels that should be given. In the case of these *vādā* prestations, as they are called, while there are certain factors that should be taken into account (such as how long the woman has stayed in her natal village, and how long it has been since her previous visit, for example), there are no ritually specified quantities that must be given; and so it is all the more likely that women will interpret the amounts that are given in terms of the closeness of their tie with their natal kin. It is also important to women that they be able to demonstrate to their husband's kin that their natal kinsmen esteem them enough to give generously. When, for example, Atri, a woman married in Pahansu, returned there to her husband's house after visiting her *pīhar*, her stepmother and her half brothers sent only six sets of cloth: five for the woman herself and one for her husband. These were judged to be of poor quality, and the fact that no sets of cloth were sent for Atri's husband's younger brother or for her husband's mother prompted some disparaging and caustic comment in the village. Upon hearing what had been sent, one of the most senior women of the village scorned the donor by saying, "What did she give, that co-wife prostitute [a potent abuse used by one woman for another]? She gave very little, and several months have passed [since the last visit]" (*kyā diyā sauk-rāṅḍ ne thoṛā diyā uskī mausī ne aur kaī mahīne ho gaye*).[9]

For married daughters and sisters, the primary significance of *milāī* and *vādā* prestations is that they signify their continuing identity as "one's own" to their brothers. In contexts in which *dān* is given, women are described as "other" (*dūsrī*) and "alien" (*parāyī*) to their natal kin, and they are referred to as *dhiyānī*, a word that has the referential meaning of "married daughter" or "married sister," and the pragmatic effect of creating distance and otherness, because it is used, in Pahansu and Hathchoya, only in contexts in which the giving of *dān* to those who are "alien" is at issue. But in contexts in which *milāī* and *vādā* are given, the term *dhiyānī* never occurs. The more usual terms *beṭī* (daughter), *laṛkī* (girl), and *bahan* (sister) are always used, and on these occasions, married women are never described as "other" or "alien" but as "one's own" to their natal kin. This shift in perspective is de-

9. Women underscore the significance of these *vādā* prestations as they celebrate the annual festival for the goddess Sanjhi Devi, during the first nine days of the bright half of the month of Asauj. The goddess is said to travel between her conjugal village and her natal home during this time. Women and young girls form elaborate images of Sanjhi (made with cow dung and various pigments) on their courtyard walls, and it is important that she be decked in the ornaments that are significant for a woman's "marital auspiciousness" (*suhāg*); in fact her body is composed almost entirely of jewelry. Appropriate *vādā* gifts are also represented around her. Jayakar (n.d.:262–63) provides several illustrations of such images from Haryana, but her description of Sanjhi Devi's identity as a "dread mother" does not correspond to the goddess's significance for women in western Uttar Pradesh. See Entwistle 1984 for an extended description of this ritual as it is celebrated in the Braj area of Uttar Pradesh.

scribed in a proverb that women use in conversations about *milāī* and *vādā* prestations: "Daughters and sons are one's own, but the daughter-in-law is other" (*dhī pūt to apne bahū begānī*). The pragmatic and emotional force of this proverb contrasts with that of the proverb "Daughter, daughter's husband, and daughter's son, these three are not one's own" that is invoked in talk about the giving of *dān*. The former proverb is clearly inappropriate as a commentary on aspects of relationships involved in the giving of *dān* and its ritual efficacy, since in that context the married daughter, the *dhiyānī*, is explicitly conceived of as alien and other. The existence of these two contradictory proverbs indicates the nature of the ambiguity surrounding women's relationships to their natal kin, and the divergent meanings attached to the gifts given to women.

Though I have argued in other contexts (Raheja 1988b, 1989) that this distinction between the two kinds of prestations is a critical one in rural North India, there is nonetheless a sense in which the contrast is blurred in everyday experience. Though the ritual meanings of the *dān* that brothers give to their sisters stress the "otherness" of the sister and her "obligation" to accept the gift to ensure her brother's auspiciousness and well-being, the degree of attachment and regard that a brother feels for his sister is often gauged by the quantity and quality of the gifts that he gives in *dān*, as well as those he gives in *milāī* and *vādā*. Thus all gift giving takes on affective significance for sisters and implicates them in considerations of the emotional valences of their relationships with their natal kin and in reconsiderations of the cultural definitions of their status as "other" to their natal kin.

IRONIC JUXTAPOSITIONS IN WOMEN'S SONGS

The representations of women as both "one's own" and "other" to their natal kin that are encoded in these two kinds of prestations are contextually distinct perspectives, and although women tend to reflect on both kinds of gift giving as indicative of their natal kinsmen's regard for them, the existence of the two perspectives nonetheless indicates a contradiction at the heart of North Indian kinship ideology.

The words of women's songs in western Uttar Pradesh configure a purposefully ironic commentary on this contradiction. As both Burke (1969: 511–17) and James Fernandez (1986) have pointed out, an intentional juxtaposition of two contradictory perspectives is the discursive prerequisite of an ironic stance. A recurrent theme of many of these songs centers on a reflexive awareness of the divergent images of women's ties to natal kin in North Indian culture. Taken together, the songs do not reject one or the other of these images in order to eliminate the ambiguity inherent in kinship relationships. Rather, a reflexively ironic awareness of the discrepancy between the two sets of representations is the predominant characteristic of the songs.

Women's songs in Pahansu and Hathchoya frequently enact a drama of competing voices and competing perspectives, thus tangibly and concretely displaying the ironic content expressed in the words of the songs. The performance context of these songs sometimes makes this particularly evident. Groups of women sing primarily at the births of sons, at weddings, and at various annual festivals. Songs are sung at two different kinds of occasions. Women sing as the ritual events of a wedding unfold, usually in close proximity to the male-dominated formal ceremony. At these times, women quite literally have to compete to let their voices be heard. At the *pherā*, the central core of the wedding ritual, at which the bride is formally transferred from her natal kin to her husband's family amid ritual acts of deference to the groom's side, women of the bride's side sit just a few feet away in the same courtyard and sing *gālīs*, songs abusing the groom's family in which obscene joking about the sexual proclivities of the groom's mother is the most common theme. It is not unusual for the men of the groom's family to become angry at this, to call for a halt, only to be rebuffed and assailed by yet more bawdy abuse. When the bride's mother's brothers come to give gifts just before the wedding is to take place, they stand just at the threshold of their sister's husband's house, and behind her the women of the neighborhood sing "songs of the mother's brother's gifts" in which their generosity, and thus their *izzat* (prestige) as well, is denigrated. Just outside the door, behind the mother's brothers, men of both sides have gathered, and there is among them, inevitably, a raucous band, playing loudly and cacophonously as if to drown out the female voices, stopping only when the women's songs are finished.

At the birth of a son, while the marriage party is away at the bride's village, and at the festivals of Holi and Tij, singing and dancing sessions called *khoṛiyās* are held, usually at night in courtyards from which males have been barred. "Dancing songs" (*nāchne ke gīt*) or "sitting songs" (*baiṭhne ke gīt*) are sung on these occasions. Unlike other genres of women's songs, both of these almost always take the form of long verse narratives in which the tragic consequences of a husband's failure to transfer his loyalties from his mother and sisters to his new wife is the most frequent theme. At the very time that the groom is accepting a bride in *kanyā dān,* according to which ideology the wife should be assimilated to and defer to the kin of her husband, his own mothers and aunts and sisters are singing of the morally problematic aspects of such a transformation.

The internal patterning and the formal structure of the songs likewise highlight the competing voices and multiple perspectives. As in Rajasthan, the verses of many songs from Pahansu and Hathchoya are "chorused conversations" in which conflicts and opposed perspectives are enacted in alternating question-and-answer exchanges among kin. Thus one song may articulate as many as five or six different points of view on a situation or relationship. These songs typically depict conversations in which the voices and differing perspectives of husband and wife, the husband's mother, his sister, and the wives of his brothers may all be heard.

The representations of women's ties to their natal villages in these songs reflexively highlight the incongruities among the possible perspectives on these ties and in doing so comment on the contradictions, emotional dissonances, and unresolvable aspects of women's experiences of these relationships. Perhaps the most powerful of these ironic evocations is a "song of the mother's brothers' gifts" that I recorded in Pahansu.[10]

10. The texts for all Hindi songs are given in the Appendix. The translations for these songs are somewhat more literally rendered than the translations from the Rajasthani, largely because I lack Ann's enviable ability to transport the poetry of women's songs into rhythmic English verse.

1. *Song of the Mother's Brothers' Gifts*
[Sister speaking to her brother]
A little pebble over a big one.[11]
Born from one mother,
I've come, now respect me,
I've come as your guest (*pāhunī*).
Born from one mother,
You too have a daughter.[12]
Born from one mother,
Sell your orchards [in order to buy the gifts].
Born from one mother,
Then come to the wedding rites.

[Brother speaking]
I won't sell the orchards.
Born from one mother,
The splendor of the orchards would be lost.

[The sister who is receiving the *bhāt* then speaks in the same way in the following verses, asking her brothers to sell their ponds, their wells, their streets, their cattle, their horses, their wives' ornaments, and their houses. The brother responds in the same way to each request, refusing to sell anything in order to give the *bhāt*. In each case he gives the same reason for his refusal, saying that the "splendor" (*śobhā*) of each would be lost. But in the case of his wife's ornament, her *haṅslā* (a heavy silver choker), he says that he can't sell it, because it came from his wife's father, and so he has no right to take it away from his wife. Following this lengthy exchange, the brother speaks again.]

[Brother speaking]
Your brother's wife (*bhābhī*) was sulking.
I was making her happy, and so I came late to you.
A little pebble over a big one.
Your brothers' sons (*bhatījās*) took time getting dressed, and so I came late to you.

[Sister speaking]
Why are you making so many excuses?
Was the rain pouring down too hard?
Was your bullock cart too far away?
Were your bullocks too feeble to walk?
Rampal's [bride's father's name] great givers of gifts,
Sister Kanta's [bride's mother] givers of gifts.

11. For an explanation of this line, see p. 190.
12. The sister is here reminding her brother that just as he has obligations to his own daughter when she marries, he also has obligations to his sister who has come to ask for the *bhāt*.

The first verses of this song represent the speech of a sister who is visiting her natal home for *bhāt nyautnā*, the "invitation for giving *bhāt*." On this occasion, a sister gives her brothers a lump of unrefined sugar, a set of cloth, and five rupees. She informs them that the marriage of her child has been arranged, and invites them to come to her *sasurāl*, her conjugal village, to give the substantial set of gifts called *bhāt* just before the wedding is to take place. A brother is always expected to give generously at this time, but the expectations for gifts of cloth, jewelry, and brass vessels will be especially great at the marriage of a sister's daughter, because these will be given onward in the dowry. The second part of the song, beginning with the brother's reference to his own wife, depicts the conversation that takes place when the brother arrives at his sister's *sasurāl*.

It is the ironic juxtaposition of the sister's identity as "guest" (*pāhunī*) to her brother, on the one hand, and as one who was "born from one mother," on the other, that gives this song its power and emotional resonance. The masculine form of the word "guest" (*pāhunā*) is in this part of North India used almost exclusively for visiting kinsmen related through marital ties, one's *riśtedārs*, and the feminine form *pāhunī* refers generally to out-married kinswomen who are visiting their natal kin. The use of the term *pāhunī* then underlines the "otherness" of the daughter or sister, her status as one who has become only a "guest" in her natal place. But just after the sister is identified as *pāhunī* in the song, she utters the phrase *merī re māīyyā jāye* (born from the same mother), which recurs forty times in the course of the performance I recorded in Pahansu. Sung in an almost hypnotic melodic line, this refrain is the most insistent phrase of the song. The text of the sister's request acknowledges the cultural logic that *bhāt* (a *dān* prestation) is to be given precisely because she is a "guest" and has become "other" to her brothers. Yet that logic is passed over, in favor of a stress on the most intimate of bonds, "born from the same mother." The brother's responses, however, indicate that for him at least, this relationship does not take first priority; he must first fulfill his own wife's needs, before he can be generous to his sister.[13] The sister knows that her brother has

13. The words that are used here are *rūsnī manātā*. *Rūsnī* (from the verb *rūsnā*

been making excuses, selfishly whining (*gin min gin min*) about the reasons why he cannot give as she asks. Yet for her the central irony is that one who is "born from the same mother" can, according to a different cultural logic, place other ties, other calculations, above that common birth.

The same situation is represented in another women's song, one sung at the time of the *bhāt nyautnā*. This "song of the *bhāt* invitation" is sung by the women who have married into the sister's natal village, those who are in the relation of brothers' wives to her. This song voices their perspective on the giving of *bhāt*, a perspective that is quite different from that of the sister herself.

2. *Song of the bhāt Invitation*
The husband's sister comes for *bhāt nyautnā*.
On the girl's head is a lump of sugar.
Girl, if you want some cloth,
Then go and live with a cloth seller, girl.
On the girl's head is a lump of sugar.
Girl, if you want some gold,
Then go and live with the goldsmiths, girl.
On the girl's head is a lump of sugar.
Girl, if you want some pots,
Then go and live with the tinkers, girl.

In this song, the brothers' wives rebuff the husband's sister's request for cloth and pots and jewelry by telling her that if she wants these things, she should go and marry someone whose business it is to provide them. In each line, the Hindi text reads "enter into" (*baṛ jā*) the house of the cloth seller, the goldsmith, and the tinker. The clear implication is that the sister should go and live as a wife there. These contemptuous insinuations stand in contrast to the sister's request, in the *bhāt* song, that she be "respected" in her brothers' house.

Many songs explicitly contrast the burdens of a woman's gift-giving obligations to husband's kin with her desire to give freely to her own natal kin. A song sung at the birth of sons in Pahansu

---

or, in standard Hindi, *rūṭhnā*) refers to a woman (*rūsnī* is the feminine form, *rūsnā* the masculine) who habitually sulks in order to press her claims on a kinsman or close friend. To engage in *rūsnī manānā* is to pacify that person, to assiduously reassure her that she is regarded with affection and esteem.

is typical in this respect. A new mother is expected to give gifts called *neg* to her husband's sister, after she provides various ritual services on the sixth day after birth. In this song, the voice of the new mother is heard refusing to give the ornaments requested by her husband's sister, precisely because of her desire to favor her own sister instead. Though the mother's sister would never in fact be the recipient of gifts at this time, what is significant is the emotional priority placed on the wife's, rather than the husband's, natal tie.

3. *Birth Song*
Fair fair cheeks and curly hair,
The newborn boy is beautiful, in his embroidered shirt.
My brother is a policeman, my brother's wife is very dear.
Ask for your gifts, Husband's Sister, today is a wonderful day.

I won't give my forehead pendant, Husband's Sister, it's an ornament for my forehead.
I won't give my forehead jewel, Husband's Sister, I've promised it to my sister.
I won't give my earring, Husband's Sister, it's an ornament for my ear.
I won't give my nose pin, Husband's Sister, I've promised it to my sister.

[The verses of this song continue in this way, naming such ornaments as the silver belt, ankle bracelets, and toe rings.]

In this song, an image of harmony and felicity is set up in the first verse, when the new mother invites her husband's sister to ask for the gift she wants, as she is customarily expected to do. But this image is undermined in the second verse, when she refuses to give the *neg*. The obligations to give *bhāt* and *neg*, however, are so well defined, the ritual reasons for giving these gifts are so compelling (Raheja 1988b), and one's *izzat* (prestige) is so much at stake that actually refusing outright to give the *bhāt* and *neg* is almost unimaginable. What is at issue in these songs, I suggest, is not so much whether to give or not to give but the particular valence to be placed on a relationship. The sister's voice in the first song asserts the priority of the brother-sister tie, the "birth from one mother," while the brother's wife in the second and third songs minimizes the importance of the husband's sister's continuing ties to her brother.[14] The "Birth Song" makes it clear that the wife's reluctance to give stems from her desire to emphasize her own natal ties rather than those of her husband. Both of these contrasting claims are set forth in the idiom of giving and receiving, and both point to an inherent contradiction in a woman's position in kinship relations: she becomes "other" to her natal kin in many respects yet longs to remain "one's own" to them. And while she longs to become "one's own" to her husband as well, his own sister may see this as threatening her tie to her brother. The women portrayed in these songs seem always to be at odds with one another, and yet groups of women, neighbors and kin of many kinds, sing these songs in unison, as if in ironic acknowledgment of their common plight.

The poignancy of women's separation from natal kin is most vividly dramatized in North India at the moment of *bidāī* (departure), when a newly married girl first leaves her natal home in the company of her husband and his male kin. Both men and women present at this time are apt to shed tears at the sight of the heavily veiled young woman being carried to a waiting automobile, tractor-trolley, or water-buffalo cart, and the women of the bride's natal village sing "departure songs" (*bidāī gīt*) at the doorway. Many of these songs are commentaries upon the ironies of a woman's relationships with natal and conjugal kin.

4. *Song of the Bride's Departure*
Refrain [Bride's natal kin speaking]
Dear girl, today you've left your father's house, today you've become "other" (*parāyī*).
The streets in which you spent your childhood have today become "other" (*parāyī*).

[Bride speaking]
My grandfather cries, my grandmother cries, the whole family cries.
My younger brother cries, your sister born from the same mother (*mā jāī*) has left and gone away.

[Verses in which the bride speaks are repeated, using kin terms for FeB, FeBW, FyB, FyBW, and so on.]

14. Commenting on marriage songs translated by Karve, Goody notes that in Maharashtra too a brother's generosity to his sister is seen as restrained by his wife (1990:224).

The second line of the refrain ends with the words *parāyī re*. (*Re* is a vocative particle that commonly appears in these songs.) The second line of the bride's verses ends with the words *mā jāī re*. The replication of the same sound pattern, the rhyme, in these two verses ironically highlights the dissimilarity in the meanings of the relationship enunciated by the bride's kin and by the bride herself. Irony is voiced in this song in this juxtaposition of the two different interpretations. *Parāyī re* and *mā jāī re* share the same sounds, but this aural similarity only serves to heighten the irony that the two perspectives on the relationship of the departing bride to her natal kin, both available in the cultural discourse, are so radically different.

5. *Song of the Bride's Departure*
Refrain [Bride speaking]
Don't let your mind be filled with sadness.
Mother, I'll meet you again.

I'll call my *dādas* (HFM) *dādī* (FM),
I'll call my *tāyas* (HFeBW) *tāī* (FeBW).
I won't remember my *dādī*,
Mother, I'll meet you again.
I won't remember my *tāī*.
Mother, I'll meet you again.

[In the following verses of this song, the bride says that she will call her husband's mother "Mother," her husband's sister "Sister," and so on.]

This second song of departure expresses an ironic perspective on cultural discourses about women in kinship not by explicitly juxtaposing two contradictory interpretations but by making an utterance whose actual intended meaning is precisely the opposite of its conventional and literal meaning. The poignant irony of a bride saying, "I won't remember my *dādī*, I won't remember my *tāī*" lies precisely in the fact that all of the women singing this song know that she will never forget, and though she may call her husband's father's mother *dādī*, as the patrilineal ideology of *kanyā dān* enjoins her to do, her experience as she utters that word in her conjugal village is worlds apart from the experience of saying it in her natal home.

These sentiments are given more direct expression, though, in a *byāī gīt*, a birth song, from Pahansu.

6. *Birth Song*
I yearned to call the midwife;
How should I know that a doctor would come running.
Give the birth gifts, it is a pleasure to give.

I yearned to call my mother;
How should I know that my mother-in-law would come running.
Give the birth gifts, it is a pleasure to give.

I yearned to call my grandmother;
How should I know that my husband's grandmother would come running.
Give the birth gifts, it is a pleasure to give.

I yearned to call my sister;
How should I know that my husband's sister would come running.
Give the birth gifts, it is a pleasure to give.

I yearned to call my elder brother's wife;
How should I know that my husband's elder brother's wife would come running.
Give the birth gifts, it is a pleasure to give.

I yearned to call my younger brother's wife;
How should I know that my husband's younger brother's wife would come running.
Give the birth gifts, it is a pleasure to give.

I wanted very much to call my father's sister;
How should I know that my husband's father's sister would come running.
Give the birth gifts, it is a pleasure to give.

In Pahansu and Hathchoya, as in Ghatiyali, women give birth in their husband's home, never in their *pīhar*s. This birth song speaks of a woman's thoughts as her child is born, and as she looks to other women for help and encouragement, and for the various ritual services she requires. Though she may expect to have only her husband's kin around her, she still yearns to have her own mother, her grandmother, her sister around her. She has not forgotten them or learned to call her *dādas, dādī*. Her husband's kin do not replace her own.

A third song of departure and a Holi song draw on a wider set of associations to evoke a sense of irony and to portray the emotions of a bride in a foreign place.

7. *Song of the Bride's Departure*
Two water pots are on my head.

A beautiful golden pendant is on my forehead.
Call me back quickly, Mother,
Beg with folded hands.
My heart is not here in my husband's mother's house,
My heart is not here with this foreign man.
Call me back quickly, Mother.
Beg with folded hands.
My friends still played with dolls together,
But I went off to my *sasurāl*.
Call me back quickly, Mother
Beg with folded hands.

[The first verse is repeated a number of times, changed only by the substitution of the names of other ornaments worn by married women.]

8. Song for the Festival of Holi

My forehead mark, the pendant there, and the wrap that covers my head, all are colored yellow.
Brother, take me away from here.
My husband's father's land is bad.
Brother, take me away from here.
For me this land is empty, there's no one to call one's own.
Brother, take me away from here.
I'm fending off the black crows.
Brother, take me away from here.

[This entire verse is repeated many times, substituting for the forehead pendant and the wrap the names of other ornaments worn by married women.]

The first two lines of the departure song invoke conventional and recurring images of desire and fulfillment, and the pleasure of attracting and pleasing one's husband. An image of a woman gracefully drawing water at a village well often, in women's songs, precedes a happy flirtatious encounter, and songs of conjugal happiness frequently include long lists of the ornaments worn by a married woman that enchant her husband and entice him to give her even more articles of adornment, the ornaments that embody her marital auspiciousness, her *suhāg*. The song of departure opens with this set of propitious images, but the desires and expectations are evoked but not fulfilled: the husband is a "foreign man," and the bride cannot bear to stay. She has become *parāyī*, foreign, to her own natal kin at the time of her marriage, but the man to whose house she has gone is a foreigner to her.

The song for the festival of Holi is patterned in the same way. The woman's wrap and ornaments have been colored yellow because she has played Holi (*holī khelnā*) in her husband's house. Holi is the North Indian festival in which hierarchies are temporarily overturned, and the norms for women prescribing deference and silence are momentarily relaxed. Nowadays, "playing Holi" involves exuberantly throwing multicolored powders and dyes—purchased from the bazaars—on friends, kinsmen, and fellow villagers, and a general sense of merriment as one's visage and one's clothes become progressively transformed as the day wears on. Before the advent of commercially prepared colors and dyes, *ṭesū* flowers from the *ḍhāk* tree were boiled to produce a yellow liquid that was used in the same way as the powders and dyes now purchased in the market. When the woman in the Holi song says that her ornaments are yellow, she is telling the listeners that she has played Holi with the *ṭesū* flower dye. The fact that it is her ornaments, the emblems of her "marital auspiciousness" (her *suhāg*), that have been yellowed suggests in a covert way that she has played Holi with her husband, a situation that suggests, if the signs are read by the husband's family, conjugal intimacy and mutuality. But as in the previous song, this image of intimacy is followed immediately by a plea addressed to the brother to take her away from a land in which there is no one she can call "one's own." And the song ends not with auspicious images of ornaments that embody a woman's *suhāg* but with the inauspicious image of the circling black crows, harbingers of death.

Both Pauline Kolenda (1990: 139) and Susan Wadley (1983: 54, 69–70) speak of an association between pleasurable erotic encounters and the throwing of colored dyes at Holi. Wadley translates several North Indian *bārahmāsā* in which the pain of separation from a husband at Holi is especially acute. These *bārahmāsā* (songs of the twelve months) are representative of a very popular poetic genre in North India, and in the examples Wadley translates a particularly poignant sorrow arises from the pain of separation from one's husband at the time of Holi because of the powerful emotional association between sexuality and the throwing of the Holi dyes. The ironic commentary evident in the Holi song from

Pahansu is emotionally charged precisely because of the very evident intertextual awareness of the *bārahmāsā*'s focus on this association and on the pain of separation a woman is conventionally represented as experiencing when her husband is away. In the Pahansu song, she has thrown the colored dyes, but she yearns, nonetheless, not for her husband but for her natal kin. It is the tension between these two textual representations that produces a sense of irony in this song.

I spoke about this particular song in 1988 with Simla, a woman who had been married into Pahansu, to Jabar Singh, about twenty years before, and who had given birth to four children, one of whom was already married and about to give birth to Simla's first grandchild. We talked about why so many women felt the poignancy of such songs, and she said to me, very slowly and deliberately as she looked around the house in which she had spent more than half her life, "You know, we never call our *sasurāl* 'one's own house' (*apnā ghar*). We only call our *pīhar* 'one's own house.'"[15] Simla's ironic tone speaks here to the fissure she seems to experience between the patrilineal convention that married women become "one's own" to their husband's family and women's continual feelings of "foreignness" in their *sasurāls*, and their feelings of longing for their natal homes. In Simla's case, her longing was particularly poignant, to me and to the other women who knew her, because her own mother had died before she could give birth to a brother for Simla. Though Simla's father had remarried, and his second wife had borne a son, neither Simla nor anyone else regarded him as a "true brother" (*sagā bhāī*), because the two were not born from the same mother. So it seemed that Simla, perhaps more than many other women, sometimes felt that there was no place she could truly call "one's own house."

In South Asia, as in most societies, kinship and gender are

15. When speaking of a married woman, other people may certainly refer to her *sasurāl* as "her own home" (*apnā ghar*). But I never heard a woman refer to her own conjugal home as "one's own home." When women use the phrase with reference to themselves, as Simla did, they almost always are speaking of their natal home. But certainly there are issues of pragmatic intent to be considered in understanding women's use of these words. If, for example, a woman wanted to make a particular statement about her authority or her status in her conjugal home, she might use the word *apnā* to reinforce her point pragmatically.

generally represented as grounded in the natural world, as the unalterable and commonsensical givens of social life. But irony, as White (1978: 6) points out, is a linguistic strategy of skepticism, and as a mode of consciousness, it attempts to explore the degree to which such given taxonomic systems are as much products of one's own need to organize reality in this way rather than some other way as they are of the objective reality of the elements placed in the taxonomy. From this perspective, irony is "metatropological" in that it signals a self-conscious, reflexive attitude toward the tropes and linguistic conventions that organize our worlds, and it signals a skepticism toward the notion that these particular tropes, conventions, and taxonomies adequately represent one's experience. Irony may play, as Michael Herzfeld (1991) points out, on the tension between an *apparent* social consensus and an inwardly experienced dissent.

For Fernandez, irony is indeed the "ultimate trope," in its deliberate though perhaps oblique voicing of an awareness of incongruities between cultural conventions and everyday experience. "To point out incongruities," he writes, "is to suggest [the possibility of] their transcendence, to suggest the passing beyond the necessarily pretentious claims of our roles in particular social organizations and institutions" (1986: 291).

In his discussion of irony as a dialectical strategy, Burke implicitly draws out a distinction between an ironic stance and a stance of subversion that would directly contest aspects of conventional discourse. He emphasizes his perception that irony generally involves a recognition of multiple voices and multiple perspectives. When one speaks in an ironic mode, he suggests, one tries to construct a dialectical perspective upon this multiplicity, "with a recognition that none of the participating 'subperspectives' can be treated as either precisely right or precisely wrong" (1969: 512).

These characteristics of an ironic discourse all seem to be present in the women's songs about natal kin I have translated here, and this ironic perspective constitutes an interrogation of some of the central propositions of the discourse of patriliny, and a critical awareness of its contradictions. The irony in these songs does not seek to displace that discourse entirely but to question its claim to exclusive moral authority.

Irony is one possible stance vis-à-vis these contradictions, but it is not the only one articulated by women in Pahansu and Hathchoya. A more potent form of interrogation, with greater possibilities of effecting transformations in women's everyday lives, is evidenced in women's talk about alternative readings of genealogically ambiguous relationships, talk that I heard daily, in nearly every courtyard in Pahansu and Hathchoya.

"DOUBLE RELATIONSHIPS": READING GENEALOGICALLY AMBIGUOUS TIES IN PAHANSU AND HATHCHOYA

Marriage in rural North India nearly always follows a pattern of village exogamy, and because marriages at a distance are generally preferred over marriages in nearby villages, a woman usually goes many miles away to her husband's house and theoretically has no natal kinsmen there. Such preferences for marriage at a distance are more frequently voiced by men than by women. Jeffery, Jeffery, and Lyon (1989: 34–36) translate a number of Bijnor residents' responses to the question of whether marriage at a distance is preferred to marriage in a nearby village. Women say that distant marriage is bad because news cannot be easily conveyed from the husband's village to the natal village and back again. Men are far more likely to remark that if a married woman lives too close to her natal kin, she is too easily able to turn to them when disputes arise in her husband's home. There would be too much interference from them, too many disagreements, and too much of a threat to the husband's rule.

At least two genres of male expressive traditions—folk dramas and proverbs—record husbands' suspicions of wives who maintain close ties to their brothers and their natal homes. In the folk dramas in the *sāṅg* or *nauṭaṅkī* popular theater of northern India, a central core of many dramatic plots is a husband's hostility to a wife's brother, and his fear and suspicion that she may harbor powerful loyalties to her natal kin that could jeopardize his own power and authority over her. But if a husband cannot fully trust his wife in these plays, brothers also frequently distrust their sisters because they have married into other families and have allegiances there (Hansen 1992: 184–88). Two Hindi proverbs, used predominantly by men, attest to the suspicions harbored by husbands about wives' brothers: "As niches weaken walls, so wives' brothers weaken the house" (*dīvār khāī āloṅ ne, ghar khāyā sāloṅ ne*); and "The wife's brother eats special fried breads, and a brother's brothers eats only peas" (*bahū kā bhāīyyā pūrī khāye, bhāīyyā kā bhāīyyā maṭar chabāye*)—that is, a wife will favor her own brothers over her husband's kin.

Despite these views of the danger that women's natal kin pose to the husband's authority, in Pahansu and Hathchoya women very frequently have natal kinsmen close at hand, though there too, just as in the nearby district of Bijnor, it is deemed appropriate if a woman is sent to a distant village at marriage. But women actively and intentionally *construct* these relationships for themselves, when their own brothers are far away. Most of the women I know in Pahansu and Hathchoya are related to a number of men and women in their conjugal village in two ways: through the marital relationship, of course, but also through previous ties they are able to trace through natal village connections, "from the direction of the natal village" (*pīhar kī taraf se*), as they always put it. These relationships traced through a woman's natal village are often quite distant in the genealogical sense—frequently there is no traceable genealogical link at all—and such relationships may also be recognized and acted upon among persons of different castes, for whom the link is simply that each has a tie, through women, to a common village. Yet any of these natal village relationships are, according to the local reckoning, "closer" (*zyādā nazdīk*, as opposed to "distant," *dūr*) than the relevant marital tie in the conjugal village, even though the latter may be genealogically quite near indeed and would otherwise be of fundamental importance according to the prevailing "patrilineal" ideology. These "closer" natal village relationships within a woman's conjugal village reorder previously existing relationships among and through men, by restructuring patterns of gift giving, deference behavior, and kin term usage among both men and women. Women's strategic invocation of these natal village ties rewrites the script of patriliny and its ideology of *kanyā dān*, in which the preservation of women's close ties to natal kin is viewed as dangerous to their undisruptive incorporation into the *kunbā* of their husbands.

It has frequently been pointed out that in many ways marriage in North India entails a complete separation between a woman's natal kin and conjugal kin, and between the natal village and the conjugal village (Vatuk 1971: 289; 1982b: 95; Sharma 1978: 221). Such a radical distinction between a woman's identity as daughter and sister in her natal village and as wife in her conjugal village is indeed powerfully marked. Apart from the distinct ritual and gift-giving roles in the two villages, a woman's everyday social identity is also grounded fundamentally in this contrast. Standards for proper behavior differ dramatically in the two villages. In her natal village, a returning married woman may visit freely and walk through the village streets with her face uncovered, and she does not bear responsibility for household work. In her conjugal village, on the other hand, a woman veils her face in a gesture called *ghūṅghaṭ* before her own husband and all males senior to him, and she must not speak in the presence of these men. She will "massage the legs" (*pāoṅ dabānā*) of the wives of these men when she encounters them. A woman never veils her face in her natal village, and it is said to be productive of "sin" or "evil" (*pāp*) if a daughter of the village should ever do *pāoṅ dabānā* there.

Powerful as this segregation of women's multiple identities may be in defining the proper relationship of gender and kinship in northern India, there are ways in which women's uses of genealogical ambiguities erase this distinction in certain limited though nonetheless important arenas, as women grant importance to even very tenuous natal village ties in their *sasurāl*s.

Ursula Sharma has suggested that, as an aspect of the North Indian patrilineal kinship ideology, *ghūṅghaṭ* functions to render women "ineffectual in the very place where their presence is most threatening to the continuous maintenance of . . . relations among men" (1978: 231). It accomplishes this by severely limiting their ability to speak in public arenas in their conjugal village, and by limiting their access to men of influence there. But Sharma also points out that *ghūṅghaṭ* and the practices associated with it are not always totally effective in this regard; she writes that women in the Himachal Pradesh village in which she worked "do not behave in a particularly passive manner in general. . . . The alliances which they form and the enmities they pursue often have a considerable effect on the course of village factional politics" and on other aspects of domestic and village affairs (229).

The following analysis of *ghūṅghaṭ, pāoṅ dabānā,* terminological usages, and gift giving in situations in which natal village relationships are traced within the conjugal village reveals some of the ways in which an emphasis on these natal ties, on a daughter's identity as "one's own" to her natal kin, facilitates a woman's effectiveness in this regard, and the ways in which aspects of North Indian patrilineal ideology are reconfigured by women in the *sasurāl* as they read relationships in this way.

Kolenda (1967, 1968) has suggested that if a woman maintains close ties to her natal kin, there is more likelihood that she will be able to effect an early separation of her own conjugal unit from her husband's joint family, thereby perhaps advancing her own interests over that of her husband's patrilineal kin. This may be possible because strong natal ties presumably enable her to escape a total submission to the authority of the husband's senior kin. I suggest, in the analysis that follows, that women actively *create* what are viewed as natal ties within their conjugal villages, in order to establish just such a site for possible negotiation, even when their own natal villages may be distant or when their own fathers and brothers are unable or unwilling to show support for them.

Women are occasionally able to utilize a kinship relationship, traced through their natal villages, that would by anybody's reckoning be viewed as a close genealogical connection. But there are many other ways that women are able to construct these *pīhar* relationships. Cases 1 and 2 are examples of the use of relatively close genealogical ties.

Case 1

Usha married Raj Kumar during my first period of fieldwork in Pahansu. She would normally be expected to perform *ghūṅghaṭ* before Mangal Singh and Sukhbir, her husband's elder "brothers" (her *jeṭhs*). She does not do *ghūṅghaṭ*, however. Mangal Singh explains why: "She is related as sister, the daughter of our mother's brother [here, genealogically, his MFZSD]. Our relationships are like this. From one direction she is our sister, and from the other direction, Amar Singh is our brother." Usha herself says that she does not do *ghūṅghaṭ* because Mangal Singh and Sukhbir are the sons of her father's sister (her *phūphī ke laṛke*). Mangal Singh him-

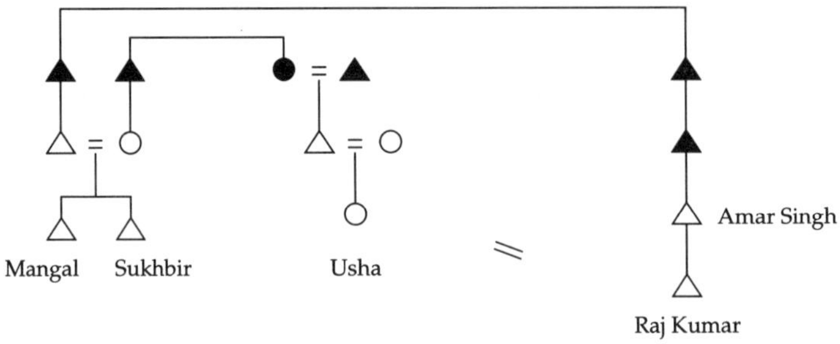

Figure 2. Usha and Mangal Singh

self went in the groom's party, the *barāt*, to Usha's natal village, as I did, but he gave her several rupees in *milāī*, as he would do for any "sister" he so encountered, but which he would never do in his capacity as patrilineal relative of the groom.

From Usha's perspective, this reckoning of kin ties stresses a *pīhar* (natal village) relationship in existence prior to the relationship to Mangal Singh and Sukhbir established through her marriage. The former relationship was genealogically traceable but never acted upon before her marriage to Raj Kumar. From the perspective of the two Pahansu men, this reckoning entails acting upon a relation through their mother's *pīhar*, which takes precedence over the genealogically closer relationship in their own village, the village of their father, and this is how Mangal Singh himself explained the situation to me.

It is not insignificant, for men or for women, that the reading that privileges the more distant natal village tie over the conjugal tie is acknowledged in such public situations. Bourdieu (1977: 41–43) has suggested that in Kabylia such "heretical" readings, which invoke connections through women, would be relevant only in the most intimate spheres of family life. But for Mangal Singh in this situation, and for all of the other Gujar men with whom I spoke about such natal village ties, relationships through women are matters of public as well as private concern.

Case 2

Descendants of Munshi by his second wife, Harikaur—Rupram and Budha—are related in Pahansu as Shanti's *jeṭhs* (HeB). According to such a relationship, Shanti should do *ghūṅghaṭ* before them and never utter their names. But because Gomi, the mother of Rupram and Budha, was Shanti's *buā* (FZ), they are also related as Shanti's "brothers," the sons of her *buā*. Shanti therefore does not do *ghūṅghaṭ*, and she pronounces their names with impunity and, often, gleeful irreverence, saying that "from one direction, the direction of the *sās* [HM], they are related as *jeṭh*s, but from my house, from the direction of my *pīhar*, they are my brothers." And of course one does not veil or remain silent in the presence of brothers, and one need not show particular deference to them.

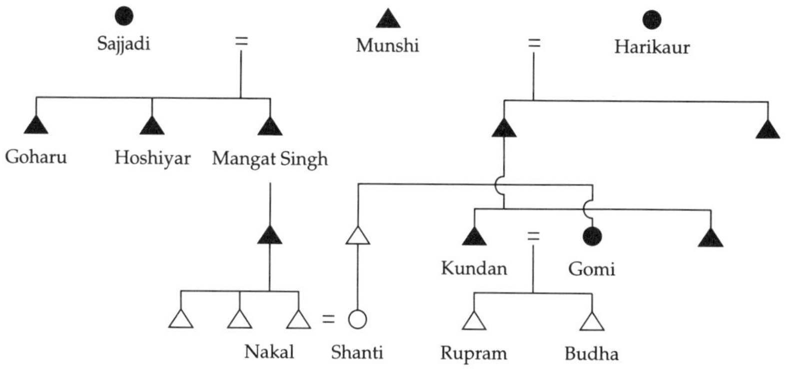

Figure 3. Shanti and Her Father's Sister's Sons

Shanti told me in this connection that Gomi, her father's sister, had in fact asked that Shanti's marriage be arranged in Pahansu, in the house of her own husband's kinsmen. "She asked for me," Shanti said. Such a pattern is quite common, and women very frequently try to have marriages arranged in such a way that there will be a *pīhar* relationship in the prospective bride's *sasurāl*, a situation that women say is infinitely desirable for a *bahū*, a wife in her husband's village, precisely because she will be able to utilize these ties to gain allies for herself should a dispute arise with her husband or his kin.

In many cases in which women trace such relationships "from the direction of the natal village," perhaps in the majority of cases in fact, there is no such traceable genealogical link at all. But these relationships are regarded by women as no less significant than actual genealogical relationships. Case 3 illustrates a situation in which a tie to a common clan (*got*) is used in this way.

Case 3

Shanti is the *chāchī* (FyBW) of Omi's husband, Raj Pal, and thus Omi's *pitas*, to be addressed as *chāchī*. Omi's mother, however, is of the same clan (*got*) as Shanti, and although the two women do not know each other, they are regarded as sisters. Omi, therefore, calls Shanti *mausī* (MZ) and does not do *pāoṅ dabānā* to her. Omi says that this is because a woman "keeps the relationship" (*nātā rākhtī hai*), that is, observes that relationship rather than any other, "from birth, from where one's birth took place" (*janam se jahāṅ apnā paidā huā*). This is so, she says, because any relationship "from the direction of the natal village" (*pīhar kī taraf se*) is "closer" (*zyādā nazdīk*) than the relevant tie traceable through the *sasurāl* (the conjugal village), even though the latter is, in this case, genealogically very near. Omi went on to say that "from here [i.e., Pahansu, her *sasurāl*], Shanti is related as *pitas*, but because of the *got*, she must be called *mausī*; she is my *mausī* from the direction of my mother" (*idhar se hamārī pitas lagtī, lekiṅ got kī vajah se mausī kahnā paṛe; apnī mā kī taraf se mausī hai*). Omi's use of the verb *lagnā* in this situation, in relation to Shanti, is very telling. As Vatuk (1969: 257–58; 1982a: 63) has indicated, the word *lagnā*, "to be related," is seldom used in conversation if the relationship at issue is genealogically close. In such a case, the usual expression would be "She is my HFyBW" (*hamārī pitas hai*), using a form of the verb *honā*, "to be." But here, in the context of Omi's discussion of the closeness of the *pīhar* tie, she has used the verb *lagnā*, which effectively emphasizes the relative "distance" of any *sasurāl* relationship, and she indicates her assessment of the "closeness" of the *pīhar* relationship by the use of the expression "She is my *mausī*" (*mausī hai*).

Omi and Shanti quarrel very frequently, however, usually over

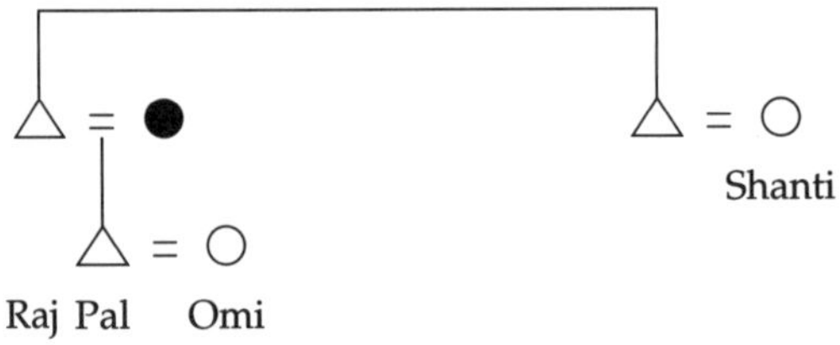

Figure 4. Omi and Shanti

domestic matters (they live in the same house but maintain separate hearths), but in such argumentative situations neighbors and relatives always comment, as did the two women themselves, that it is "the fighting of a HM and SW" (*sās-bahū kī laṛāī*), presumably because it would be inappropriate amid such dissension to emphasize the *pīhar* relationship.

Another way that women establish *pīhar* ties is by acting upon relationships that involve only a link to neighboring villages. Case 4 is such an instance.

Case 4

Gendi is Nakli's *chāchī* (FyBW) and thus the *pitas* (HFyBW) of Taravati; the latter would normally call Gendi *chāchī*, massage her legs, and show her great deference, but because the *pīhars* of the two women are "neighboring villages" (*guwāṅḍ*) to each other, Taravati calls Gendi *buā* (FZ)[16] and does not do *pāoṅ dabānā* to her. Thus both women give priority to a *pīhar* relationship over a genealogically very close *sasurāl* relationship, even though they previously did not know each other, and the *pīhar* relationship itself is, by usual standards, very distant indeed. But for both the tie is a significant one.

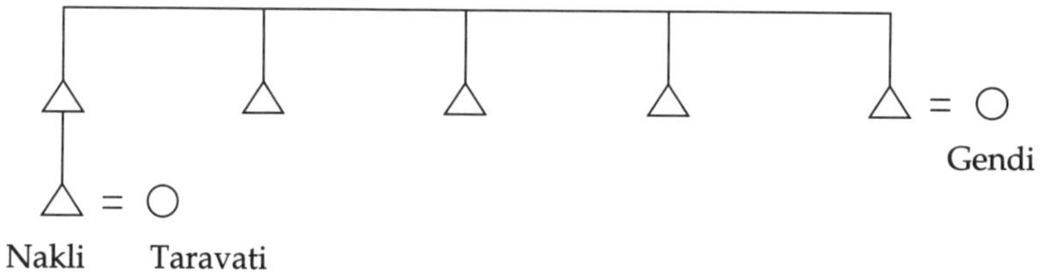

Figure 5. Gendi and Taravati

In a number of cases that I observed in Pahansu, women observe the importance of natal village ties even when the person to whom they trace a relationship is of another caste, and actual genealogical relationship is therefore not at issue. Cases 5 and 6 illustrate this point.

16. Kin terminology, reckoned according to "generation" (*pīṛhī*), is used not only for all the people of one's own village but for the people of "neighboring villages" (*guwāṅḍ*) as well.

Case 5

Prithvi is a Water-Carrier man who works as an agricultural laborer for Telu Ram, a Gujar farmer. His wife, Parkashi, frequently assists Telu's mother, Asikaur, in the cultivation of a small cotton crop and in various household chores. Parkashi would normally, according to "village kinship," call Asikaur *dādī* ([H]FM), but because she herself is from the village of Hathchoya, where Asikaur's daughter Tara is married, she calls Asikaur *mausī* (literally, "mother's sister," but also, as here, BWM), because, as she says, she "keeps the relationship from the direction of the natal village" (*pīhar kī taraf se nātā rākhtī*), and from that perspective Asikaur is not *dādī* but *mausī*.

Case 6

Prithvi, Parkashi's husband, is himself not a native of Pahansu but immigrated there from another village in the district. Nevertheless, he has been incorporated into the village kinship "genealogy," and wives of Pahansu are expected to do *ghūṅghaṭ* before him accordingly. Telu's wife, Rajavati, however, calls him *bhāī* (brother) and does not veil her face before him because his village of origin is a "neighboring village" (*guwāṅḍ*) of Titron, her own natal village, and she therefore "understands him to be a brother, a neighboring-village brother" (*bhāī samajhtī hūṅ, guwāṅḍī bhāī*).

Women frequently act upon ties traced through their mother's natal village. This considerably widens the opportunities for tracing *pīhar* relationships that may be of use to them. In some cases, as in the following, this may involve deemphasizing a relationship through their own natal village.

Case 7

Tara's daughter Pushpa came to Pahansu, her mother's *pīhar*, for a visit and remarked to me one day (without my asking about it) that she and Raj Pal are related in two ways. "From one direction" he is her brother (*bhāī*), the son of her mother's brother, because Amar Singh is related as Tara's brother. Her own natal village, Hathchoya, is the same as that of Raj Pal's wife, who is related to Pushpa there as *buā* (FZ). Raj Pal is thus related to her "from the direction of Hathchoya" as *phūphā* (FZH). Pushpa

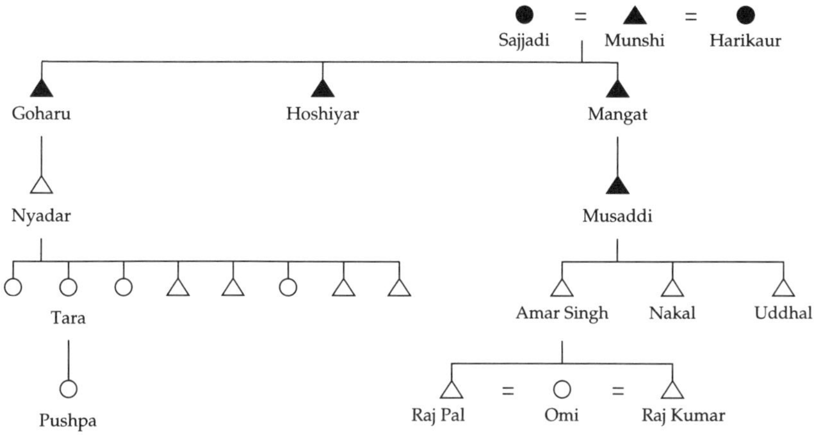

Figure 6. Pushpa and Raj Pal

calls Raj Pal *bhāī,* thus emphasizing the relationship through her mother's *pīhar* rather than that through her own natal village.

Another way in which a woman's *pīhar* relationships reconfigure relations within her husband's village is in the context of intravillage reciprocal prestations exchanged by families within a *kunbā,* or lineage group. Important among these is the distribution of food packets (*parosā*) on festival occasions. When men talk about the distribution of these packets, they always say that they are given to one's "brothers" (*bhāī*) within the *kunbā*. Now the terms *kunbā* and *bhāī* have both restricted meanings that mark the boundaries of fairly shallow lineages and broader meanings that may at times embrace a very large segment of the population of a caste within the village. Because the average number of *parosā*s that are distributed by a household generally does not exceed fifteen to twenty, the referent for the term *kunbā* in such contexts is in fact a rather small group of kin. Yet the actual distribution of these gifts is not predicated simply on the genealogical closeness of patrilineal kin, as village rhetoric about them would suggest.[17] In nearly all of the distributions I witnessed, a woman's prior

17. Vatuk and Vatuk (1976:225, 230) describe *parosā* gifts as one of several gifts given in "direct and balanced exchange among peers, typically between neighbors in a village or among agnatic kin." This is an apt characterization, except for the fact that women's ties to natal kin may redefine who is to be classed within the network of "peers."

pīhar ties redefined the limits of patrilineal connection within her husband's village, as in cases 8 and 9.

CASE 8

Parosās were sent from a Gujar household at the festival of Gugga's Ninth because a wife in the first household is from the *pīhar* of a wife in the recipient household. The two households were only distantly related through patrilineal ties, and in the absence of the common *pīhar* tie the *parosās* would not have been sent.

CASE 9

Parosās from a Gujar daughter's wedding feast were sent to another Pahansu Gujar household, in which a wife was related as FZD to the mother of the bride, only because of this *pīhar* connection.

Thus even though the overt meaning of these *parosā* prestations lies in the reciprocal relation of *bhāīchārā* (brother conduct) and patrilineal kinship ties within the village, they are not sent to everyone who could potentially be counted as a "brother." Discriminations are made, and it is significant that the existence of *pīhar* relationships among in-married women may serve to activate an otherwise contextually unstressed "brother" relationship and thus reorder gift-giving patterns among members of the patrilineal *kunbā*.

Although the "patrilineal idiom" of a wife's transformation at marriage, and her "one's own" relationship to her husband's family, is what one might call a "dominant ideology" in the sense that it has very important material consequences for women's lives and in the sense that it would certainly be invoked more frequently in abstract discussions like anthropological interviews, we see here, in this ethnography from Pahansu and Hathchoya, another sort of ideological construct existing in counterpoint to it. We find in these cases of double relationships a very strongly articulated notion that natal ties can never be supplanted by conjugal ones, that even genealogically very distant natal ties are really "closer" than any tie to the husband's kin.

How are we to interpret the relationship between these two sets of ideas about kinship and gender in North India? When Omi says that a woman always maintains the relationship "from where one's birth took place," and when so many other women say that ties "from the direction of the natal village are closest," these words may appear to represent, for them, a cultural template, a set of rules according to which women and men must order their daily lives. But if we look at the uses to which such words are put in Pahansu and Hathchoya, we may begin to understand the extent to which the variant readings of genealogically ambiguous ties represent, as in the similar cases from Algeria that Bourdieu has discussed (1977: 30–71), strategic negotiations of one's social world, and not enactments of a fixed and determinate cultural structure.

A bride who, because of *pīhar* ties, need not veil her face before a few senior male affinal men in her conjugal village may frequently use this advantage successfully to gain allies for herself in the course of disputes with her husband's family. Such strategies sometimes lead to quarrels and the disruption of the "solidarity" of patrilineal relationships in her husband's village. Yet even in these cases, a woman is deemed morally justified in marshaling the support of the men to whom she traces a natal village tie, and these men in turn generally feel an obligation to aid and perhaps give shelter to her, much as they would if it were their own sister who needed their help.

The extent to which women may invoke these ties in particular contexts for particular purposes and ignore them when it is expedient to do so is illustrated in the following case from the village of Hathchoya.

Case 10

Tara, the daughter of Asikaur, who figured in cases 5 and 7, is married in the village of Hathchoya. Since the time of Omi's marriage (about ten years after her own), Tara maintained little connection with Omi's natal family in Hathchoya, despite the fact that Omi had been married into Tara's natal *kunbā*, in the house next door to her own in Pahansu. (We have already encountered Omi in case 3.) There was little "coming and going" (*ānā-jānā*) on Tara's part, mostly because of factional cleavages that divided her conjugal family from that of Karta Ram. Yash Pal and Dillo were close to this family, however, because Dillo's daughter Anjali had

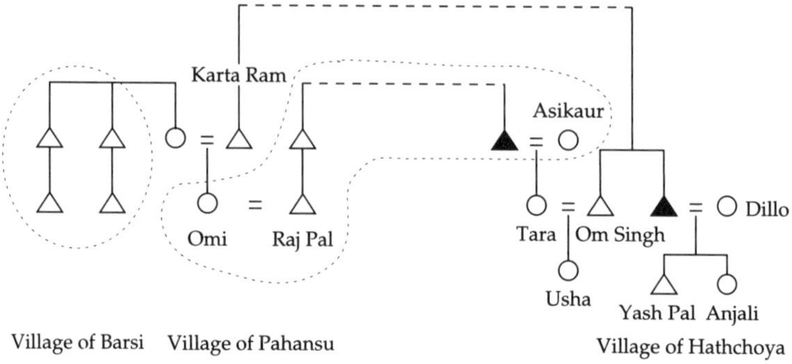

Figure 7. The Families of Tara and Omi

been married to Omi's mother's brother's son in the village of Barsi. Yash Pal had even arranged for Omi's brother to obtain a much sought-after position in a local Gujar college. Internal disputes arose within the joint family of Om Singh and Yash Pal, and when Omi's natal family failed to support Yash Pal in a village election, Yash Pal and Dillo stopped all "coming and going" with them. Just after that, Tara began to solidify her relationship with the women of Karta Ram's house. She said publicly that this was because "from the direction of the natal village" she had a close tie to that household, but it was clear to everyone in Hathchoya who observed her actions that she was cultivating this *pīhar* connection specifically in order to influence the internal politics of the patriline in which she had married, and to widen the rift that had developed between Om Singh and Yash Pal.

Sometime later, Tara's daughter Usha was also married in the family of Omi's mother's brother. Anjali and her brother Yash Pal were opposed to the arrangement of this marriage because, they said, they felt that two "sisters" (i.e., two women from the same village) marrying in the same household could possibly cause dissension and disharmony there. (Such marriages are in fact generally avoided in western Uttar Pradesh precisely for this reason.) But the marriage was arranged nonetheless. As a result, Tara is now connected in yet another way to Omi's natal family, and the people of Yash Pal's household say that their own position and influence within the Barsi household are consequently weaker, because they have only one route by which to trace a relationship with Barsi, while Tara has two. Tara's strategic use of her natal village tie has thus played a significant role not only in reconfiguring relationships within her conjugal village but also in building up and cementing her own network of affinally related kinsmen beyond the village. (It was generally agreed in Hathchoya that it was Tara's intentions and Tara's actions, and not those of her husband, that had shaped the course of these events.) Because of the importance placed on one's position in such networks in rural North India, Tara's deployment of her natal ties to Omi's family has been of critical significance to herself and to a wide network of kinsmen in Hathchoya and beyond.

Both Vatuk (1969, 1982a) and Das (1976b) have analyzed instances from North India of multiple genealogical links between two people, and the strategies through which choices are made as to which relationship will take precedence in any given context. In analyzing North Indian kinship terms of address, Vatuk considers several such cases and finds that in situations involving multiple affinal relationships the most important considerations are that preexisting relationships take priority over newly established ones, and that relationships defining one as a giver of gifts should take priority over others (Vatuk 1982a: 70; on the latter point, see also Das 1976b). Vatuk also observes that in cases in which both the conflicting ties are consanguineal precedence in this patrilineal milieu might be expected to be given to the patrilateral tie. Her data indicate, however, that closeness of consanguineal connection, whether patrilateral or matrilateral, is the decisive consideration (1982a: 68–69). This in itself can be seen as an indication of the limits of patrilineal ideology in northern India, like the bilateral (rather than strictly patrilateral) definitions of the categories of "daughter" and "sister" that Vatuk elsewhere describes (1975: 178, 193–94).

The examples of double relationships from Pahansu and Hathchoya seem to go even farther in documenting women's specific resistance to certain aspects of patrilineal ideology. These examples demonstrate that women's *pīhar* ties supersede a husband's patrilateral ties not only when they are genealogically closer but even when they are significantly more distant, thus demonstrating to an even greater degree than Vatuk's data an alternative to the "patrilineal bias" of North Indian kinship. They also demonstrate that women may utilize such calculations, and the ambiguities of their relationship with natal kin and natal village, to negotiate and renegotiate identities and relations of power within their conjugal villages, and to reconfigure, to some extent, the pattern of kinship relations there.

Margery Wolf has written that rural women in China learn early in their lives to regard many of the conventions of patrilineal kinship as burdens and as obstacles to be maneuvered around rather than as ideals to be upheld or values to be embraced. Wolf has also shown how women utilize uterine relationships, ties to their children and ties to their own natal kin, to subvert some of those conventions (1972, 1991). In Pahansu and Hathchoya, women's talk about gift giving, the songs they sing about natal kin and natal places, and talk in their *sasurāl*s of the importance of relationships "from the direction of the natal village" similarly demonstrate that women have only partially and incompletely internalized the ideals of patrilineal kinship. The ironic detachment from these ideals, voiced in song but observable also in everyday life, allows them to see that the system of marriage, familial relations, and power in which they live is not so fixed, unyielding, and monolithic as their men might sometimes wish them to believe.

Plates

(*above*) During Ann's first month in Ghatiyali a baby boy was born in the house where she lived. For the ritual of Sun Worship, Pushpa, the new mother, sits veiled with her baby in her lap while the Barber's wife holds a tray with offerings to the Sun God before her.

(*right*) Pushpa and her husband, Gopal Singh, with their new baby boy, Durgesh, in Ghatiyali. Both Ann and Gloria found that many young wives eagerly desired to be photographed by their husband's side, face unveiled, although it was clearly an unaccustomed and strained pose for them to take.

(*above*) In Pahansu, Pahel Singh, his wife, Kalavati, and their children worship at an ancestral shrine in the fields. Kalavati is veiled both because of her husband's presence and because women customarily cover their faces as they approach these shrines dedicated to their deceased male affinal kinsmen.

(*left*) Shanti's legs are massaged by a young Gujar bride in Pahansu. Women are expected to perform this act of deference for the wives of their husband's senior male kinsmen.

(*above*) An image of Sanjhi Devi is constructed at the home of a Sweeper woman in Pahansu for the Nine Nights festival. Like the women who form her image, the goddess is adorned with ornaments that embody her *suhāg*, her marital good fortune. At the festival in the month of Asauj, the goddess is said to travel between her conjugal village and her natal home. Women speak sorrowfully of how Sanjhi's brother stays in one place, but the goddess must go away to her husband's place. Like ordinary women, the goddess returns only for a brief visit; she cannot remain at her *pīhar*.

(*above*) In Ghatiyali at the home of Ratan Lal Mehta, a well-to-do Brahman whose son is about to be married, women enjoy singing wedding songs while the groom-to-be is anointed with turmeric.

(*opposite left*) The icon of a powerful goddess at her pilgrimage spot called Kuchalvara Mataji. Like Rajasthani women, the goddess too is wrapped in a glittery veil, although it does not cover her face. Such wraps are offered at shrines like this by pilgrims grateful for the goddess's boons.

(*this page and opposite*) These three photographs were taken at the same *khoṛiyā*, in a Gujar courtyard in Pahansu in March 1988. Women sang and danced as a young man from the house was married in a nearby village.

(*top*) Gujar women sing in chorus during a funeral celebration in Kalera, a village not far from Ghatiyali. Photo by Joseph C. Miller, Jr.

(*bottom*) Women sing and dance at a religious fair at the shrine of Dev Narayan, called Puvali ka Devji, just outside of Ghatiyali. Photo by Joseph C. Miller, Jr.

(*above*) A group of women, neighbors, gather in front of Four Armed Vishnu's Temple in Ghatiyali for the story of Cow Worship told on the morning of that festival day.

(*above*) Three older women, all Gujars, gather together for a visit in Pahansu.

(*right*) In Shobhag Kanvar's courtyard, with the ongoing construction of her new house as backdrop, she and Sohan, a Brahman woman, pray before a shrine to Dev Narayanji. Sohan has come for help in conceiving a child.

(*above*) Simla and Santroj with Santroj's infant daughter in Pahansu. Though women often sadly murmur, "Ah, whatever God has given has been given" at the birth of a daughter, and though girls do not receive many of the advantages accorded to sons, girl children are usually treated with love and affection.

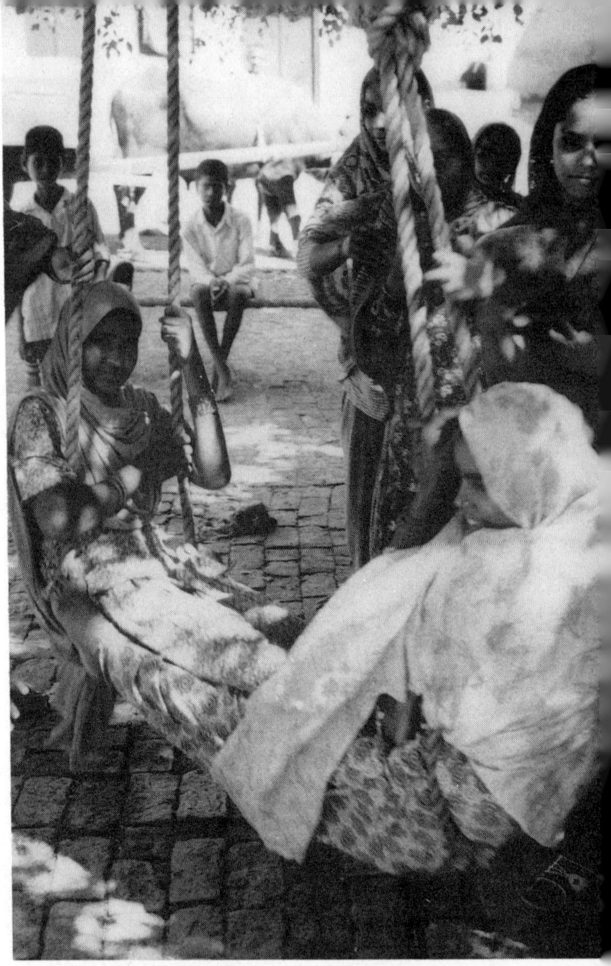

(*top, right*) Women swing on rope swings and sing at the festival of Tij in Pahansu. Perhaps the most powerful examples of resistance to norms of wifely submission that we recorded are voiced in these Tij songs.

(*bottom, right*) Shobhag Kanvar worships Diyari Ma, represented in this Rajput home by the ancestral family swords. Diyari Ma is worshipped within families during the semiannual Nine Nights of the Goddess.

(*above*) Shobhag Kanvar participates in celebrating the birth of her husband's elder brother's first grandson; in her lap is her own son's daughter. She smiles as she pours *bhāng*—a drink made with hashish.

Tara, on a visit to her natal home in Pahansu.

4

On the Uses of Subversion: Redefining Conjugality

The ability of a married woman to disrupt relations between her husband and his patrilineal kin is viewed with some uneasiness, both in anthropological studies of North Indian kinship and in many indigenous perspectives that find expression in everyday talk and in some genres of oral tradition. Both the anthropological and the indigenous unease result from an expectation that the most significant kinship bonds are those through males, the "patrilineal" and "agnatic" connections that are indeed of pivotal importance in many respects, particularly insofar as landholding and inheritance are concerned. Allied to the theme of wifely devotion associated with the figure of Sita are the injunctions placed upon a married woman to remain obedient and subservient to her husband's parents and other family members, and, perhaps most important, to subordinate her desire for intimacy with her husband to his preexisting bonds of loyalty and affection with his natal kinsmen. Kakar (1978) suggests that in this regard the wife represents a pernicious threat to the unity of her husband's family, and her intimacy with him must not be allowed to disrupt or weaken his ties to his parents and siblings. The ideal wife, then, is unquestionably loyal to her husband even if he rejects or slights her (1978:66), and she accepts the patrilineal assumption that her husband's natal ties take precedence over the conjugal relationship, and accepts, in consequence, her subordinate position in her *sasurāl*. A common Hindi proverb speaks of this assessment of wives and of their position in the husband's house:

> Whoever kicks [i.e., offends or displeases] his mother and father to strengthen his relationship with his wife,
> His sin will not go away even if he wanders through all the pilgrimage places [where sins are said to be removed].

māī bāp ke lātan māre meharī dekh juṛāy,
chāroṅ dhāmeṅ jo phir āve tabhuṅ pāp nā jāy.

The songs that I consider in this chapter challenge this devaluation of women as wives and articulate a differing set of perspectives on kinship relations, particularly relations with the husband, his mother, and his sisters. The voices we hear in these songs are the voices of women positioned in a particular way within a system of relationships, and the perspective that is constructed from the vantage point of wife is quite different from that found in the songs sung from the perspective of women as sisters and daughters translated in the previous chapter. But these two perspectives are alike in that both express acute awareness of the tensions and contradictions within North Indian kinship relations that result from a woman's movement from natal home to conjugal home. Both comment critically on these contradictions, though the voice of the wife speaks not of remaining "one's own" to her natal kin but of apprehending the significance of the husband-wife bond in a patrilineal milieu in which it is precisely relationships among men, rather than the sexual and emotional ties between spouses, that are given moral priority.

Nandy (1990: 42–43) has written of the way in which a widening of women's identity in the West has generally meant defying the limits of conjugality, while in India it may mean underscoring conjugality within a web of kinship relations. I would suggest that this is precisely the locus of much of rural North Indian women's compelling commentaries on kinship and gender. I certainly do not mean to assert that rural North Indian women resist the conventions of patrilineal kinship only to gain the affection and love of their husbands. When women's expressive traditions place this emphasis on the husband-wife bond, they are envisioning, I think, a rather dramatic alteration in the relations of power within the family. They are envisioning a world in which relationships among and through men are not always given moral primacy. It is this fact that gives women's songs their status as a "hidden transcript" (Scott 1990) that challenges some fundamental tenets of the dominant discourse. When women in Pahansu and Hathchoya sing of conjugal intimacy, they do not substitute submission to the husband for submission to his senior kin; the hidden transcript of women's songs is not radical enough to envision a world without marriage and the family, but it is subversive enough to suggest that marriage ought not to deprive a woman of intimacy or reduce her to the status of a passively submissive and powerless interloper in a household of patrilineal kin.

The evidence from the oral traditions I discuss here suggests that the often-observed instances in which in-married women precipitate disharmony and the partitioning of households and coparcenary units are not necessarily viewed as unambiguous moral transgressions. It suggests that women see a diminution of the strength of those patrilineal relations as a valid resolution of conflicting kinship expectations, and as a condition of their own agency.

Taken together, five interconnected themes, found particularly in dancing songs sung at weddings and at the festival of Tij, comprise a powerful revaluation of conjugality and a critical commentary on the set of images of the "ideal wife" associated with the figure of Sita. The first four of these themes concern the relative valuation of the husband-wife bond, on the one hand, and the solidarity of the husband with his natal kin, on the other. Together, these four themes undermine conventional North Indian assumptions about the necessary subordination of a wife to her husband's natal kin and about the threat that a wife poses to the solidarities of patrilineal kinship. I will examine these themes as they appear in a number of women's songs from Pahansu and Hathchoya. The fifth theme I will take up concerns varying representations of gender, agency, and dependency in the context of kinship relations and conjugality, as they appear in women's oral traditions and in other North Indian folklore genres performed by and primarily for males.

CONJUGALITY AND PATRILINEAL SOLIDARITIES

The first of these recurrent themes appears at first sight to be congruent with the depiction of Sita as the ideal wife, yet it represents a revaluation of the roles of mother and wife found in other South Asian discourses and practices. In most such discourses, the mother is characterized as a "master of the earth" (*Laws of Manu* IV: 183, trans. Doniger 1991); she willingly undergoes great pain in giving birth and willingly makes any sacrifice for the welfare of the sons she bears. Das has written of the relative valuation of mothers and wives in Punjabi kinship ideology: "People often say that a wife is replaceable since one woman is as good as another for purposes of procreation, but that a mother is irreplaceable. As proof of this they often quote the fact that when in pain a person calls his mother (*haay maan*) but never his father or his wife" (1976b: 4). A common North Indian proverb has it that "one does not find a bad mother" (*ku-mātā*) (Khare 1982: 157–60; Das 1976b: 5). A mother, in this view, need not be enjoined to love her son and devote herself to him, because there is a cultural assumption that she cannot do otherwise. The burden is shifted to her offspring, who must honor her precisely because of her unswerving devotion. Wives, on the other hand, are regarded with a great deal of ambivalence. Mythic and epic texts, as well as male-dominated local traditions such as the *sāṅg* drama performances of northern India, tend to portray wives either as unambiguously devoted and subordinate to their husbands or as scheming, lustful deceivers who treacherously betray their husbands and destroy the honor and solidarity of their husbands' kinsmen.[1] The love of a wife, desirable though it may be, is often suspect in male discourse, as a Punjabi proverb illustrates: "A woman who shows more love for you than your mother is a slut" (Kakar 1990: 19).

The dancing songs from Pahansu and Hathchoya that are sung, paradoxically, by the groom's mother and sisters while he is being married in his bride's natal village portray wives and mothers from a vastly different perspective. One often reiterated theme in these songs is that while a mother may be treacherous to her son, a wife will defend her husband against such disloyalty. One of the most often heard dancing songs among the dominant caste Pahansu Gujars concerns the Gujar *rājā* of the Landhaura estate in Saharanpur district who was said to have been poisoned by his mother in the nineteenth century so that his mother's lover could rule in the dead son's place. In the song, the *rājā*'s wife refers in a veiled and sorrowful way to the murder in address-

1. See, for example, the discussion of *sāṅg* dramas in Vatuk and Vatuk 1975 and Hansen 1992.

ing her mother-in-law, but the *rājā*'s mother denies that the death has even occurred.

1. *Song of the Landhaura King*

[Wife speaking]
Mother-in-law, I won't wear it, without my king I won't wear my forehead ornament.

[Mother speaking]
He's coming back, Daughter-in-law, he's coming back. Your Landhaura king is coming back to you.

[Wife speaking]
He's not coming back, Mother-in-law, he's not coming back; those who have died don't return to this world.

[Mother speaking]
Daughter-in-law, don't speak these poisonous words to me, don't speak these words.

[Wife speaking]
You've lost it, Mother-in-law, you've lost it. You've lost the Landhaura throne.

[The same lines are repeated for many verses, substituting for the forehead ornament the many ornaments, embodiments of *suhāg* (marital auspiciousness), that are worn by a woman as long as her husband is alive.]

From the very elaborate oral history of this Landhaura king recounted by Saharanpur Gujars, it is significant that the women's rendering of the story focuses on just this depiction of his female kin: the treachery of his mother and the loyalty of his wife. That this depiction of the cold and treacherous mother is not confined to the specificities of the Landhaura story is evident from the fact that this theme is echoed in several other Pahansu dancing songs. In one song I recorded, a wife again refuses to adorn herself with ornaments, because she fears that her husband has died, far away from her in the army. But her husband's mother shrugs this sentiment off, saying, "Don't think in this way, daughter-in-law, I have four other sons," thus implying that the death is inconsequential since the daughter-in-law could take one of those other sons for her husband.

Though representations of such wives may appear to validate dominant conventions concerning the duties of a wife, from another vantage point they undermine them. The depiction of the mother as treacherous and the wife as loyal subverts the usual representations of "women's character" (*strī charitra*) and women's sexuality that result in the subordination of a wife's interests to that of her husband's natal kin and the solidarity of her husband's patriline.

A second major theme found in women's songs concerns the deception that is deemed necessary if a wife is to gain intimacy with her husband. It is evident that from the perspective adopted in these songs such deception is both desirable and morally justified. In one such dancing song, it is the wife who entreats her husband to come stealthily to her in the night.

2. *Dancing Song*

I've made myself beautiful, and I'm standing in our room.
Invent some excuse and come, my husband.

I can't bathe alone with soap and warm water.
Invent some excuse and come, my husband.

I can't eat warm breads and sweet pudding alone.
Invent some excuse and come, my husband.

I've set out the chess pieces in the moonlight, and now I can't sleep alone.
Invent some excuse and come, my husband.

This song and many others like it assume an awareness of the restrictions placed upon the development of an intimacy between husband and wife, and of the role played by the husband's natal kin in these restrictions, and they seem to question their moral validity. In this song, the wife has arranged various comforts and amusements for herself and for her husband: a warm bath, festive foods, and a chess game, and she expects that her husband will join her, even if he has to lie to his family to do so. Many such songs put the words of resistance not in the wife's voice but in the husband's. The following is a "song of the young bride" (*banī kā gīt*), which is sung at the bride's house before and after the actual wedding rites:

3. *Song of the Young Bride*

The groom calls, the bride doesn't come.

[Husband speaking]
Come, my beloved, today the house is empty.

[Bride speaking]
How can I come to you? Your grandfather is standing there.

[Groom speaking]
Veil yourself heavily and take off your ankle bracelets.
Come, my wife, today the house is empty.

[These lines are then repeated many times, substituting for "grandfather" the terms for other natal kin of the husband.]

In this song, it is significant that the deception of the husband's kin is effected through the use of *ghūṅghaṭ*, the veiling, which in other contexts is emblematic of the wife's subordination to her husband's male kin. Here, far from rendering her ineffectual and powerless, it provides her with an anonymity that enables her to assert herself against the wishes of those senior males, and it figures as a sign of resistance rather than of submission. This reversal of the meaning of the act of veiling parallels that observed in chapter 2, where the veil functions as a sign of erotic allurement rather than of male control of female sexuality.

In many songs, it is not simply deception but an active confrontation that is necessary and, indeed, desired by the husband. In other North Indian expressive genres performed by males, a man is expected to thwart any attempts by his wife to fracture the solidarity of his own natal kin, to which she herself is often seen as posing a threat. But here in these women's songs, the husband encourages her to challenge his kinsmen.

4. *Song of the Young Bride*
[Bride speaking]
How can I come, how can I come near you?
Husband, your grandmother is very cunning.
She fights with me and then puts her own cot down next to our bed.

[Husband speaking]
Beautiful one, take the sword from my hand.
Come waving it, come brandishing it, come near me.
The drum will sound, the cymbals will sound, they'll sound the whole night through.

[These verses are repeated, substituting for "grandmother" other terms for the husband's female kin.]

In many dancing songs, the same valorization of the solidarity and intimacy between husband and wife is evidenced in the fact that, from the wife's point of view, oppression by her husband's kin may be possible only in the husband's absence. The following song from Hathchoya is typical of this sort of perspective:

5. *Dancing Song*
I'll go with you, brother of my *nanad*.[2]
As soon as you go, your mother will give me work to do.
But I won't do any work, brother of my *nanad*.

I'll go with you, brother of my *nanad*.
As soon as you go, your brother's wife will give me work to do.
She'll have me scrub all the family's pots.
But I won't do any work, brother of my *nanad*.

I'll go with you, brother of my *nanad*.
As soon as you go, your sister will give me work to do.
She'll have me wash all the family's clothes.
But I won't do any work, brother of my *nanad*.

I'll go with you, brother of my *nanad*.
As soon as you go, your brother gives me work to do.

Many women's songs, particularly dancing songs, speak of the possibility of the husband's joint family becoming partitioned, and in these songs the valuation placed on the conjugal bond is greater than that placed on the solidarity of the patrilineal kinship group, as in the following song from Hathchoya. It is the marital bond that is to be maintained, even if all other relationships disintegrate and the patrilineal family is divided. I recorded this song on a quiet and sultry August afternoon, when a group of women had gathered for a visit in Prem's courtyard in Hathchoya. Women normally wouldn't sing on such an occasion, but, knowing of my interests, they decided that day to sing some dancing

2. *Nanad* is the most common Hindi term for "husband's sister." The husband is thus being addressed as "brother of my husband's sister." In women's songs in which the relative valuation of the conjugal tie versus the husband's tie to natal kin is at issue, the husband is often addressed in this way, as *nanadī ke bīrā*. This mode of address has the pragmatic effect of emphasizing the fact that though the husband is brother to the *nanad*, he is nonetheless expected, by the wife, to de-emphasize this natal tie in comparison with the demands of conjugal solidarity.

songs for me. A young wife was present in the group who was known throughout the village for her independence and her aggressiveness in standing up to her mother-in-law and others among her husband's kin. During a brief lull in the group singing, she began this song. Women often begin a song alone in this way, singing a few words themselves until the others recognize the melody and the lyric and join in. But it seemed to me that there was an air of deliberate ostentation as she sang alone of quarreling with a mother-in-law, with a just barely detectable note of defiance in her voice. With knowing expressions on their faces, everyone turned to look at her as she sang, and they took up the song themselves after the first verse.

6. *Dancing Song*
I don't like to fight, Mother-in-law.
Even if you divide our family in the morning,
Even if you take all the rooms in the house, just give me my husband's room.

I don't like to fight, Mother-in-law.
Even if you divide our family in the morning,
Even if you take all the jewelry, just give me my husband's ring.

I don't like to fight, Mother-in-law.
Even if you divide our family in the morning,
Even if you take all the clothes, just give me my husband's handkerchief.

I don't like to fight, Mother-in-law.
Even if you divide our family in the morning,
Even if you take all the pots and pans, just give me my husband's glass.

One of the most common themes, represented in a number of songs that I recorded, goes much further in its depiction of the necessity for the husband to reorient his loyalties upon his marriage. This third theme suggests that a husband's allegiance to and faith in his own natal kin lead to disaster.

7. *Dancing Song*
[Wife speaking]
I picked up a small water pot, I picked up a big water pot.
I went to fill them with water, there was a crowd at the well.
My husband-lord came home, after being away twelve years.

My *sās* was sitting at the door.
He saw his mother, he saw his sister.
But he didn't see his wedded wife.
When he wielded his dagger the first time,
It caught her in the ankle.
When he wielded his dagger the second time,
It caught her in the chest.
When he wielded his dagger the third time,
It cut her all to pieces.

[Husband speaking]
O Mother, first wash my hands,
And then wash my dagger.

[Mother-in-law speaking]
Have you killed a deer, Son,
Or have you killed a rabbit?

[Husband speaking]
No, Mother, I haven't killed a deer
And I haven't killed a rabbit.

[Wife speaking to her husband, at the time of her death]
Don't listen to your mother and your sisters,
Or your house will be destroyed.

Pahansu women explained this tragic and rather elliptic dancing song to me in this way. The husband had been away for twelve years, and just before his unexpected return, his wife had gone to the village well simply to draw water. But when the husband returned and didn't see his wife, his mother and his sister insinuated that she had gone to the well to meet a lover. In the midst of the violence that ensues, the wife is killed, but as she dies she tells him that this tragedy has happened only because he put his faith in the malicious words of his mother and his sister, rather than trusting in his wife.

I recorded a number of songs in Pahansu in which a wife is killed by her husband after she is wrongfully accused, by the husband's natal kin, of being unfaithful to him. In one song for the festival of Tij, for example, a woman dawdles over the array of bangles in a bangle seller's pack, because the colors of her husband's eyes and hair and lips come to her mind as she looks at the multicolored glittering bracelets spread out before her. Her mother-in-law and her husband's sister then tell her husband that she has "made friends with the bangle seller," implying that she has struck up an illicit relationship with him. In this song too, the husband brandishes his dagger and kills his wife. But the wife appears to him in a dream, revealing the truth to him, that she had been betrayed by his mother and his sister. Hearing his wife's words, the husband is filled with anger and remorse:

> He climbed up to the roof of the house, and he shouted out,
> "O men, don't listen to your mothers and your sisters.
> She lost her life because of a bangle."

Another song for the festival of Tij narrates a similar story of betrayal and death.

> *8. Song for the Festival of Tij*
> [*Bahū* to *sās*]
> *Sāsū*, someone has come selling fish.
> *Sāsū*, everyone is buying some fish.
> *Sāsū*, buy some fish and give some to us too.
> You give us sweet pudding and fried breads (*halvā-pūrī*) every day, *sāsū*.[3]
>
> Hearing of the husband's coming, a cup of poison.
> She drank the cup of poison, and she felt so very sleepy.
>
> [*Bahū*, who has just drunk the poison, to *sās*]
> Tell me *sasu*, where should I sleep?
>
> [*Sās* to *bahū*]
> Sleep on the top floor, *bahū*, in the room with the red door.
> Lie down and sleep on your bed, *bahū*.
>
> Away for twelve years, the beloved husband came home.
>
> [Husband to his mother, the *sās*]
> I see my mother, I see my sisters too.
> There's one I don't see, Mother, my wife, the daughter of a gentleman.
>
> [*Sās* to her son, the husband]
> On the top floor, Son, in the room with the red door,
> She's sleeping there, Son, the daughter of a gentleman.
>
> [Husband to the *sās*]
> I called her once, Mother, I called her twice,
> But still she didn't speak, Mother, the daughter of a gentleman.

3. This verse is not entirely clear to me. It seems apparent though that the mother-in-law is angered by the *bahū*'s suggestion. The next line indicates that upon hearing that her son would soon return (after a long absence), the mother-in-law poisons the *bahū*.

[*Sās* to the husband]
Go into the garden and bring in a branch.
Hit her and wake her up, the daughter of a gentleman.

[Husband to the *sās*]
I hit her once with the branch, Mother, I hit her twice.
But still she didn't speak, Mother, the daughter of a gentleman.

The husband took off her veil, to have a look at her.

[Husband to the *sās*]
Is she dead or asleep, Mother, the daughter of a gentleman?

[*Sās* to the husband]
Go to the garden, Son, and cut some sandalwood.
Burn her body, Son, the daughter of a gentleman.

He burnt her body, and he came back to the house.
The husband sat at the threshold, wailing out of grief.

[Sās to the husband]
Why are you crying, Son, wailing so loudly?
I can have my son married four times.
Two fair brides, two dark ones,
I can have my son married four times.

[Husband to the *sās*]
You can throw all four down a well, Mother.
I don't have that one, the daughter of a gentleman.

The husband spread out his scarf and lay down to sleep.

[Husband addressing his dead wife]
Come in a dream, fair one, and tell me all that happened.

[*Bahū* speaking in the dream]
Husband, every day she gave bread and pudding.
She heard that you were coming, and she gave a cup of poison.
I drank the poison, and I felt very sleepy.
Where should I sleep, *sāsū*, tell me the place.
On the top floor, Husband, in the room with the red door.

Go up to the roof, my husband-lord, and shout out to everyone.

[Husband]
Don't listen, men, to your mothers and your sisters.
My mother and my sisters have laid waste to my home.

In this song, after his wife is poisoned by his mother, the voice of the husband is twice heard resisting the assumption that a particular woman as wife is replaceable and indeed dispensable. When the mother suggests that her son can easily marry four more times if he wishes, the husband rejects this portrayal of the woman, his wife, as an anonymous cipher, as either irreducibly "other" to her conjugal kin or as so assimilated to them that her own particular identity is dissolved. And finally, at the end of this Tij song, as he climbs to the roof and proclaims that a man's loyalty to his natal kin must often be subordinated to his loyalty to his wife, he subverts a fundamental tenet of North Indian kinship.

But how frequently does a man really shout from the rooftops in such subversive tones? The fourth theme that appears in dancing songs from Pahansu and Hathchoya embodies in fact a metacommentary on women's representations of men's speech and men's stances toward patrilineal solidarities. While men appear in some songs as publicly defying patrilineal dicta, they are portrayed in others as feigning, before an audience, adherence to norms concerning the priority to be placed on patrilineal solidarities rather than on intimacy and solidarity with the wife, while at the same time privately undermining them.

In the following dancing song from Hathchoya, as in several others that I recorded, public conformity to the requirements of patrilineal solidarities is at odds with a man's private subversion of them:[4]

9. *Dancing Song*
My mother-in-law is very cunning.
I am my husband's beloved.
I sat at the grinding stone, I ground the grain coarsely.
She rubbed the flour between her fingers, to see how coarse it was.
I am my husband's beloved.
When she rubbed her fingers together, she told her son about it.
I am my husband's beloved.
When she told her son about it, he brought a stick with knobs, and he beat me gently gently (*dhīre dhīre*).
When he beat me gently gently, I went up to the room and slept.
I am my husband's beloved.
When I was sleeping in the room, he brought a *ser* of *laḍḍūs*.[5]
I am my husband's beloved.

4. My reading of this song owes much to Das's analysis (1976b) of similar ambiguities in Panjabi kinship.

5. A *ser* is a unit of weight, about two pounds. *Laḍḍūs* are sweetmeats made from chick-pea flour and sugar that are often distributed at weddings and other festive occasions.

When he brought a *ser* of *laḍḍūs*, I threw them back at him.
I am my husband's beloved.
When I threw the *laḍḍūs* back, he hand-fed them to me, and I ate one or two.
I am my husband's beloved.
When I ate one or two, I became very thirsty.
I am my husband's beloved.
When I became very thirsty, he brought some water to me.
I am my husband's beloved.
When he brought the water to me, I drank a drop or two.
I am my husband's beloved.
When I drank a drop or two, I became very cold.
I am my husband's beloved.
When I became very cold, he brought a red quilt to me.
I am my husband's beloved.
When he brought a red quilt to me, I became very warm.
I am my husband's beloved.
When I became very warm, he brought a red fan to me.
I am my husband's beloved.
When he brought a red fan to me, I waved it gently gently (*dhīre dhīre*).
I am my husband's beloved.

In this song, the husband makes a show of beating his wife to present a public image of acceding to his mother's claims on his loyalty, but he beats her "gently gently," and then in their own room, away from the gaze of his mother, he brings her food and drink and engages in sexual intimacy, as the last lines of the song strongly suggest. I have elsewhere pointed out that *bījanā* (embroidered fans) appear, for a number of reasons, in women's songs and in North Indian folk art as signs of sexual intimacy (Raheja n.d. [forthcoming]). The private sexual intimacy is read by the wife as a negation of the significance of the public beating, since the beating was a sham one staged for the benefit of the husband's mother. In this song, both the beating and the figurative sexual intercourse are done "gently gently" (*dhīre dhīre*). This rather prominent linguistic equation in the song might be read as an ironic commentary on another kind of equation that is often made in Hindi between beatings and sexual intercourse. A contemptuous way of describing intercourse is, in Hindi, *chūt mārnā*, literally "beating the vagina." *Mārnā* is the usual word for "beating," the one that is used in this song. But the equivalence between beating and sexual intimacy (both are done "gently gently") that is drawn in the song underlines the fact that a man's adherence to a public and "normative" devaluation of sexuality and women as wives may be only a cover behind which other perspectives are given moral credence, overtly by women, though perhaps covertly and furtively by men. "I am my husband's beloved," the wife's voice insistently proclaims, and this declaration appears as her summation of the tale, but it is an assertion of her own authority as well.[6]

As I thought about this question of women's metacommentaries on their own representations of men's speech, I realized that I had come across only one song in which a man tells a woman not to sing or dance. But his reasons for asking her not to dance, in a song from Pahansu, have nothing to do with silencing her subversive speech. In this song, only the husband's voice is heard.

10. Dancing Song

Don't wear a forehead jewel, my fair one, and don't wear a
  pendant there.
Don't dance, my fair one, or the evil eye will come.
We are a couple now, and you'll leave me all alone.
And you'll leave only darkness where the moon once shone.

[Other verses follow, in which the husband asks his wife not to wear other ornaments that might attract those evil glances.]

In this song, the husband begs his wife not to dance, because he fears that her beauty and grace will attract the envious glances of others, and she may sicken and die. He does not fear the resistance to patrilineal solidarities he may find in her dancing and singing; he fears only that their "two-person pair" (*do janoṅ kī joṛī*) will be threatened.

Perhaps women wish to convince their men to think in this way, of the *do janoṅ kī joṛī* and its implications for power rela-

6. It is of course obvious that the limits as well as the power of women's resistance appear in this song. It is tragic to hear in these words that women perceive that they must sometimes endure a public beating for the sake of appearances, even when their husbands are reluctant to administer such punishments. And it is even more tragic if women at times come to regard beatings as an intrinsic part of a conjugal relationship. In the novel *Ek Chadar Maili Si* by Rajinder Singh Bedi (from which a Hindi film was made), a woman is convinced that her husband cares for her when he finally beats her "like a husband"; only after that beating was he able to consummate the marriage (Kakar 1990:9–14).

tionships in the *sasurāl*. Kakar has discussed the longing, felt by slum-dwelling Delhi women he interviewed, for the *joṛī*, a "single two-person entity" in which they would live in intimate oneness with their husbands. He suggests that the *ardhanārīśvara*, the god Siva merged with his spouse Parvati as half man and half woman, provides a cultural image that underlies these yearnings for the *joṛī* (1990: 65–84). While such cultural images are no doubt important, I would suggest that women's insistence on the importance of the *joṛī* also represents a critique of the power relationships inherent in the conjugal family, which result in a denial of the importance of the *joṛī* in favor of a subordination of the wife and her interests to the demands of patrilineal solidarity. Or perhaps women know that their husbands do in fact share this perspective on the *joṛī* at least some of the time, but that men are as much victims of the prevailing ideology as they are themselves, and are constrained to speak one way to their wives, of the *do janoṅ kī joṛī*, and another way before their senior kin.[7]

GENDER, AGENCY, AND DEPENDENCY IN NORTH INDIAN EXPRESSIVE GENRES

An extremely common theme in a wide variety of North Indian textual and oral traditions involves the banishment or scorn of barren women, of women whose husbands decide for one reason or another to take a second wife, and of women accused of engaging in illicit sexual relations. Representations of women's responses to such treatment, and the moral valuations of these responses, differ dramatically in the epic traditions, in popular North Indian folk dramas (*sāṅg*) performed by and largely for males, and in the narrative dancing songs from Pahansu and Hathchoya. It is in these differing valuations that I locate some polyvalent, rather than monolithic, discourses on gender, agency, and dependency in northern India.

The ethnographic context of *sāṅg* folk drama in western Uttar Pradesh has been described in detail by Ved Prakash Vatuk and

7. This is not to say that women or men would always favor the abolishing of joint-family arrangements in favor of nuclear families; nor do I wish to imply that women's position in North Indian society would be improved if joint families came to an end. Women's critiques are focused, in these songs, on specific relations of power within such families, and not on the joint family itself.

Sylvia Vatuk (1979a, 1979b). *Sāṅg* troupes usually consist of nine to twelve men serving as instrumentalists and as actor-singers who perform all female as well as male roles in the dramas. Dramas are staged on open-air platforms in towns and villages upon invitation by the village as a whole or by individual wealthy patrons. Vatuk and Vatuk describe separate seating areas for men and women, but in my own experience it is often the case that attendance at these dramas is deemed inappropriate for women, and the audience is predominantly male. *Sāṅg*s are musical plays, and much of the dialogue is sung in verses called *rāginī*s, the form of which is described in detail by Vatuk and Vatuk.

The stories enacted in *sāṅg* dramas are widely known in this region, and they are enjoyed in other forms as well. Cheaply printed pamphlets containing the text of a particular drama are available for a few rupees in any market town of western Uttar Pradesh, and they appear to be purchased primarily by men for the purpose of learning the words of *rāginī*s. These individual *rāginī*s are sung, with or without simple musical accompaniment, at evening gatherings of men in the village and by semiprofessional singers at weddings and other occasions. Recent years have witnessed, perhaps, an increase in the popularity of *sāṅg* dramas, as they are being recorded on cassette tapes in greater numbers, sold for relatively modest sums in district towns, and played more and more frequently on radio.

The first *sāṅg* drama to be considered is *The Legend of Raja Dhru*, a well-known North Indian story that is discussed briefly by Vatuk and Vatuk (1979b). The full Hindi text and translation of a performance from western Uttar Pradesh appear in R. C. Temple's *Legends of the Panjab* (1884–1900). The drama opens with Uttanpat, the king of Ayodhya, being urged by his barren queen to take a second wife so that a son and heir might be produced. The king warns her that "a co-wife is evil and sets fire to the heart,"[8] but he arranges nonetheless for a magnificent wedding to the daughter of another royal house. When she arrives at Uttanpat's palace, he is so smitten by her that he promises to do anything she asks of him. The new queen demands that the king turn the first queen out of the palace. The king agrees to her request,

8. In this and in other cases that follow, I have amended Temple's translations in light of my own readings of the Hindi transcriptions.

but "with sorrow in his heart." He follows the co-wife's order to "give her ill fortune" (*dījo us se duhāg*) by forcing her to take off the clothes and ornaments of an auspiciously married woman (her "good fortune," *suhāg*) and to "put on the clothes of a widow" (*abhran paharo rāṅḍ ke*). Both the king and the first queen speak of these actions as "the writing of fate" (*kartā kī aṅk*) that cannot be circumvented, as "ill fate" (*burī kismat*) that cannot be undone by the husband or the wife. Yet it seems to be the king who most vociferously attributes the turn of events to "fate." The queen's assertion that it is simply her evil fate that has brought her to these circumstances seems tinged with irony as she addresses the absent second queen: "Deceitful co-wife, may good fortune be yours. What is your fault in this? It is only my ill fate." Yet she submits silently and without protest to the order of her husband.

Stripped thus of her "marital auspiciousness" (*suhāg*) and the garments that embody it, the first wife is banished to a hut in the forest, provided only with old and worn-out bedding, and barley for her food. Some months later, the king is hunting in the forest and stops at the hut and spends the night with his first queen. Thereafter, sons are born to each of the queens. Drums are played, and lavish gifts are given to mark the birth of the son of the second queen, but the first queen and her son Dhru remain in the forest alone.

As a young boy, Dhru asks his mother about his father. The queen replies that the king did an injustice (*anrit*) in sending her away from the palace, but that the son should not go to the palace of his father to redress the wrong that was done. Dhru, however, cannot understand this acceptance of "fate": "Such trouble as this is unbearable," he tells his mother. And so he goes to the palace. When the king sees his son, he repents of his actions toward his first wife and tries to give Dhru whatever he desires. Dhru refuses his father's offer and instead retires again to the forest to practice austerities. But when he amasses ascetic powers, he reenters the city in triumph, accepts the throne from his father, and restores his mother to the palace.

In this tale of barrenness, co-wives, and the workings of "fate," we find a number of parallels to events recounted in the *Ramayana*. A king of Ayodhya banishes his wife not out of his own conviction but because he succumbs to the pressure of public opinion or a hastily made promise. In both the epic and this *sāṅg* drama, the banished queen is portrayed as an ideal wife whose attention to her husband's well-being sets into motion a course of events that leads to her own subsequent misfortune. In both cases, this ideal wife endures her banishment silently and without protest, though she knows herself to be blameless. And finally, both Sita and Uttanpat's queen endure their exile until an outraged son returns to the palace and demands the vindication of his mother. While they actively seek the welfare of their husbands, the virtuous wives in the *Ramayana* and in the drama passively submit to an unjust fate and in so doing embody potent images of the obedient wife, dependent on male kin for protection and exercising only a limited agency in relation to a tragic course of events.

Temple presents a transcription of a performance of *The Legend of Sila Dai* from Ambala district, and this *sāṅg* drama exhibits a similar set of parallels to the plight of Sita in the *Ramayana*. The drama opens with a conversation between Raja Rasalu and his minister Mahita, in which the latter praises the virtue (*sat*) of his wife, Sila. Rasalu replies to Mahita's words with a proverbial utterance, "To praise a woman is the action of a fool," and with a remark that prefigures the events to follow, he tells Mahita that there will never be another "virtuous woman" (*satī*) to equal Sita, and he observes that even Sita herself ignored Ram's command and stepped out of the line drawn by Lakshman around her, within which she could come to no harm, thus bringing about her abduction by Ravana.[9] Mahita persists in his praise of Sila, however, and Rasalu devises a plan for sending him on a mission to a distant land so that he can test Sila's virtue or cast doubt upon her faithfulness in her husband's absence. Before he leaves, Mahita warns Sila about the cleverness and treachery of Rasalu, much as Ram and Lakshman warned Sita before leaving her alone, and he admonishes her to stay awake at night and to bolt all the doors at sunset. Sila accepts his counsel but asks him, "Who can circumvent the lines of fate?"

9. For a discussion of the import of Sita's stepping over "Lakshman's line" (*lakṣmaṇ rekhā*) and the use of this image in ordinary conversations in northern India, see Das 1982:198.

After Mahita's departure, Rasalu contrives by trickery to gain admittance to Sila's chambers. Sila rebuffs him, but he manages, unobserved, to leave behind his ring in Sila's palace. (Rasalu makes advances to Sila, but just as Ravana did not attempt to seduce Sita against her will, neither does Rasalu force himself upon Sila when she spurns his suggestions.) But Sila fears that even this nocturnal visit will destroy her honor and bring shame upon her. So she asks the doorkeeper and her servant girls not to tell Mahita of Rasalu's visit. When Mahita returns, he asks Sila if Rasalu came to the palace. She denies it, whereupon Mahita discovers Rasalu's ring and knows that Sila has lied. He asks her how the ring came to be in palace, and out of fear she tells two different stories, that the ring came into the palace in a bowl of curd, and that a crow dropped it within the walls. Mahita then threatens to flail her with a whip. Sila is forced then to tell the truth, that Rasalu entered the palace through trickery and placed the ring secretly in her bed as she rebuffed his advances and sent him away.

Mahita ignores her assertions of innocence and orders that she remove the ornaments and clothes signifying her "auspicious wifehood" (*suhāg*) and put on "the clothes of ill fortune" (*bheṣ duhāgan*), "the clothes of a prostitute-widow" (*bheṣ rāṅḍ*). Sila accedes to this dishonoring demand without protest, though she clearly recognizes it as a grave injustice. Her response is to ask Mahita's family bard (*bhāṭ*) to take the news of her distress to her father and mother.

When they hear of Mahita's actions, Sila's brother and father are outraged, and they go to Sialkot, Mahita's city, to find Sila and take her back to her natal home. In Sialkot, they attempt to persuade Mahita that he has erred in casting blame on his wife, but Mahita refuses to believe in her innocence, and so they go to Rasalu to ask him to convince Mahita of his wife's virtue. He suggests that Sila's honor be proven through a dice game between Mahita and Sila's brother. The dice are thrown, the outcome is in Sila's favor, but Mahita refuses to place faith in the test when he sees this result. Sila's brother asks him to suggest another way of ascertaining truth, and Mahita proposes that Sila bathe in a cauldron of burning oil; if she survives the ordeal, he will believe in her virtue. Sila steps into the oil, calling upon God to defend her honor in the way that Draupadi's honor was preserved when her clothes were stripped from her in the royal assembly of the Kauravas.[10] Sila emerges unharmed from the cauldron, but Mahita is now convinced only that Rasalu has cooled the fire through magical charms.

Asserting only that "what is written in one's fate cannot be wiped away," Sila leaves Sialkot and returns to her natal home with her brother and her father. Mahita then becomes a wandering *jogī*, approaches Sila's father's house, and dies there begging alms. Sila asserts that she will mount his funeral pyre in order to attain "unalterable good fortune" (*aṭal suhāg*), but as she does so Siva and Parvati intervene, restore Mahita to life, and the two are married again.

The events leading to the banishment of Sila Dai are foreshadowed in the first scene of the drama, when Raja Rasalu tells Mahita that there can be no second Sita in the world. The phrase "She is a second Sita" is, in northern India, an appreciative acknowledgment of wifely self-sacrifice, of faithfulness and steadfastness even when she is treated unjustly by her husband (Kakar 1978: 64–66). Sita's response to being exiled from Ayodhya and Sila Dai's from Sialkot demonstrate these characteristics of the ideal wife, the ideal woman: "chastity, purity, gentle tenderness and a singular faithfulness which cannot be destroyed or even disturbed by her husband's rejections, slights or thoughtlessness. . . . The moral is a familiar one: 'Whether treated well or ill a wife should never indulge in ire'" (66). Of critical importance in this image of the ideal woman is the fact that she herself submits to her husband's will even in such adversity, and she is thus dependent on her male relations—father, brother, or son—to redress the wrong done by her husband. These epic and folkloric portrayals of the characters of Sita, Uttanpat's queen, and Sila Dai valorize this sort of dependency and are thus congruent with the prescriptions set forth in the *Laws of Manu*: "A girl, a young woman, or even an old woman should not do anything independently, even in [her own] house. In childhood, a woman should be under her father's control, in youth under her hus-

10. The connection between the dice match and a subsequent ordeal that is likened to Draupadi's disrobing is interesting in light of the connection between the dice game and disrobing in the story of Draupadi itself (Hiltebeitel 1988:6–7).

band's, and when her husband is dead, under her sons'. She should not have independence" (V: 147–48, trans. Doniger 1991).

Kathryn Hansen (1992: 171–207) analyzes a number of *nauṭaṅkī* or *sāṅg* texts and describes similar portrayals of "women's nature" (*triyā charitra*). She finds in these plays a pervasive abhorrence of female sexuality and female agency, and the same splits between the dependence and asexuality of the ideal woman as mother and the independence and threatening sexual voraciousness that must be curbed and kept under control by fathers and brothers before marriage, and by the husband and his kinsmen thereafter (185).

These are indubitably powerful images in North India. Yet Kakar's perception of a "formidable consensus" among Indian women concerning the power and persuasiveness of the image of Sita and figures like Sila Dai and Uttanpat's queen seems to be founded on the supposition that women are the passive assimilators of a monolithic set of cultural discourses on gender, in terms of which their own lives are either unambiguously morally exemplary in the manner of Sita and the *sāṅg* heroines or morally flawed and reprehensible.

Dancing songs and "sitting songs" from Pahansu and Hathchoya frequently narrate stories that parallel in many ways the opening scenes of many *sāṅg* texts. They tell of the banishment or scorn of a wife or depict, what from the wife's point of view is a similar fate, a husband's decision to take a second wife. I read these songs intertextually, that is, in relation to the epic and *sāṅg* narratives that begin with strikingly similar situations yet represent the wife's responses and the issues of gender, agency, and dependency in dramatically different ways; and I would also suggest that women's songs are composed and sung with an awareness of this intertextuality, of the ways in which these poetic genres speak to and interrogate other textual representations of the ideal wife.

Such interrogation of dominant conventions is particularly striking in the following narrative songs from Pahansu:

11. Song for the Festival of Tij

From which direction did the clouds come,
In which direction will it rain now?

Indar Raja comes down in the garden.[11]
The clouds have come from the east,
And it's about to rain in the west.
Indar Raja comes down in the garden.

[*Bahū* speaking]
Mother-in-law, I heard a surprising thing,
That your son will marry again.
Indar Raja comes down in the garden.
Mother-in-law, have I come from a bad family,
Or did I bring a small dowry?
Indar Raja comes down in the garden.

[Mother-in-law]
No, *bahū*, you aren't from a bad family,
And you didn't bring a small dowry.
Indar Raja came down in the garden.
Your color is a little dark, *bahū*,
And my son wants a fair wife.
Indar Raja comes down in the garden.

[*Bahū*]
Sisters, I went to ask my father-in-law,
Is your son to marry again?
Indar Raja comes down in the garden.
Father-in-law, have I come from a bad family,
Or did I bring a small dowry?
Indar Raja came down in the garden.

[Father-in-law]
No, *bahū*, you aren't from a bad family,
And you didn't bring a small dowry.
Indar Raja came down in the garden.
You are a little dark, my *bahū*,
And my son wants a fair wife.
Indar Raja comes down in the garden.

[*Bahū*]
Sisters, I went to ask my husband's sister,
Is your brother to marry again?

11. The god Indra is associated with the rains in many Indian myths. The festival of Tij is celebrated in the rainy month of Savan, hence the lines about the rains and the god Indra who presides over the monsoon rains. In North Indian oral traditions and pictorial art, the rainy season is represented as a time of erotic encounters and the reunion of lovers. (See, for example, Wadley 1983.) The repeated references to the rains in this song thus function in the same ironic mode as the references to the throwing of colored dyes in the Holi song explicated in chapter 3; they create an expectation of conjugal intimacy that is thwarted by the wife's realization of her husband's plan to marry again.

Indar Raja came down in the garden.
Husband's Sister, have I come from a bad family,
Or did I bring a small dowry?
Indar Raja comes down in the garden.

[Husband's sister]
No, Brother's Wife, you aren't from a bad family,
And you didn't bring a small dowry.
Indar Raja comes down in the garden.
Your color is a little dark, Brother's Wife.
And my brother wants a fair wife.

[*Bahū*]
Sisters, I went to ask my husband-lord,
Tell me, are you to marry again?
Indar Raja comes down in the garden.
Husband-lord, am I from a bad family,
Or did I bring a small dowry?
Indar Raja comes down in the garden.

[Husband]
No, you aren't from a bad family,
And you didn't bring a small dowry.
Indar Raja comes down in the garden.
Your color is a little dark,
And I want a fair wife.
Indar Raja comes down in the garden.

[*Bahū*]
Husband-lord, who will do the women's rites at your marriage,
And who will sing the auspicious songs?
Indar Raja comes down in the garden.

[Husband]
Wife, my mother will do the women's rites,
And my sister will sing auspicious songs.
Indar Raja comes down in the garden.

[*Bahū*]
Husband-lord, who will send off the marriage party,
And who will bear the expense?
Indar Raja comes down in the garden.

[Husband]
Wife, my brother will send off the marriage party,
And my father will bear the expense.
Indar Raja comes down in the garden.

[*Bahū*]
Sisters, I went to the roof [to see the marriage party return, after the husband has married again].

And how many came in the marriage party?
Indar Raja comes down in the garden.
Sisters, there were 150 of them, without feet and hands,
And the bald ones were uncountable.[12]
Sisters, when I heard that the co-wife had come,
I was trembling and feverish from anger.
Indar Raja comes down in the garden.
Sisters, I went to see the co-wife.
I took a bent and worthless coin.[13]
Indar Raja comes down in the garden.
I went to the feast for the new wife,
Sisters, I slipped poison in the pudding.
Indar Raja comes down in the garden.
Sisters, I heard that the co-wife died,
My fever went down right away.
Indar Raja comes down in the garden.
Sisters, I went to the lament for the co-wife,
I veiled myself heavily.[14]
Indar Raja comes down in the garden.
Sisters, outside I was lamenting, but inside I was laughing.
And my heart was joyful.

A sitting song from Pahansu, like the Tij song, defies conventional ideas of the docile wife who quietly submits, without protest, to the dictates and the whims of her husband.

12. *Sitting Song*
[Husband speaking]
O fair one, I'm going away to search for a job in the morning, and in twelve years I'll come back.

[Wife speaking]
Husband-lord, go in the morning, even if you're gone for eighteen years.
From there he sent a letter saying he'll bring a Panjabin[15] with him.

12. The wife is here ridiculing the men of the marriage party.

13. When a new bride is brought to her *sasurāl,* the women there lift her veil to see her face for the first time, and give small cash gifts to her called *mūṅh dikhāī,* "showing the face." In the song, the first wife expresses her revulsion by giving a coin without value.

14. It is customary for women to gather together to lament a death. As they wail, they sit in a circle with their faces covered.

15. The detail that the husband will bring a Panjabi woman to live with him seems to heighten the outrageousness of his behavior: it is bad enough for a husband to bring home a co-wife, but to bring such a "foreign" woman seems to be doubly offensive to the wife.

My husband's younger brother was eating his meal when the letter came.
Husband's Brother, eat your meal later, read this letter to me now.

[Husband's younger brother speaking, as he reads the letter]
My brother writes he's doing fine,
He'll bring a Panjabin with him.

[Wife speaking]
After twelve years he came back, he brought a Panjabin with him.
He went upstairs at once, the Panjabin went up with him.
I went right up behind them, a cup of milk to give him.

[Husband speaking]
O fair one, go downstairs away from here, I've brought a Panjabin with me.

[Wife speaking]
I went downstairs at once, and I took up an ax in my hands.
I went back up, I killed my husband-lord, and I killed the Panjabin with him.
And I sat down on the bed and wept.

In both these songs, the wife is placed in a situation not unlike that of Uttanpat's wife in *The Legend of Raja Dhru*. Yet in contrast to the submissive posture assumed by that queen in the presence of a co-wife and in the face of banishment, and in contrast to her dependence on her son for vindication, the heroine in each of these two songs takes immediate and decisive action in the face of a threat to her position in her husband's house.[16] In the Tij song, the appeal made by the wife to "sisters," the women listeners who hear her tale, makes it evident that the wife's actions are indeed valorized. It is not necessarily the violence, the poisoning of the co-wife, or the axing of the husband and his lover that is being extolled but the ability to act decisively when a wife is treated unjustly. There is no talk of a powerless submission to "fate" here or of ineradicable ill fortune, as is found in the *sāṅg* dramas.[17] There is, rather, in these songs, a definitive moral judg-

16. Both of these songs end with a line that reveals the feelings of the wife after she takes her fateful actions. In the Tij song, the wife rejoices because she has eliminated her rival, but in the sitting song, she weeps because in order to avenge the wrong done to her, she has killed her "husband-lord" as well. Perhaps this sitting song expresses again, more poignantly, the limits of women's resistance: sometimes exercising agency has dire consequences in Northern India.

17. I do not mean to suggest here that women *never* speak of fate and the in-

ment and an immediate and potent response to the injustice. In addition, as in the other songs considered in this chapter, in the Tij song, a woman is represented as having to struggle against the interests and wishes of her husband's natal kin in her efforts to establish and maintain intimacy within the conjugal bond and to preserve her own position. Finally, the heroines do not wait for a son or brother or father to rescue them from their predicaments; there are no such male rescuers in this text, and there are very few indeed in the songs I recorded in Pahansu and Hathchoya.

Mohanty (1984) has written incisively of the difficulties involved in predicating an invariant homogeneous category "woman," existing prior to and outside of a system of kinship relations. Women cannot be assumed to be undifferentiated subjects prior to their entry into kinship systems; while they may in many ways resist the cultural discourses associated with these systems, they are nonetheless produced as sisters, wives, and mothers within these relations (342), and women's perspectives on kinship systems may shift in relation to these varied positionings. Thus, while the women's voices in the songs I have considered in this and the previous chapter do in fact interrogate pervasive and powerful North Indian discourses on kinship and gender, these voices do not coalesce into a single homogeneous female perspective. The voices of women as sisters and daughters tend to speak in an ironic mode of the ambiguities in their relationships with natal kin, and in so doing they stress the importance of the brother-sister tie over and against the brother's tie to his own wife. The voices of women positioned as wives speak in a more openly subversive fashion of the expectation that conjugal bonds will be far less important than relationships through men. Yet both positions subvert the ideal of the silent submissive wife, and they subvert the idea that it is dangerous to patrilineal

---

evitability of its denouement in human life. In other situations, such as the birth of daughters or the death of a loved one, women may indeed draw upon ideas of fate and ill fortune to interpret and comment upon events in their lives. Women draw upon these and other cultural discourses selectively and strategically (Raheja 1993). Das (1986:203), for example, shows that women's taking up of a "fatalist" or "voluntarist" outlook on death, in ritual laments, may depend on the closeness of kinship connection to the one who has died, and Daniel (1983) discusses men's and women's contextually fluid use of ideas of fate and human action in Tamil Nadu.

solidarities for a woman to be either too close to her brothers or too close to her husband. Songs sung from the point of view of sisters challenge these patrilineal ideals by rejecting their requirement that women distance themselves from brothers who might side with them against their in-laws in times of crisis. Songs sung from the point of view of wife challenge them by rejecting their requirement that intimacy with the husband should be controlled so that his ties to his patrilineal kin are not placed in jeopardy, and their requirement of wifely obedience to the husband's senior kin. Despite the obvious incongruities between these two perspectives, the voices of both sisters and wives converge in their critique of the *contradictions* within North Indian kinship that produce them as sisters and wives having divergent expectations and contradictory claims on brothers and husbands. And because all these women—sisters, daughters, wives, mothers-in-law, and daughters-in-law—sing these songs together and in unison, their taking up of each other's voices in performance tells us, perhaps, of their ironic apprehension of the oppressiveness of a kinship ideology that splits their identities and pits one woman against another.

5

Devotional Power or Dangerous Magic? The Jungli Rani's Case

The story of the *janglī rānī*—which could translate as "queen from the jungle" or by strong implication "uncivilized queen"—offers further insights into the ways female identity may be split and yet stay whole, not only in relation to particular kinship roles but beyond these always partial facets of a woman's total career.[1] When I first began to think about this story, it was as integral to the argument against the split-image approach to Indian women elaborated in chapter 2. But the "jungli rani" eluded my focus on the conjunction of motherhood and sexuality in women's self-images because her story's central concern is neither fertility nor erotic satisfaction. Even though, as we'll soon see, the king marries her because her food is so delicious—an attribute perhaps equatable with sexual attractions—and even though she bears him a son in just nine months, these matters are peripheral. The source of the jungli rani's problems is more basic still: the people around her assume that female virtuosity cannot coexist with female virtues, at least not without a supporting male lineage.

The jungli rani, it seemed to me, was about a dichotomy that could be formulated as opposing stereotypes of the clever, auspicious, and blessed bride who brings prosperity to her husband's home and the dangerous female "black" magician whose power is

1. Another version of this chapter entitled "The Jungli Rani and Other Troubled Wives" will appear in *Hindu Marriage from the Margins*, ed. Lindsey Harlan and Paul Courtright (New York: Oxford University Press, n.d. [forthcoming]).

Throughout this chapter I persist in using the anglicized spelling "jungli"—not an accurate transliteration—because I wish to sustain in English the same evocative powers *janglī* has in Hindi and Rajasthani.

threatening and ultimately destructive. But the story poses this explicitly as a false dichotomy between whose poles the heroine must find her inner balance while maintaining an outer act. There is indeed in men's minds an important "split" between approved womanly skills and disapproved black magic. What truly clever brides should do is perform wonders without drawing accusations of performing magic. This implies an externally imposed, judgmental dichotomy straddled by a female person self-consciously trying to sustain her integrity. If issues of erotic and reproductive capacities are secondary here, the idea that an independent, powerful woman is intrinsically dangerous certainly looms large. It looms, however—and this is the crux of my argument—not as cosmic reality but as human obtuseness. The jungli rani's power, acquired through proper worshipful acts, is mistaken for black magic or witchcraft. Thus externally imposed and false assumptions about female nature threaten her life more than once.

The jungli rani's story is one among many stories that North Indian women tell as an integral part of domestic rituals. Although filled with unlikely events and supernatural interventions, these tales realistically portray household roles and relationships. They also articulate the conflicts and anxieties entailed by those roles and relationships. The persons, both male and female, who populate such stories are almost never named but rather referred to in kin categories: "There were seven sons' wives"; "There was a sister's brother"; "There was a Brahman's daughter." Some stories focus on relationships in a woman's natal home, where she is daughter or sister; others on her married roles, most often as a brother's or son's wife. In several stories a transition from one setting to the other is central: these begin with a daughter and end with a wife.

The jungli rani's story contains a daughter-to-wife transformation that is exceptionally problematic. Her tale is a favorite among village women. Told in the context of worship, it is received with more animation than many other rote-told tales. Her situation—especially her lack of natal kin and besiegement by antipathetic co-wives—inspires sympathy. The jungli rani's world, however weird the events that take place in it, is not perceived as remote. Parochial as she appears, emerging from her hollow pipal tree, there is something elementary and moving in her story. And that something reflects on the nature of female identity.[2]

The jungli rani's tale should help us understand how women respond to the predicament of being perceived as split when they are really whole, and of being perceived as threatening when they are only acting according to moral and devotional convictions. This understanding includes the obvious but elusive fact that although marriage changes a woman's life in many ways, her identity as a person is continuous from girlhood into the marital state. The jungli rani always refers to herself as a "Brahman's daughter," thus sustaining her valued natal identity—as we have seen women in Pahansu do—rather than acknowledging subsequent disjunctions and transformations. It is her co-wives and the residents of her husband's kingdom who dub her "jungli rani" in a distinctly negative tone. But the storyteller and her female audience use the same rubric with sympathetic affection. As we listen to or read the story it is clear that despite the very different connotations in Hindu society of "Brahman's daughter" and "uncivilized queen," they are incontrovertibly a single human being.

Without much further preamble, I give the jungli rani's story. I then draw some comparisons and contrasts between it and a few others of the same genre—women's worship tales—where approved, clever-bride heroines predominate. I also briefly examine the lady magicians who appear in the epic tale of King Gopi Chand as sung and explicated by a male bard of the Nath caste in the same village where the jungli rani's story is told. These villainous females have genuinely nefarious goals and questionable characters. I hope, then, effectively to contrast the way that women may sympathetically portray unsupported women as viewed with unjust suspicion by men, and by women aligned with men, with the ways that men zestfully describe independent, saucy, "bad" women whose rebellion is enjoyable because it inevitably ends in defeat. In conclusion I will suggest some connections, posed by these oral traditions, among women's worship, women's magic, and women's power.

2. When I called up my colleague, anthropologist Margaret Trawick, eager to learn her scholarly opinions on the very first draft of this chapter, which was composed for a panel where we were both to present our work, her first comment was, "Oh, I feel like a jungli rani all the time."

THE JUNGLI RANI'S TALE

Although everyone calls the tale in question "the story of the jungli rani," according to villagers' usual classification system by performance context, it is a "story of the Sun God" (*Suryā Rāj kī kahānī*) and is told on the first Sunday after Holi as part of a fast for that divinity.[3] As described in the story, a cow-dung worship space, raw whole grains, and *roṭ* (thick, unsalted bread prepared for offerings to the gods) compose the simple ritual paraphernalia.

I give here a composite of two tellings of the jungli rani's tale, recorded from the same Rajput teller—a grandmother in her fifties whose repertoire of religious stories was the largest in the village. One version I recorded on March 2, 1980; that year the Sunday following Holi happened to be the very day after Holi, a ritually busy one for village women even when not a Sunday.[4] Joseph Miller's recorded text of the jungli rani's story, made the year before my arrival in the village, supplied some details lacking in mine. Perhaps because the storyteller had so much ritual work to accomplish the year I recorded the tale, she abridged it somewhat.

The Jungli Rani: A Story of the Sun God

There were two, a mother and a daughter. They both said, "Yesterday was Holi," and so prepared a cow-dung worship place: "We will tell the Sun God's story." On that Sunday after Holi, mother and daughter plastered the courtyard with cow dung. And then the mother said to the daughter: "Daughter, I am going to bathe, and you roll out the bread."

3. Surya Raj is also worshiped, and a different story of his told, on Makar Sankranti, the day celebrating the winter solstice (for that story see Gold 1982:58–61). His vow, or *vrat*, may be performed by devotees on any Sunday, but the "published story" (*vrat kathā*) that accompanies that undertaking is not the jungli rani's. In a Marwari manual of "the festivals of twelve months," a very truncated fragment entitled "Story of the Sun God's bread" (*Suraj roṭ kī kahāṇī*) is included as part of a Sunday vow falling within the major festival of Gangaur (Rajgarhiya n.d.:174–75).

4. It is the prescribed occasion for the worship and story of Brother Second and for the first of the ten-day series of Dasa Mata's worship, as well as an auspicious time for various life-cycle rituals. For the story of Brother Second see Ramanujan 1991b:62–69; for the worship of Dasa Mata—a form of Lakshmi—see Gold n.d. (forthcoming). In the household where I was living, on this particular second day of Holi, a *ḍhūṇḍanā*, or protective ritual for a first son, was also performed and celebrated.

So the mother went to bathe, and the daughter was making bread. First she rolled a bread made of 1¼ seers [of flour]. Then the Sun God arrived, disguised as a holy man. He said to her, "Give me a small piece of that first bread you have made, as alms."

She said, "Great King, this bread is reserved for my mother. You can take some alms of raw grain, or whatever you want to take, but the first bread is reserved."

"Give me some of it."

"O Great King, it belongs to my mother. You can't have that bread."

"Brother, I'll have the first bread; I'll take some of it, or else there will be trouble. If you don't give it to me, I'll curse you."

"So take it," and she quickly tore up the bread and gave one-fourth of it to the holy man. That's what happened. Then her mother came and said to her, "Daughter, bring the bread, bring yours and bring mine too. And light the lamp on the cow-dung square and put some whole grains down there and then tell the story."

At once, she did all these things.

"But, Daughter, what happened? My bread, why did you break it? Why is it broken?"

"Mother, a holy man came and asked me for alms, and I said, 'Great King, I'll bring grain.' Then he said, 'What need do I have for grain? That first bread you are making, that first bread, give it to me.'

"'So, Great King, feast on my bread; that one is my mother's.'

"'But I want you to give me some of your mother's. I will take some of the first bread, and if you don't do as I say, then I'll curse you.'

"So I tore your bread and gave him one-quarter of it."

The mother began to scream like a crazy person, "Give me my whole bread!"

She screamed, *"Dhī roṭo da roṭā māṭī kor da, dī roṭo da roṭā māṭī kor da."*[5]

When her mother began carrying on in this way, the daughter became deeply disturbed. "And now what will I do?"

Because of her mother, she went wandering this way and that in the forest. Then she came to a banyan tree and a step well, and nearby was a pipal tree[6] with a hollow niche in it. She climbed into the hollow, and there she sat and sat, and the Sun God gave her his grace. He gave her nine kinds of treats, thirty-six sauces, and

5. This mad cry is not readily translatable. Its rhythmic nonsensicality indicates that the mother has become irrationally upset about her broken bread.

6. Pipal trees are proverbially famous for offering shelter to small animals in danger; they are also personified at times as female, and their weddings may be performed by those inclined to religious actions (Gold 1988a).

thirty-two treats, and in a small clay pot he gave her good water. Who? The Sun God, he gave her his grace. So there she sat and ate bread and drank water. Right there in the hollow tree she lived. Twelve months passed.

Now a king was out hunting in this forest, accompanied by his barber. But he got lost. Coming upon the step well and the banyan tree, he went there and lay down. He went to sleep, and his mouth fell open in his sleep. A crumb fell into his mouth from one of her nine kinds of treats. He had never tasted such food, the kind of food that if you eat one crumb, your soul is utterly satisfied.

The king thought, I have never tasted such delicious food. I am a king, but I have never eaten anything like it. The king was astonished. How could there be food this good in the jungle? Then another crumb fell. And she was drinking water, and a drop fell into his mouth, and he said, "Oh, I was so thirsty, and with one drop my thirst was extinguished." And another fell, and his soul was satiated.

So he told his companion, the barber, "Climb that pipal tree and see who is there, who is there that has such food as I've never tasted and such water as I've never drunk."

When the barber climbed he looked everywhere but found nothing.

Then the king himself climbed up and looked in every direction carefully, but he saw nothing. Just as he was descending he glimpsed the girl, and he understood. "Oh ho ho, who is this? Brother, is it a witch, is it a ghost, is it a deceptive illusion, or a spirit seductress?

"Who are you? Explain this mystery."

"I am not . . . not . . . I am not a witch, not a ghost, not a deceptive illusion, not any kind of spirit seductress at all. I am a Brahman's daughter." [She narrates all that has happened up to now.] She was talking to the king.

"God has had such grace on me that every day I receive all kinds of good cooked foods, and today I was eating, and one piece slipped from my hand and fell in your mouth. In this way, from this sign, you have found me."

The king said, "If you are a Brahman's daughter, then I will marry you." In that jungle the king made a dharma marriage with her. The king already had six queens. And she became the seventh. When the king arrived in his kingdom, then the news spread everywhere: "The king has married a seventh queen, a jungli one."

People said, "Oh, the king has married a jungli rani. Oh, he has married a jungli rani, he has married one more queen and brought her here." She began to live in the palace, and after just nine months she had a son, and the Sunday after Holi came. The seventh queen prepared for worship; she plastered the courtyard with cow dung, she made a cow-dung worship space with a thousand rays and kept the fast of the Sun God and began to tell his story. Then the other queens, seeing this queen's method, began to say, "This jungli rani is doing some kind of magic on the king."

Another queen said to the king, "That queen is a magician (*kāmaṇ gārī*), a magic knower (*jāṇ jugār*), a magician, doing magic on you."

The king said, "Oh, you're just talking."

"This jungli rani is doing magic on you."

The king said, "You're just saying this."

"Every day, sir, what does she do? She lights a lamp and sets it in a cow-dung worship space and sprinkles around golden grains, and she also places bread, 1¼ seers of it, and tells the story. The other queens say that she is completing her magic on you today. So go, you had better go and see what she is doing."

The king went to the place. Just as he came, the jungli rani covered up the bread, and she also covered up the offering flowers. At that time the king had a sword in his hand. The king lifted the cover and looked beneath it. The bread was of gold, and the flowers were diamonds and pearls. Seeing this, the king raised his sword and confronted her: "Queen, what are you doing?"

"King, from where did you bring me? I tell the things of the Sun God, and then I will eat bread. From where did you bring me?"

The king said to the queen, "We will go to your mother's home."

The queen said, "Hey Maharaj, I am the daughter of a poor house, a starving natal home."

"But I want to see it."

"I am from a starving natal home and lineage, such a starving natal home."

"I too will see it, whatever kind of a starving natal home it is."

At this the queen became angry and went to bed. She didn't eat food or drink water. In the morning her crazy mother came from somewhere, selling grain sifters. The jungli rani thought, We should buy one for ourselves; so she went out from the palace. As soon as she went out, her gaze fell on her mother. The mother also recognized her. The mother, recognizing her daughter, began calling for that same bread. All these things the other queens were watching, and the queens began to say, "The jungli one has called her mother here too." The jungli queen heard this, and the jungli one shut her mother up inside the house. Having shut up her mother, her mother became a golden icon. Those other queens told the king about it: "This queen isn't good. She is a witch, a magician. A woman came, and this jungli rani ate her." At this the king became angry.

That jungli rani went to bed. She was very worried. When midnight came, the Sun God arrived: "You're awake, you're not sleeping, what's the matter?"

Then she said, "Great Lord, I'm not awake and I'm not asleep and I'm very worried."

"Go, I will give you a natal family and home for three hours, over there by the banyan tree and the step well. Go over there."

"Great." So she said [to the king the next day], "Yes, let's go, sir, let's go, sir, to my natal home, if you desire it, let's go." So they went; they took a chariot with horses, and they went. They took their baby boy, and they took the barber with them too. They went there and found a nine-story mansion, and in it were aunts and uncles, mother and father, brothers and brothers' wives and all. And when they got there these relations sang son-in-law songs for the king, and they seated them.

They served them nine kinds of festive food. An entire, populated city has appeared there. But the three hours were over, and the jungli rani's soul was sorrowful. Then she pinched her little son very hard [so he started howling] and said, "Let's go!" She said to the king, "The child is sick, we ought to return." The king agreed.

To the jungli rani her brother and father's brother gave many things of gold and silver. All three then set off to return to their kingdom. On the way the barber said, "I left my riding crop behind."

The king said, "We have much gold and silver, we will have another made." But the barber insisted on going back to get his whip. When the barber reached the pipal tree place, he saw that there was nothing, no castle and no garden. All that met his gaze was a desolate jungle.

The barber took his whip and came to the king and said, "Hey King, this queen is a very big magic worker. Everything over there was the play of her illusional art. I have just seen it. Over there now is neither castle nor family."

At this the king took out his sword and prepared to kill the queen. And he said, "What is all this? First you made bread into gold. Then you made a woman into a golden icon. Then in this way you made a castle and a family. Reveal the full mystery; if not I am going to kill you."

The queen said, "Hey Maharaj, don't ask me this mystery, because you took me from a hollow pipal tree. I am a poor Brahman's daughter. In this world I had nothing but my mother. But I worshiped the Sun God, I kept his fast, and this is the miracle. All this work was done by the Sun God. For this reason, he gave me both wealth and a natal home."

Hey Sun God, if it's a little short, then complete it; if it's complete, witness it. Four names short or four names too many, hey

Grain-Giver, hey Sun God, as you gave to her so give to the whole changing world!

THE JUNGLI RANI'S TROUBLES

The same storyteller from whom I learned the jungli rani's tale had a number of others in her repertoire concerning resourceful brides who, against all odds, triumph over adversity in their husbands' houses. But in no tale, with half an exception, does this adversity include suspicion of practicing "magical arts" (*jādū, kāmaṇ*). Rather, most of the other stories are about young women who overcome poverty, unkind in-laws, and so forth through a combination of a chosen deity's blessings, native intelligence, and good fate—in proportions that vary from case to case. Their success is more often praised by kin and neighbors than subject to hostility and disapprobation.

For example, there is a Brahman's daughter who, married off (by a cruel stepmother) to one among five ill-mannered, bachelor brothers, effectively brings order and religion to their chaotic household through her own unstinting labors and by enlisting the sympathy of neighbor women. Eventually she devises a foolproof plan to coerce the goddess into granting them infinite prosperity. Public opinion dubs this clever bride not "magician" but "Lakshmi"—goddess of auspiciousness and wealth (Gold n.d. [forthcoming]).

There is a sister who renounces her own hearth and home to save her brother's life. The peculiar actions she must perform to achieve this end lead others to judge her mad for a time. But she is never maligned for evil intentions or threatened physically, even though she pronounces vile curses on her brother (retold in Ramanujan 1991b: 62–69).

When a girl tricked into marrying a sword becomes pregnant (the goddess having miraculously produced a husband-prince for her in a secret room), although there is some scandalmongering about her condition, there is certainly no talk of black magic. In the end her mother-in-law touches her feet and praises her for the good fate that granted existence to a long-desired son (Gold 1982: 32–38).

Besides the jungli rani's tale, only one other women's story that I know from my area includes the motif, expressed far more obliquely than in the jungli rani's case, of suspected magic. That is the story of King Nal, told on the last day of worship of Dasa Mata, the Mother of Well-Being (Gold 1982: 15–23). Nal notices a cotton string—Dasa Mata's emblem—on his queen's neck. The implications of their interchange about this string are that he finds her wearing such a thing, among her golden necklaces, suspicious as well as ugly. She forthrightly informs him, "This is my special women's power." The string represents, indeed is, the goddess of well-being. But the king, because he doesn't like its looks, rashly and brutally destroys it, bringing endless misfortune upon himself and his wife. Only her return to the goddess's grace, when the annual worship comes round again, restores their former prosperity and undoes all the disasters that have dogged both king and queen since his violent folly.

Why, when the majority of worship stories show women's power, acquired through devotion, accepted without question as an indication of great virtue, do a few describe such power as attracting violent suspicions? The jungli rani acts only according to moral precepts, both in her mother's house when she gives the bread to the holy man and in her husband's palace when she worships the Sun God. Yet she incurs abuse, distrust, and accusations of magical practice.

Before speculating on the reasons for the jungli rani's troubles, let me introduce another set of females of a very different type from those portrayed in women's worship stories. Neither Brahman's daughters nor queens, but low-caste artisans and traders, this group includes a female yogi, a potter, an oil presser, a wine seller, a laundress, and their ilk. These are the lady magicians of Bengal as presented in the Rajasthani folk epic of King Gopi Chand. They are "spicy" characters; indeed, the yogi Charpat Nath refers to the guru of them all, Behri Yogin, as "a bag of hot chilis."

These ladies have husbands, and they make some pretense of performing women's typical domestic chores when there is nothing more interesting to occupy their attention, but such drudgery is not their true avocation. Thus, although we meet them on their way to fetch water—the paradigmatic female task—the first to note the presence of a yogi near the water place exclaims, "Burn up all other matters and listen to me. . . . Many days have gone by since we've played a contest, but today's our lucky day. So burn up all other matters, and let's hurry to the waterside, for today we'll have a contest with this yogi." They quickly abandon their unfilled pots and surround the hapless yogi and former king, Gopi Chand.

The tale presents this readiness to drop household chores—whether filling water jugs, nursing babies, or making bread—as a dangerously contagious one; for although only the seven magicians themselves go to play with (and easily to best) Gopi Chand, when the first rescue team of fourteen hundred yogis arrives in search of the lost disciple, each of the seven lady magicians brings seven hundred more women to the contest. The bard describes this antagonistic mob as looking "like clouds mounting in the rainy season." And, hearing about the grand female victory that concludes *this* encounter, all the rest of the city's women clamorously beg, "Take me with you next time, take me with you. Next time, Sister-in-law, don't leave me behind."

The low-caste lady magicians of Bengal seek their own pleasure and power and appear to be without loyalties, whether to gods, husbands, or one another (for they blatantly lie to one another in competing over who should possess their victim). Even though Behri Yogin is repeatedly described as the guru of the other six, they are quite capable of attempting to lie to her too, demonstrating an amorality truly beyond the Hindu pale. Although a few of their husbands are mentioned, Behri Yogin is the only one of the seven actually portrayed interacting with her husband; her demeanor on this occasion is certainly not that of an ideal wife. She hopes to impress Asmal Yogi with her accomplishment of transforming Gopi Chand into a parrot. But her husband chides her for playing an ill-advised, foolhardy prank, warning her of its potentially dire consequences should Gopi Chand's guru Jalindar come to save him. Instead of accepting criticism or advice, she defies Asmal boldly and insultingly. Her parting lines as she stalks away are "My pockets are filled with many such as Jalindar Baba. I keep them in my pockets." The husband, not insignificantly, has the last word, calling after her, "Ho, Lady-Yogi, one day your pockets will split, and Jalindar Baba will emerge. Your pockets will burst, and on that day I won't come to help you."

Behri enjoys some sweet moments of triumph until Shiva's own disciple, Jalindar Nath himself, does indeed arrive in Bengal and, as predicted by Asmal, takes the wind out of her sails. Jalindar Nath sends all the Bengali women, transformed into braying she-asses, into the wilderness, where they starve pathetically because the yogis they have previously turned into donkeys and camels have already stripped the terrain of edible plant life. For all their impudence, independence, and irresponsibility toward hearth and home, it is the wife and mother role that saves them by making their absence difficult to endure: bread burns, babies howl. Accordingly their husbands miss them, and eventually the king is persuaded to control the magicians and restore normalcy to society (Gold 1992: 219–64).[7]

How might this excursion into a male oral tradition help to illuminate the questions raised by the women's tale of the jungli rani? In both genres indigenous distinctions are made between "magic" and "religion" (a partitioning that has often vexed anthropologists attempting cross-cultural definitions). In the Rajasthani view, magic—a manipulation of deliberately cultivated power for selfish or destructive purposes—is threatening and dangerous to particular victims and, when it gets out of hand, to the social order. Dharma—acting according to biomoral duties that, in relation to a grace-granting divinity, can bring special powers and boons—is by contrast beneficent and helpful, not just to the actor but to community and cosmos.

The chief characteristic of the lady magicians in Gopi Chand's tale would seem to be their selfishness. They have no higher purpose in life than the dubious aim of playing power contests for fun. To enjoy this sport they drop all pretense of serving domestic needs. A suggestive if undeveloped antipathy emerges here between women ready to abandon hearth and home for the selfish motives of exercising power and male yogis who also leave their families for the (perhaps equally) selfish cause of spiritual development. Such social irresponsibility, the tradition implies, is fine for male devotees; but female adepts are "sluts" (*rāṇḍ*). A familiar double standard is at work here.

7. For a more extensive description and discussion of women in the Gopi Chand epic see Gold 1991; a complete translation of the lady magicians episode is provided in Gold 1992.

Aloof, independent, and uncompromising, the jungli rani clearly values her relationship with the Sun God above all human connections, much as the Bengali magicians value their magical sport. The transformation of the crazed mother into a golden icon speaks quite strongly for the priority of devotion over kinship, as does her giving the fatal bread in the first place. The Bengali magicians and their female followers abandon their babies when an opportunity to joust magically with yogis presents itself; the jungli rani does not mind pinching her baby hard in order to get her husband to leave the illusory natal home before the time allotted by the Sun God's grace expires. Those attributes that the jungli rani has in common with the lady magicians may reveal why her devotion is perceived as dangerous. It fosters independence from, rather than submission to, familial demands—whether natal or marital.

The clever bride who manages the five bachelors puts her energies not into worship but into cooking and cleaning. The sister totally dedicated to her brother's well-being averts fate itself without evident recourse to a deity.[8] The wife of the sword-husband misbehaves a bit in her daughter-in-law role (snitching the keys to the inner room when her mother-in-law is dozing) but only toward the approved end of perfected wifehood. But the jungli rani's devotion to God overrides her domestic attachments. It appears to be selfishly inspired and thus is perceived as magic, not religion. This is the main source of her troubles. If all women's worship stories have a foundation of devotional emotion and action, the jungli rani's is unusual in giving these concrete priority over the family (although that of King Nal's wife being well justified in spoiling the looks of her golden ornaments with the goddess's white string might also be said to do this).

Connected to the public misperception of the jungli rani's character is the ambiguity attached, in her case, to both daughterly and wifely roles—an ambiguity deriving from her devotional prowess. Such indeterminacy in one woman's identity has no place in Gopi Chand's epic. Where split images prevail it is never hard to decide what kind of woman you are dealing with. The females connected to Gopi Chand by kinship may be loving impediments

8. On Brother Second, it is said, the brother is the deity.

to his renunciation but are of unassailable virtue; the rest—dangerous, defiant "bags of hot chilis"—threaten his life and passage and insult his person. All the latter types, including servant girls and slaves as well as the magicians and their followers, are often referred to by the male bard as "sluts." The jungli rani is never called a slut, but for her to be called a lady magician means that her devotion and character have been misunderstood, if not without cause.

Whenever she is accused of magical practices by her husband, the jungli rani responds, "From where did you bring me?" as if demanding that the king himself acknowledge her as a jungli rani. She, however, consistently describes herself as a Brahman's daughter—that is, as high-caste and part of a family. Others dub her "jungli" with its implications of tribal castelessness and uncivilized kinship patterns. In fact her daughterhood is quite problematic. She has no brothers or father. When the story opens she has a mother. (Indeed, the tale begins: *Do māṅ beṭyā hī* . . . , "There were two, a mother and a daughter. . . .") But the initial episode concerns her total rejection by that mother, and soon enough there is only one, the daughter, alone in the jungle. After she becomes the king's wife—one of seven—she is still isolated, bearing the stigma of her jungli origins.

In chapter 2 I described a prevailing dichotomized view that depicts Hindu women as tamed, paired, matched, motherly, and safe or else untamed, single, unmatched, unmotherly, and dangerous. I also showed how women's songs offered far more unified self-images. In the case of the jungli rani and in a few other worship stories a homologous opposition between women's miraculous manifestations of power as divinely bestowed or as acquired through black magic seems to exist within women's own performance traditions. But, this chapter argues, women's tales define such splits as externally imposed, and work against acceptance of their validity. The jungli rani's troubles come from false, externally imposed splits that are magnified and exacerbated by her lack of a family, especially her lack of male kin. In reality, the barbaric jungli rani and the innocent Brahman's daughter are one. Village women speak the words "jungli rani" with fond approval rather than insultingly, as do the citizens of the story kingdom.

Definitions of the self in women's lore are probably in part responses to male labeling and in part expressions of self-knowledge. In examining the jungli rani's tale, we have seen some interplay between these two modes—an interplay reflecting something of the ambivalence aroused in the Hindu world by manifestations of women's power when divine gifts are not immediately channeled into domestic bliss. Presumably, as the story ends, the king lowers his sword and takes his seventh queen home vindicated, but his recognition of her innocence is never verbalized. It would be easy to imagine her troubles continuing, yet the closing prayer, a standard one, brings the jungli rani's somewhat odd gifts within the circle of blessings sought after by all women. After all, through the Sun God's grace, she has a wealthy husband, a palatial home, and a son, and this is far more than a virtual orphan, from a starving kind of natal home, could reasonably expect.

The jungli rani is not afraid to remind the king that although she is a Brahman's daughter, he took her out of a tree. She maintains her integrity as devotee first; daughter, wife, and mother second. The Sun God blesses her for just this. Perhaps the implicit happy ending to the jungli rani's tale gives expression to women's visions of themselves as persons empowered by divine beneficence as well as maintaining familial bonds—stretched, but not split, by characterizations of female duplicity.

6

Purdah Is As Purdah's Kept: A Storyteller's Story

The heroine of chapter 5 was a story heroine; the heroine of this chapter—Shobhag Kanvar—is a storyteller.[1] But the two are intimately linked, for Shobhag Kanvar is the woman who narrated the jungli rani's tale. The relations between tales and tale tellers, songs and singers, is at the heart of this book. The textures of verbal art, such as Shobhag Kanvar's storytelling language, and the bounded frame of a defined event, such as the Sun God's worship, set emergent performative realities apart from lived realities (Bauman 1977). Nonetheless, narrative realities always interact with tellers' and audiences' everyday experience. Through stories, persons link their own lives simultaneously with cosmological frames and interpersonal networks. A storyteller, as Roma Chatterji comments, knits "his own and other people's diverse and disparate experiences into a coherent narrative" (1986: 95–96). In the process, both stories and the experiences they transmit are subject to manipulation.[2]

Shobhag Kanvar is now a widow in her sixties, but when I first knew her she was a married woman about fifty-five years old with two grown sons and two married daughters. Her life course has been much like that of thousands of high-caste women in rural India. She is a mother, mother-in-law, grandmother, and

1. When I realized how close this book was to publication, I began to worry a lot about using the life and art and photographic portraits of Shobhag Kanvar without consulting her. I wrote her a long letter in Hindi describing this book and the things I wanted to tell in it and mentioning that it was likely her grandchildren or great grandchildren would some day read the book. Because Shobhag herself cannot read, I asked Bhoju to deliver my letter to her and read it out loud in private. Bhoju wrote back her response, which was very favorable: she was happy that such a book would exist. One minor aspect of the way I had described her life troubled her, and I have revised the chapter according to her wishes.

2. For one very powerful exploration of the relation between life and art in a South Asian oral performance see Trawick 1991.

sister—and was for many years a wife—and these kin relationships play a major part in defining her identity, just as they do for most South Asian women.

There are, however, ways in which Shobhag Kanvar is not ordinary: although totally illiterate, she possesses more knowledge about rituals and traditional lore than most women in her large, multicaste village, giving her a certain status there as a religious expert. Thus she is one of a handful of women to whom others come for various kinds of assistance and information. On particular festival days neighbors flock to her house to hear the worship stories properly told, sometimes in front of meticulously executed wall paintings. She also possesses a few healing spells, for muscular aches and such; and barren women seek her out for a series of stomach massages said to prepare the womb for conception. Shobhag Kanvar's is an authoritative, powerful, and deep personality, and I make no claims to represent it here fully, still less to analyze it. I present only fragments of her life story and her tales, selected and assembled to illustrate some aspects of purdah, or the seclusion of women, in Hindu India that have been ignored by most academic accounts.

Like the jungli rani's tale, the story with which I preface Shobhag Kanvar's own is another favorite with teller and audience, but for different reasons. Rather than strong empathy, it evokes hilarity. Teller and listeners laugh together. Shobhag Kanvar tells this story, as she does the jungli rani's, in a ritual context: a small group of women gathered together to worship the goddess and other deities. The tale concerns a Brahman girl and an icon of the beloved elephant-headed deity, Ganeshji. While Hindus often describe stone icons as nothing but partial representations of a formless god, when imbued with divine presence by a devotee's faith lifeless statues can come to life.[3] To those unfamiliar with the ambiguities surrounding icon worship in popular Hinduism, this story may seem strange; but its content displays some ideas about the interrelationship between purdah and women's worship and devotion that help to illuminate the storyteller's own story.

3. See Ramanujan 1991b:33–38 for a South Indian story of a similarly feisty young woman whose bad/good behavior moves an icon to change its position twice.

Ganeshji and the Brahman Girl

There was a Great Ganeshji, and there was a Brahman girl. Now this Brahman girl worshiped Ganeshji every day. But how? She brought burning coals from the cremation ground; and she took the clarified butter from Ganeshji's navel [accept the minor miracle that Ganeshji's navel contains a perpetual supply of butter] and put it on these cremation ground coals for a burnt offering. She did this every day.

This went on until one day Ganeshji thought, Oh ho, how clever this Brahman girl is! She brings fire from the cremation ground and she gives us our offering from our own navel. Then Great Ganeshji was very happy, and he put his finger on his nose, for a joke.

But the villagers got worried: "Oh, this is inauspicious for the king: Great Ganeshji has put his finger on his nose."

They went to the king to complain: "Sir, Great Ganeshji has put his finger on his nose, and it is inauspicious. What should we do?"

The king said, "Set up a sacrificial area, and send for Brahmans from Banaras. Call astrologers."

They did all that, and the Brahmans poured oblations of clarified butter on Ganeshji's nose, but Great Ganeshji didn't take his finger down.

That Brahman girl, she knew, so she said to her husband's mother: "O Mother-in-law, go to the court and ask the king what he will do if your daughter-in-law gets Ganeshji's finger down."

The mother-in-law answered, "Daughter-in-law, for many years I have never gone to the fort, but you are sending me, so I will go."

She went and said, "King, if my son's wife gets Ganeshji's finger down, what will you do?"

"I will give her villages and make her great."

She went back and said, "Daughter-in-law, the king said he would give villages and make you the greatest of all."

At Ganeshji's place the Brahmans from Banaras were still sacrificing, but Great Ganeshji didn't take his finger down from his nose.

Then the girl said, "Hang up a curtain (*pardā*) in front of Ganeshji, and I will come over there."

She took a short stick and double water pots, and she filled her pots with water and bathed Ganeshji. And she ran to the cremation ground and brought fire, and from Ganeshji's navel she took clarified butter and made an offering.

Behind the curtain she said, "Ganeshji, I have bathed you; I have brought fire from the cremation ground, and I have given you an offering of your own butter, and you have put your finger on your nose. Now take your finger down; if you don't, then I will take this stick and break your icon into little pieces."

Great Ganeshji understood. "Yes, it's true, this girl is telling the truth." Then Ganeshji started laughing, and blooming flowers fell of their own accord, and his hand came down. She removed the curtain, and all the world saw.

"Oh ho, look! Ganeshji took his finger off of his nose, Ganeshji is laughing, and heaps and heaps of flowers have piled up."

The king put his hand on her forehead and said, "Lady, you are my dharma daughter [morally adopted daughter]," and he gave her five villages.

O Lord, Great Ganeshji [the storyteller concludes with prayer], as you satisfied that Brahman girl, so satisfy me, and satisfy the world, O Lord.

This story demonstrates three linked ideas:

1. In Hinduism, women's devotional actions may diverge considerably from codified practice, established and maintained by high-caste males, and nevertheless succeed in pleasing God. In the context of Hindu worship, the deviant nature of the young woman's acts is self-evident. First, offerings should be pure and auspicious, but substances secreted by the body are repugnant and polluting, while cremation coals are fearsomely inauspicious.[4] Second—and here lies the girl's special "cleverness"—worship should involve expense, but hers, although performed with devotion, costs her nothing. Moreover, since a god's bodily substances may be transvalued just as a god's leftover foods are, and since a god should not be subject to death's terrors, Ganeshji is forced to uphold his divine status by admiring her trickery.
2. Women may think of purdah (the word means literally "a curtain") as a cover behind which they gain the freedom to follow their own lights, rather than as a form of bondage or subordination.
3. The South Asian social and religious hierarchy in which male kings and male priests appear to hold all the cards may be profitably manipulated by a clever woman (with a little help from God).

4. See Holly Baker Reynolds's discussion (1988) of a South Indian women's worship story in which a virtuous woman is instructed by the goddess to bring "a firebrand from the cremation ground" to light her cooking fire. Reynolds interprets this as women saving "their male kin from the funeral pyre by transferring the cremation fire to the domestic hearth" (27). For women's power over death see also Gold 1988a:123–31.

While preceding chapters have highlighted one or another of these themes in the texts of oral performances, in this chapter I begin to show that women's lives and women's stories, women's strategies and women's self-portrayals, overlap in many ways. In offering just one woman's partial life story I hope that these overlapping, mutually defining qualities of story and life will emerge.

Much of Shobhag Kanvar's story has to do with her "devotion" (*bhakti*) and how it does and doesn't conflict with her adherence to the codes of confinement or curtaining of women practiced in North India and known as purdah.

The literal meaning of "purdah" is, as already noted, "a curtain." In rural Rajasthan for a woman to observe purdah (in Hindi, *pardā rakhnā*, "to keep purdah"; *pardā karnā*, "to do purdah") usually includes these behavioral components, adhered to with highly varying degrees of strictness: in her marital village she doesn't leave the house, and she veils her face in front of all strangers and certain categories of male kin. Husband's father, husband's elder brothers, and, in public, husband himself are the figures before whom a woman most strictly observes purdah. While among the wealthy nobility keeping purdah involves having a separate women's part of the house (the *zanānā*), for ordinary village folk —my subjects here—all spaces are shared. Women effect (and affect) purdah with their garments, eyes, and voices. For instance, when the storyteller's husband was seated near her, she kept her face covered, looked in the other direction, and whispered.

Scholarly definitions and analyses of purdah are plentiful, but I have not found any better than some of those advanced in Hanna Papanek and Gail Minault's anthology, *Separate Worlds* (1982). There Jacobson writes:

> The most important single common feature of all forms of purdah observance is that they are part of a larger cultural pattern of behavior effectively limiting women's access to power and to the control of vital resources in a male-dominated society. The basic essentials of purdah as perceived by both its practitioners and academic observers are restriction and restraint for women in virtually every activity of life.
>
> (Jacobson 1982: 82)

This is true, and yet, as much of Jacobson's own sensitive ethnography and many other descriptions of South Asian women reveal, purdah for them is not a monolithic prison but a subtle, fluid, and often highly manipulable bundle of practices and precepts.[5]

Another common use of the term *purdah* in the area where I worked is to refer to spreading a large piece of cloth in front of a deity when some practice displeasing to that deity is performed. For example, the god Dev Narayanji doesn't like liquor, but Bhairuji—a lesser deity who shares Devji's shrine—requires it. So, when liquor is offered to Bhairuji, two worshipers spread a large cloth, called a purdah, between Devji and Bhairuji. Presumably this protects Devji from the unpleasant sight, or perhaps it shields Bhairuji and his worshipers from Devji's displeasure. The aspect of purdah stressed in this context of worship is opacity, even to divine vision—an opacity that gives license to perform displeasing or insubordinate acts.

In the story presented above, both implications of purdah are simultaneously evoked. Does the Brahman's modest daughter-in-law demand a curtain to hide herself from public view? Or is it to conceal her intimate and wholly unorthodox encounter with the deity from the Banaras Brahmans and their ritually potent fire sacrifice?

Bhakti is regularly translated as "devotion" and occasionally as "love," with the qualification that it is a worshipful love that flows up. If *bhakti* as religious practice teaches humans to adore superior deities, *bhakti* in society is associated with antihierarchical ideas and movements. These include the understanding that priestcraft is unnecessary to mediate between the true devotee and divinity; and that with love any human, regardless of caste or sex, can touch God and receive a bountiful grace.[6]

Some Rajasthani women's lore explicitly elevates *bhakti* in relation to purdah. Lines such as these occur in devotional songs:

> Father-in-law, don't forbid me to go and bow to Devji,
> Father-in-law, those who forbid are marked with fault.
> I will go to the Brave Lord.

The singer speaks directly to her father-in-law, the paradigmatic figure before whom she should veil and keep quiet, defying his

5. Illuminating accounts of the realities of purdah are found in Jacobson 1977b, 1978; Mehta 1981.

6. The literature on *bhakti* is vast. For some insights into the experiences of women devotees, see Kinsley 1981, Ramanujan 1982, and Wulff 1985.

authority over her. Indeed, he becomes a sinner in his opposition to her going out to see her chosen god.

Other women's songs describe how inner devotion can compatibly exist with external adherence to purdah practice:

> Hey Radha, there's a company going to Ganga,
> Let's both make the journey, O Lord,
> Let's go paired on pilgrimage, O Lord.
> Hey Radha, your husband's father is going too,
> How will you praise God, O Lord?
> . . . .
> Hey Ramji, I will veil my face slightly,
> With my mouth I will praise God, O Lord,
> In my heart I will praise God, O Lord.
>
> (Gold 1988a: 272–73)

The first of these texts tells us that *bhakti* gives a charter to break purdah; the second that, with care, one can manage both. Shobhag Kanvar has combined these approaches in her life but given precedence to the latter.

From the early days of our acquaintanceship, Shobhag Kanvar gave me many lessons in the fluidity of the purdah concept, as she kept it. She told me more than once that married women of her caste simply don't leave the courtyard: not to bathe in the pleasant water tank, not to fill water pots at the well. Yet, wishing to instruct me in the art of bathing in the tank (which required deft modesty in changing clothes, which I at first lamentably lacked), she went there with me, saying, "I never go."

Shobhag Kanvar frequently described her unorthodox actions according to the given proprieties. During my first weeks in her village her husband's brother's son's wife gave birth to a much desired boy child, and there was a great celebration during which most male but few female participants quaffed quite a bit of intoxicating *bhāng* (a liquid hemp preparation). When, several weeks later, I showed Shobhag Kanvar a picture I had taken of her boldly raising a foamy glass of this brew and said, "There you are, drinking *bhāng*," she replied, "I'm drinking tea, tea." She was correcting me; from her voice I sensed there was no argument to make. Now, the celebration past, it surely was tea.

Shobhag Kanvar was my mentor in many aspects of religious behavior and decorum, but I knew her best as a storyteller. She was proud of her knowledge and of my recording (and later transcribing) her words. Told on festival days to small groups of female worshipers, many of the stories I collected from Shobhag Kanvar concerned spunky heroines who, out of devotion to husbands, brothers, or deities, suffered disapproval from parents, inlaws, and community but were finally justified and rewarded.

There was, for example, the daughter-in-law who worshiped the goddess of well-being despite the mocking of her husband's family; she eventually won a kingdom for her husband, and a son and sweet revenge for herself. There was the girl, tricked into marrying a sword, who found a God-given husband, became pregnant by him, and had to endure the abuse of her in-laws, who believed her an adulteress; in the end her mother-in-law touches her feet. And there was, of course, the Brahman daughter-in-law who offered Ganeshji butter from his own belly button and received great blessings. Shobhag Kanvar told these, among many other stories, prayerfully on particular ritual occasions. However, their humor and social implications didn't escape her. She and her audience laughed most heartily at the Ganeshji story, enjoying both the ludicrous image of a stone icon raising its finger to its nose (trunk) and the triumph of the resourceful young woman who bested the priests from Banaras.

Certainly the most extraordinary factor in Shobhag Kanvar's character and life is her devotion to Dev Narayanji, a regional epic hero-god who is largely worshiped by the middle peasant castes —Farmers, Gardeners, and Cowherds—rather than by her Rajput community, traditionally higher-ranking warriors and landlords. This passionate devotion has moved Shobhag Kanvar well beyond the circumscribed patterns of action that characterize the lives of Rajput women living in purdah in their husbands' villages. I shall explore just how she has managed to follow freely her religious inclinations while maintaining her reputation as a good Rajput wife.

As a devotee of Dev Narayanji, Shobhag Kanvar was deeply involved in his worship at a shrine just outside her village and equally involved with a mixed-caste group of that deity's devotees. The central figure among this group was the shrine's charismatic priest—a Cowherd man of about Shobhag Kanvar's age. Over the years, her affiliation with this god and place and these people had led her gradually to revise the standard configurations of purdah in a number of ways. For example, the Dev Narayan priest and several of his male followers came to her courtyard every day for tea and sat often for more than an hour, talking freely with her. Shobhag Kanvar did not, indeed, go to the well for water, but whenever hymns to the formless lord were performed, whether on the other side of the village or at a shrine in the jungle, she attended.

As a proper Rajput wife she should never have gone on pilgrimage except "paired" with her husband; but during my stay in the village she made two four- or five-day journeys to distant rivers and temples in the company of men of the Cowherd and Gardener castes who worshiped the same god she did; before my arrival she had taken a much longer pilgrimage in the same company.

This freedom to converse and to travel with unrelated males had not been gained all at once, nor was each fragment of it achieved without struggle. Shobhag Kanvar's husband did not live in the village but in a nearby city where he worked for a salary. This fact does not necessarily imply estrangement but is part of the economic realities that affect ever greater numbers of households in present-day rural Rajasthan. He had held his job for many years and returned home regularly for important festivals and family events.

Rumor had it that once, when they were all much younger, Shobhag Kanvar's husband had indeed objected to his wife's involvement with the group of Dev Narayan devotees. Regularly she welcomed them in her cloistered courtyard and served them the finest spiced tea. Their battle over this issue had attained mythic dimensions in village gossip, and the victory had gone to Shobhag Kanvar. By the time I moved into the village, overt conflicts were long past; purdah does slacken as a woman ages. But Shobhag Kanvar had managed her greatest triumphs when, as a young matron, issues of sexuality were still relevant.

During my initial period of fieldwork in Shobhag Kanvar's village, I spent a lot of time with her, recording her stories, observing her worship and healing arts, accompanying her to the shrine where she regularly advised female pilgrims on Saturdays.

I asked her many questions about her actions but few about her life.

In January 1988, I revisited the village. During the close to seven years that had elapsed since my departure, Shobhag Kanvar had lost her husband, married off two granddaughters, and had some serious quarrels with her eldest son; but I found her personality unchanged. She had, of course, stopped wearing the colored bangles and gold forehead ornament of the auspiciously married woman: indeed, the only verbal reference she made to her widowed status was accompanied by a sweeping gesture that eloquently encompassed these losses. But she had not stopped worshiping Dev Narayanji. In fact, she had built a new, exquisitely painted household shrine for him and continued her regular participation in the public shrine's activities. Nor had she given up serving tea every day to the priest and his followers.

I asked Shobhag Kanvar if I could talk with her about her life, and frankly directed my initial questions to the seeming contradictions between *bhakti* and purdah. My research assistant later told me that I had been presumptuous and risked offending her greatly by asking such questions, for by doing so I implied that she might have been lax in her observation of purdah. However, she understood my drift immediately, and the flow of her ensuing narrative followed it so appropriately, without further prodding, that I am convinced she herself had already interpreted her own development along these lines. In any case, she did not take offense, indicating that she had perfect confidence in her unassailable virtue. Never did Shobhag Kanvar describe herself as "breaking" or "coming out of" purdah; rather, she continuously redefines purdah as she stretches its cover; or to put it another way, she stretches the meaning of purdah, as she keeps it.

Shobhag Kanvar began by asserting, "From my childhood I had *dhyān*"—*dhyān* meaning "meditative attention, concentration on the divine." In her natal home lived a widowed aunt who influenced her, turning her mind to worship. Shobhag Kanvar was married at thirteen, and during the early years of her marriage, when her children were coming along, some living and some dying, her *dhyān* was less, as she put it. Two sons and two daughters survived, and as they grew older, Shobhag Kanvar's concentration, her interest in devotional practices, gradually returned and increased. Several encounters with special persons and several miraculous events punctuated this increase.

These are the decisive incidents in her later career as a devotee, as she recalled them:

1. There was a woman of the Cowherd caste, called Auntie Chand. Auntie Chand's characteristics stand in total opposition to purdah: she left her husband, put on men's clothes, wandered with holy men, did *bhajan*.[7] The term *bhajan*, used almost as synonymous with *bhakti*, has an important dual significance, for it can refer both to inner meditative devotional practice and to singing devotional hymns, usually done by groups of men. Arriving in Shobhag Kanvar's village, this unusual person heard that Shobhag Kanvar was devotionally minded, and sought shelter at her house. Note that although this is the first major incident Shobhag Kanvar offered, it already presumes her strong interest in "doing *bhajan*" and her public reputation for this.
2. A buffalo gave birth, and its milk kept curdling. Accompanied by another Rajput woman and Auntie Chand, Shobhag Kanvar made her first pilgrimage to the shrine of Dev Narayan called Puvali ka Devji, located a short distance outside her village, to find out what the problem was. This is the shrine in which Shobhag Kanvar is deeply involved even today. After the pilgrimage the milk was all right; so Shobhag Kanvar kept going there.
3. The shrine's regular sessions for healing and consultation take place on Saturday afternoons, and the priest otherwise lives at home in the village. But during the semiannual Nine Nights festival, when much divine power is loosed in the world of mortals, Dev Narayan's priest, attended by a few staunch devotees, spends all his time at Puvali. On one of these nights, a Cowherd man, a Potter, and an Oil Presser (all known devotees) were there. The Cave-Baba, deified spirit of a long-

7. In all these traits Auntie Chand appears to follow the model of the sixteenth-century Rajasthani poet-saint, Mirabai—a princess who confounded her royal in-laws by consorting with holy men and eventually abandoning her palace home altogether.

deceased holy man and guru to the priest, showed himself—gave *darśan,* or a divine vision—to them. First they saw only his form, but then the vision spoke, calling out, "*Bachchī Bachchī*!" (Girl! Girl!), but they didn't understand his meaning. The Cave-Baba called again, "The girl from my *rāvalā*!" (that is, the Rajput girl, *rāvalā* being the Rajput neighborhood). Later the Cowherd man and the Oil-Presser man came to Shobhag Kanvar's house and asked, "Did you have *darśan*?" and she said, "I did," for at the exact time that the men at Puvali had heard the spirit cry, "Girl! Girl!" Shobhag Kanvar, too, had seen him in her home in the *rāvalā*.

After this simultaneous *darśan* experience Shobhag Kanvar offered a feast at the shrine and continued to attend its Saturday afternoon sessions. But still she did not attend all-night hymn-singing parties around the village.

4. As she put it, "When they were singing hymns, my soul was sorrowful that I couldn't go and hear; I felt that I was suffocating. Sometimes I cried. When this happened I sat beneath the Cave-Baba's shrine [she had established a place to worship Dev Narayanji and other deities in her home] and thought, and the thought came to me that if I were some other caste, I too could go to hear the *bhajans*." (Rajput women are the most strictly constrained by purdah.)

Her temporary solution to this problem was to make a vow to hold a hymn-singing party every month at her house for one year. But still she was restless and wanted to attend those at other people's homes.

One day a *bhajan* party was getting under way at Ganga Ramji Mina's house, and at this time other devotees of Dev Narayan's shrine, including the priest himself, were there. Shobhag Kanvar's husband also was present. The other devotees, after consulting among themselves, finally asked him to give permission for her to attend. Their argument was "Shobhag Kanvar gets *darśan* (has divine visions), so she too should come." He agreed. Then two of them came to Shobhag Kanvar's house and found her sitting beneath her home shrine.

"At this time I was praying to the Cave-Baba to let me go. If I was in a caste that could go out, then I would go there. I was imagining going, and just then I heard them calling, 'O Shobhag Kanvar.'

"They said, 'You come, Thakur ["overlord," referring to her husband as a powerful Rajput; also a term used for God] is calling you.'"

From that time, Shobhag Kanvar explained, she started to go out. But she insisted here on making the distinction that she does not attend *bhajan* sessions in other villages: "I go only to a few houses where there is love; if I went to other villages, then it would be bad for my family and caste."

This is where Shobhag Kanvar chose to conclude her story (which I have condensed but not reordered). It is certainly not the whole story, as many village tongues would tell. She has omitted not only the dispute with her husband but another major conflict with the priest's wife and mother, which resulted in her temporarily boycotting the shrine. What Shobhag Kanvar gave me was a narrative that above all stresses her maintenance of purdah, even while, moved by *bhakti*, she redefines its limits.

My research assistant noted, while we worked together at transcribing this interview, that Shobhag Kanvar does indeed go to other villages; she would no doubt have explanations of these instances, in terms of compelling devotional or kinship connections. But that is not the point. The point is that she does as she pleases, making up the rules as she goes along. She also makes money, receiving a share of the Dev Narayan shrine's not inconsiderable profits. And she also thoroughly enjoys herself.

Shobhag Kanvar and her audience of women laughed delightedly at various moments throughout her telling of the story of the Brahman girl and Ganeshji, a story distinctly concerned with feminine manipulation of the discourse of religion. Let me conclude by returning briefly to that tale, where *bhakti* and purdah go hand in hand to win the favor of deity and king, but both are curiously rewritten.

Devotional acts are performed with polluting substances, and no expense. This should be doubly objectionable, because ideally the gods are offered pure and costly stuff. But Ganeshji is delighted, not offended, by the Brahman daughter-in-law's trickery, just because it proves her cleverness. One of the story's messages, then, might be the radical one that impure, cheap offerings from smart, imaginative women are more acceptable to God than pure and costly oblations from Brahman men who follow their ritual learning without inspiration. Such a message is in fact consonant with the persuasions of *bhakti*, if the way it is conveyed seems comically unorthodox.[8] Similarly, the humor inherent in the girl's threat, "I'll break your icon to pieces," also delights Ganeshji. This humor is based on a simple-hearted if complexly construed faith both in the actuality of Ganeshji's embodied presence (he cares about his icon) and his superiority to any perishable representation (allowing her to threaten his form with impunity). "This girl is telling the truth" is the divinity's response to her threat, confirming her deeper insights into cosmic realities.[9]

As for purdah, in this story curtaining offers license rather than imposing restraint. When, behind the purdah, the Brahman girl threatens to break the icon, God "understands," takes down his finger, and rewards her worship by pouring down flowers upon her—flowers that are as pure and auspicious and proper for worship as cremation ground coals and navel butter are not. Then she removes the purdah and shows the world God's pleasure. Perceiving God's happiness as a public good, the king rewards her service to his kingdom with a gift more substantial than flowers.

Shobhag Kanvar too has developed an intimate relationship with a powerful deity; in doing so she has risked the disapproval of the community and defied the wrath of her husband. But these are not the points she herself stresses in telling her own story. Instead she offers a tale of singleminded devotion confirmed at critical junctures by miraculous events revealing divine attention to and love for her.

Like the women in her stories, Shobhag Kanvar too has prospered as a direct result of her innovative religious path. If she has

8. There is, for example, a well-known story about Rama preferring an offering of saliva-polluted fruit from an untouchable devotee to any pure or costly gift. The theme of polluted offerings provides powerful imagery in early South Indian devotional poetry (Ramanujan 1973) and emerges as a subversive message with potential political power in later North Indian *bhakti* traditions—particularly of the untouchable saints (Gokhale-Turner 1981; Zelliot 1981).

9. Jane Atkinson (personal communication 1988) has suggested a sexual interpretation of the imagery of Ganeshji putting his finger on his nose and the girl, behind the curtain, bringing it down. It is certainly possible, indeed attractive, to speculate along these lines. However, I have no cultural confirmation for such speculations. Ganesh is not a sexually active god, with designs on his devotees, as some regional Hindu deities are.

not received castles or whole villages, she has entirely rebuilt, in costly brick and stone, dwellings for herself, her two sons, and their families. She also believes herself to have spiritual gifts (such as reading the future from the palm of her hand). Brahman priests have played no part in her development, and she has told me that she is equal (*barābar*) to the Cowherd shrine priest in devotion and knowledge, conducting Devji's worship at her home shrine with full authority. Shobhag Kanvar keeps purdah, but purdah is, as Shobhag Kanvar keeps it, a curtain draped according to her own design. As her stories teach, a woman who defines patterns that differ from those set by authoritative males may please God and better her own existence too.

EPILOGUE

A few days after I returned home from the annual meeting of the Association for Asian Studies in San Francisco in March 1988, where I had delivered an early version of this chapter, I received a letter from my research assistant in Rajasthan. I translate some passages of this letter from his Hindi.

> There is some very bad news. You know that I always tell you the truth, and I can't hide anything from you. One day before Holi, on March 2, 1988, Gopal Singh came to Ghatiyali from Jaipur, and Ram Singh came from Kekari. [Holi is a raucous harvest festival celebrated with abandon throughout North India. Gopal Singh is Shobhag Kanvar's nephew, and Ram Singh is her younger son; both men, in their early thirties, work at city jobs—Gopal Singh in Jaipur and Ram Singh in the nearby market town of Kekari—while their wives and children live in Shobhag Kanvar's compound in the village of Ghatiyali.] They came to Ghatiyali bringing meat and liquor. . . . They were cooking meat and drinking liquor in the sitting room [a showpiece "guest room" built on the street]. At this time, I don't know why, Gopal Singh and Ram Singh went over to Shobhag Kanvar [across two courtyards] and began to insult her. [The young men's accusations had to do with Shobhag Kanvar's involvement in the worship of Dev Narayanji at Puvali ka Devji.] In this way there was a big fight, and Ram Singh began threatening to beat Shobhag Kanvar with the sword. On the next day Shobhag Kanvar left Ghatiyali and went to Kekari [where her elder son maintains a family house]. I met her there, and as soon as she saw me she began crying hard and saying, "Now I will not live in Ghatiyali." So, Ann, now look, what will happen? Will Shobhag

> Kanvar come back to Ghatiyali or not? Whatever happens, just now she is very sorrowful.

As I read these words remorse and shame swept over me. Even while I was receiving praise for my lively portrayal of Shobhag Kanvar as an expert if subtle subverter of gender hierarchies, these young men had abused her and driven her from the place she loved. Why had this happened now, after so many years? Irrationally, I wondered if it could be my fault, if by analyzing and exposing Shobhag Kanvar's delicate maneuvers to a laudatory audience of Western feminists I had somehow undermined them, leaving her subject to this terrible attack by her drunken son and nephew. (That the incident had occurred about three weeks prior to my presentation was no consolation.)

Irrational guilt gave way to academic rationalization soon enough. Obviously Shobhag Kanvar's problems had nothing to do with me. I even experienced, although I attempted to repress it, a certain pleasure at receiving this confirmation of my argument that Shobhag Kanvar's lax purdah practices were not simply a privilege of her advancing age. Here was proof that her continuing freedoms rankled the family men's sense of honor even now.

Reviewing my assistant's narrative of this event, I was struck by how symbolically laden were the elements composing it. Moreover, all their force converged strongly to suggest Shobhag Kanvar's eventual relief from her current distress, as did my correspondent's quizzical conclusion. First, the incident was precipitated by consumption of meat and liquor. It is appropriate to the nature of Rajput males, as warriors and hunters, to indulge in such consumption. Confined to a separate "guest room" built to accommodate just these indulgences on the part of visiting sons-in-law, such polluting activities might be tolerated. However, to carry their taint to Shobhag Kanvar's domain, where the abstinent and exacting deity Dev Narayanji was enshrined, was sin. Shobhag Kanvar held the morally superior position here.

Then there was the sword. This sword is a family relic, dating from a more glorious and lamented past when Rajput men fought heroically in the service of local overlords. The weapon is emblematic of an era when male power among Rajputs had deeper foundations than it does today. But, in terms of family politics, the sword held an entirely different significance, as it played a critical part in the fight between Shobhag Kanvar and her husband that I described as having "attained mythic dimensions in village gossip." The story, whispered to me by several male and female friends but never alluded to by Shobhag Kanvar herself, went as follows.

One day, many years ago, Shobhag Kanvar's husband decided to put a stop to her active involvement with the group of Dev Narayan devotees. They had strong words, and she appeared to accept his authority. However, that night, after he was asleep in his bed, Shobhag Kanvar took down the family sword from its place on the wall, climbed astride her husband's chest, and poised the weapon over his neck. "Let me continue to worship Dev Narayan as I have been," she demanded. He complied. Obviously, in threatening her with that same sword Ram Singh aspired to reestablish masculine authority in their domestic circle. But I could not imagine that he had a chance of succeeding.

Unless I was severely deluded in my perception of Shobhag Kanvar's character, and of the balance of power in her household, she would not stay exiled in Kekari for long. Her son Ram Singh himself was not a completely stable person, and he and Shobhag Kanvar normally had a very close, tender relationship. She had spoken frankly to me on this most recent visit of the "love" (*prem*) between them, contrasting it with the distance she felt from her more educated and successful elder son, at whose home she took refuge after leaving the village. As for the nephew, Gopal Singh, there was a history of rivalry and conflict between his household and Shobhag Kanvar's. Surely the temporary alliance of two inebriated young males would dissolve under the weight of more enduring loyalties.

I begged my research assistant in several subsequent letters to tell me further developments. But it was another three months before I received a brief answer: "In the village all are fine, jolly and happy, living in pleasure. Shobhag Kanvar is back with Ram Singh, living happily; there is no trouble at all." The details of their reconciliation I have yet to learn, but my faith in Shobhag Kanvar's ability to manipulate her social environment is confirmed.

Shobhag Kanvar's return to happiness relieved me, by and large, of my lingering fears of personal accountability. But the whole episode gave me cause to consider my enterprise as an interpreter of someone else's life story. At the original oral presentation of this and other papers on "ordinary women," Chandra Mohanty, the discussant, asked us, the authors, if we had shared our own life stories with the women who told us theirs, implying that our enterprise as tellers of lives should be grounded in mutuality.

Shobhag Kanvar and I, despite the gulfs that lay between us, forged a mutuality on many levels and in many modalities. I know that she often entertains her guests with vivacious imitations of a weak-minded, inept foreign woman even as I further my career by spinning tales of—and drawing conclusions from—her power and grace. Although we thus take advantage of each other in several ways, we have also cared about and helped each other, learning throughout these sometimes painful negotiations. To paraphrase a prayer that Shobhag Kanvar often makes at the end of her traditional tales: as this has enriched our lives, so may it satisfy the world.

7

Conclusion: Some Reflections on Narrative Potency and the Politics of Women's Expressive Traditions

THE POETICS OF RESISTANCE AND THE POWER OF WORDS

The women we know in Pahansu and Hathchoya and Ghatiyali reimagine their lives and their worlds in the songs they sing and the stories they tell. As anthropologists and linguists come more and more to regard texts as instruments and as products and as modes of social action (Hanks 1989), we find that the boundaries between words and lives are fluid and permeable, and they are sites of contestation and of struggle. The poetic genres that we have translated in these pages—dancing songs, songs of birth and marriage and festivity, ritual narratives and the narrative frames women use to tell of their own experiences—are South Asian discursive forms that have very long histories. Yet these "traditional" expressive genres bear witness not to a cultural consensus about gender and kinship but to a "dissensus," to reflexive cultural criticism embedded in many kinds of textual performance. In South Asia as elsewhere, protest and tradition, as Lakshmi Holmström reminds us (1991: xiii), slide together, instead of being at odds with each other.

But do these story worlds, the narratives sung and spoken by women in Uttar Pradesh and Rajasthan, flow into lived worlds? Do these words interact with everyday realities and transform them, or does their power reside only in the imagination, only in the telling? While in hiding from the Ayatollah Khomeini's death sentence, the Bombay-born novelist Salman Rushdie wrote a children's book dedicated to his son, called *Haroun and the Sea of Stories*. Toward the climax of this multiply-allegorical work filled with cross-language punning and polycultural meanings, Haroun, the child-hero, confronts the evil Cultmaster, Khattam-Shud (in Hindi, meaning "Completely Finished"), who is busy concocting dreadful poisons designed to pollute the Ocean of Story. Haroun is naively appalled:

> "But why do you hate stories so much?" Haroun blurted, feeling stunned. "Stories are fun. . . ."
>
> "The world, however, is not for Fun," Khattam-Shud replied. "The world is for Controlling."
>
> "Which world?" Haroun made himself ask.
>
> "Your world, my world, all worlds," came the reply. "They are all there to be Ruled. And inside every single story, inside every Stream in the Ocean, there lies a world, a story world, that I cannot Rule at all. And that is the reason why."
>
> (Rushdie 1990: 161)

Khattam-Shud knows that stories contain unruly, multiple, moving worlds, alive worlds, and worlds capable of challenging the powers that be. And that is why he is "the Arch-Enemy of all stories and of Language itself." He is the "Prince of Silence and the Foe of Speech" (39) because he wishes to silence all voices of protest. If he brings stories to an end, dreams and life itself will come to an end as well.

Haroun ponders one question over and over again: "What's the use of stories that aren't even true?" And we have asked ourselves, What is the use of the songs and stories from Uttar Pradesh and Rajasthan that tell of women's power and agency when more authoritative and hegemonic voices speak only of women's submission to powerful males? But when Haroun asks his question, his father, a master storyteller, hides his face in his hands and weeps. Later in Rushdie's novel, when Rashid the storyteller is confronted by the power of Khattam-Shud, he too speaks of such a gulf between story worlds and "somewhere real." "And when Haroun heard his father say *only a story*, he understood that [he] was very depressed indeed, because only deep despair could have made him say such a terrible thing" (48). Perhaps he weeps because if he accepts that stories have no power, he accepts the inevitability of control and of domination.

Visions of the power of speech and of stories abound in contemporary Indian fiction. Sometimes it is the potency of hegemonic and authoritative words that is at issue. In the short story

"Raja Nirbansiya" the Hindi writer Kamleshwar juxtaposes a folktale of a childless king and his wife to the story of Jagpati, a poor village man, and his wife, Chanda. In the folktale, the king finds reason to doubt the wifely virtue (*satītva*) of his queen, and he demands proof that the sons she finally bears are truly his own. The queen undertakes an ascetic regime to demonstrate that her *satītva* is unbroken, and the gods in turn provide miraculous proof of the queen's devotion to her husband. In the interwoven parallel story of an ordinary village man, Jagpati doubts the virtue of his wife when she becomes pregnant, and his doubts are fueled by village gossip and by proverbial comments about the unsteadiness of "women's nature" (*tiriyā charittar*, in the Hindi dialect that Kamleshwar recreates). The story ends tragically, because although "Chanda had no divine powers, and Jagpati was not a king," Jagpati falls victim both to his poverty and to the terms of a discourse that defines female nature as unruly and in need of male surveillance.

Kamleshwar's short story traces the potency of a hegemonic narrative about wifely virtue and "women's nature."[1] In the very act of descrying a final difference between a story world and the real world of Jagpati and Chanda, the author tells of the power of a dominant discourse, lodged in a simple folktale, to frame people's lives and expectations, and he speaks of the enormous burdens it forces them to bear.[2]

Beyond such literary depictions of the power of discourse to perpetuate hierarchical relations in India, there are also depictions of the subversive projection of story as rhetorical force into a world of listeners and readers. The incorporation of political messages into a traditional form of oral storytelling is vividly fictionalized in the opening scenes of Raja Rao's compelling novel *Kanthapura*—a portrayal of how Gandhian ideology, introduced in

1. Tales of husbands demanding proof of their wives' virtue, followed by divine vindication of their claims to be *pativratā* (faithful to one's husband), are legion in Indian oral traditions such as the *sāṅg* drama *The Legend of Sila Dai*, examined in chapter 4, and in written texts such as the *Ramayana*.

2. Kamleshwar's perspective, however, is by no means a completely feminist one. When Jagpati, for example, speaks of the danger that follows the wiping out of "Lakshman's line," which is drawn by men to protect women, one does not sense that the author has totally abandoned the notion that women are in constant need of protection by powerful males. This is a theme that surfaces in several of his short stories. Yet the stories do cast a critical eye on the unthinking internalization of ideas about "female nature" and female duplicity.

the performance of *harikathā*, brings awareness of the struggle for independence from colonial rule to a South Indian village.[3]

The Bengali short stories translated by Kalpana Bardhan in *Of Women, Outcastes, Peasants, and Rebels* (1990) portray the complex struggles of marginalized and oppressed peoples as they variously resist, transcend, or submit to the ideologies and social arrangements that constrain and dehumanize them. As Bardhan points out, such struggles sometimes take the form of overt rebellion, but more often they are struggles in the realm of consciousness, struggles in which women, untouchables, and impoverished tribal people gradually come to recognize that their oppression is neither inevitable nor unquestionable. Some of the most powerful fictional representations of resistance in these stories are richly permeated by styles and motifs from oral traditions. In Mahasweta Devi's story "Paddy Seeds," for example, a landless laborer gives voice, in a Holi song, to the suffering he has witnessed as a result of the avarice of powerful landowners, and those who hear his song are moved to revolt by his words. And in Rabindranath Thakur's "Letter from a Wife," a woman who finally flees the confines of an oppressive conjugal home ends her introspective and critical narrative with an invocation of the songs of Mirabai, the sixteenth-century poet-saint who rejected conventional definitions of the ideal wife in favor of a life spent in the pursuit of her own religious aims. In these fictional worlds, social contexts determine, reflect, interpret, and are changed by the meanings and voices produced in expressive forms.

Such expressive forms are not of course always or regularly successful in permanently altering the structures of dominance or deprivation they critique. Nonetheless, the existence of subversive poetic genres—as Khattam-Shud's project dramatizes—remains an affront to any enterprise of domination or suppression.[4]

3. Anticolonial discourse in Uttar Pradesh folklore has been documented by Vatuk (1969).

4. We write these concluding words in December 1992, just days after the tragic destruction of the Babri Masjid in Ayodhya by militant Hindu fundamentalists and as hundreds of Muslim lives and Hindu lives are being lost in the violent aftermath. We are thus made more aware than ever of the political uses of stories, of the potential for narrative texts—in this case, the *Ramayana*—to be used for political ends of many different kinds. The human creative capacity exemplified in narrative performance is as likely to foster hatred, bigotry, violence, and death as to promote awareness of oppression, resistance, and liberation.

It is not only in fictional worlds that expressive traditions are deployed as modes of political resistance. In Rajasthan in 1992, village women trained as *sāthins* (voluntary workers in a program aimed at educating and organizing rural women) sing folk songs in which themes of resistance and equality have been interwoven (Baweja 1992). Here "tradition" is consciously reformulated to serve in struggles to end gender inequities. In many other feminist groups throughout India, puppet shows, songs, and traditional forms of street theater convey messages of social transformation to groups of urban and rural women alike. In the film *No Longer Silent*, which documents the work of activists for women's rights in Delhi, Bina Agarwal, Kamala Bhasin, and other prominent Indian feminists compose and sing lyrics, patterned like women's folk songs, to use in rallying women to protest gender inequities in India. Yet even in the far less overtly political genres that we have examined in these chapters, resistance is inextricably embedded in women's expressive traditions.

That there is a continuity between ordinary expressive forms heard throughout India and these versions specifically adapted as tools of political struggle is evidenced by instances in which "traditional" forms are used spontaneously in moments of crisis, to communicate desperation and protest to those in positions of power. In the aftermath of the violent and murderous riots in Delhi that followed the assassination of Indira Gandhi in 1984, a group of bereaved Sikh women, slum dwellers, were able to meet with the Chief Secretary of Delhi to protest the lack of protection afforded them by municipal authorities. As their grievances were presented, one woman began to sing a lament in the traditional style, expressing her view that if the government is to be thought of as mother and father, then it should not fail to protect those whose security is in jeopardy (Das 1990b: 373–74).[5] Here again, tradition slides into protest, since women's competence in such

5. Yet it is the case that suffering can be so extreme and so incomprehensible as to render the performance of such traditional expressive forms impossible. Das also describes how some women who had lost husbands, sons, and brothers in the riots were unable to mourn their dead in the traditional manner, by singing laments. But they did use certain practices connected with the observance of death pollution to resist publicly the silence about the tragedy that Das says was imposed upon them (Das 1990b:362–65).

expressive genres may confer the ability, in times of tragedy, to give voice to their discontent in wider political arenas. As Das writes, "The division of labour in the roles played by men and women in the work of mourning during normal deaths stretches into the field of political deaths and makes women the special interlocutors between the worlds of kinship and politics" (1990a: 29). Ordinary women know the power of words, and they know well the experience of speaking of their grief and their resistance in sung and spoken narrative, and thus, as Davis (1975) and Scott (1990) have argued, poetic and ritual forms of protest can enable women to articulate a resistant stance and then to raise their voices when more practical forms of protest become possible.

CHANGING SONGS AND CHANGING WORLDS

As the nineteenth century drew to a close and the twentieth century began, women in northern India sang, as they do now, of the sometimes conflicting loyalties a man owes to sister and to wife (Luard n.d.) and the enmity that may exist between a wife and her husband's sister (Grierson 1886: 249–50); they sang of the pain of seeing daughters leave their natal homes, "this custom of the degenerate times" (*kālī kī rīti yahī*) (Crooke 1910: 338); women in Saharanpur district sang lamentations at the deaths of their husbands, mourning the loss of their *suhāg* and the bangles and the earrings that betoken it (Crooke 1910: 336–37); in Sirsawa, a few miles from Pahansu, women sang of the labor of grinding grain and the labor of childbirth (Cunningham 1882: 84–85); and women sang, as they do now, of the pain of separation from husbands and from lovers (Grierson 1884; Tharu and Lalita 1991: 187–90). In some ways, women's critical assessments of these elements of their experience in kinship relations have undoubtedly remained constant over the years since colonial administrators like Luard, William Crooke, and Alexander Cunningham had such songs recorded by Indians in their employ. Songs we recorded in Pahansu, Hathchoya, and Ghatiyali speak profoundly of these continuities.

But women's spoken and sung narratives have not remained untouched by time. Songs sung by Gujar women in Saharanpur district at the end of the nineteenth century speak of their perceptions of the revolt against the British in 1857 (Crooke 1911: 123),[6] and a women's song from Central India recalls a brother's visit to a British imperial *darbār* in Delhi (Luard n.d.: 106). Songs from Pahansu and Hathchoya, recorded in 1988 and 1990, acknowledge the arrival of many consumer goods in these villages: they tell of grooms enjoying breezes from electric fans,[7] of a husband who's a "radio fiend" (*raiḍiyo bāj*), of a groom appearing at his wedding on a green motorcycle, and of wives demanding watches from admiring husbands. In one song from Hathchoya, a brother sets out with *bhāt* gifts in an airplane, his landing hampered only when his plane runs out of fuel. And in a song from Ghatiyali, the god Dev Narayan is described as walking in the bazaar and listening to his transistor radio, only to find that his batteries have gone dead. Songs recorded in Ghatiyali in 1980 included many references to modern transportation—buses and cars—and to household items like electric light bulbs. Some commented on current political events, such as Sanjay Gandhi's ill-fated family planning campaign of the late 1970s. Several songs lamented the loneliness of a young bride left in the village at her in-laws' house while her husband works in the city. The very first song Ann heard in Ghatiyali when she returned there in 1993 reflected perhaps a change in attitude: in it a young girl wishes for a husband with a job and contrasts the easy life she would have with such a spouse to the hard daily toils of a farmer's wife.

Women's songs acknowledge changing educational expectations as well. In a dancing song from Hathchoya, a wife's voice lists her complaints about her *sasurāl*, and she implores her friend to listen to how she has been told to go to college, only to find that "my book bag is torn, and the teacher's too old." In a wedding song from Pahansu, the voice of a twelve-year-old bride protests that she's too young to be married, that she'd rather join the Congress party and become a goddess of learning. In another wonderful wedding song from Pahansu, women of the bride's side sing, "There are ever so many B.A. pass grooms, our girl wants a groom who's an M.A. pass."

6. For a brief discussion of Gujar participation in this revolt, see Raheja 1988b: 255 n.3.

7. Pahansu was electrified only in late 1987, several months before I returned for my second visit.

When I returned to Pahansu in 1988, after an absence of nine years, I saw a number of hand-painted signs in towns in the vicinity proclaiming that "an educated woman is the light of the home" (*paṛhī likhī nārī ghar kī ujārī*). It was my impression that girls in Pahansu were attending school for a few years longer than they had in the late seventies. And in between Ann's first and second visits to Ghatiyali, a girls' school had been established in the village. Certainly in 1988 there were more young women in Pahansu who could read and write than there had been in 1979. But some of this inclination to allow girls to remain in school has to do with the idea that dowry expectations would be lower for girls with a little education, a domestication of female learning that seems to be echoed in the phrase "light of the house." Could it be that the dancing song that complains about the incongruity between conjugal expectations and the college as the young bride finds it in fact represents a nascent critique of the limitations and the uses of such female education? Though women value education and literacy, for themselves and for their daughters, they also see that it is sometimes used only to enhance male honor or as one more "qualification" for an acceptable bride.

We have not focused in this book on historical transformations in women's performance traditions. The historical record of women's voices appears now to be too scanty and too heavily edited by powerful males writing in pencil so that the forthrightness of women's songs and narratives "should be struck out if considered befitting" (Luard n.d.: 160) for a completely satisfactory analysis to be feasible. Yet it is possible to discern that women's songs have never stood outside of history. And it is just this historicity and transformability of tradition that provides us with additional grounds for suggesting that women's expressive genres might possibly serve as catalysts in more highly charged and more widely ranging demands for change on the part of rural women.

But the direction of change in women's oral traditions is as yet far from clear. Commercial influences are legion, and the danger is that the voices and the styles in women's expressive genres may be further marginalized by such influences. Some of these influences seem relatively benign. The melodies of some songs, for example, are taken from film music. When I was translating the "Song of the Mother's Brothers' Gifts" in chapter 3, for example, I spent an enormous amount of time asking women for the meaning of the first line, "a little pebble over a big one." Expecting to discover at last that it had some profound symbolic meaning in relation to the *bhāt* gifts, I must admit that I was a bit chagrined to find that this was simply the first line of a film song, inserted into what appears to be a very old set of lyrics, to introduce a *philmī* melody.[8] Edward Henry (1988: 111–12) reports that in eastern Uttar Pradesh song booklets are sold in the bazaars, with film song melodies suggested for the commercially composed songs. Such commercial booklets have not yet made their way to Pahansu. But in 1988, I came upon two printed collections of folk songs from Saharanpur and Muzaffarnagar districts, compiled by a teacher of Hindi at a local college (Sharma 1983, 1984). I had copies of these with me in Pahansu, and when a few literate young women discovered them in my room, they read them avidly, pointing out to me which songs they had heard in Pahansu, performing some of them for me, and adopting others, selectively, into their own repertoires.[9]

These kinds of influences do not seem to marginalize women's expressive genres, and they may even foster some kinds of creativity; but others may go much farther in diluting women's distinctive perspectives. This is not a simple issue of "authenticity." As Arjun Appadurai (1991: 473) points out, this notion is suspect if it involves an assumption of a past simplicity and fixity of folk traditions, or if we counterpose a notion of "authentic" tradi-

8. Three months after the electrification of the village in November 1987, there were already thirty television sets in Pahansu, and televisions had become important dowry items. The sets were most avidly watched on Sunday evenings, when Hindi films were aired, and the film songs were always particularly appreciated. The women in our house would cook the evening bread and lentils before the film began, and set them aside until the intermission, when everyone would eat a hurried meal before the film resumed. I had never before seen people willingly consume cold *roṭis*, but even the men seemed unconcerned, in their haste to return to the television set. For most women, this was the first opportunity to see Hindi movies, since expeditions to the town for such a purpose would have called forth cries of *beśaram*, "No modesty!" On one occasion in 1988, a television and videocassette recorder were rented from a nearby town so that a Hindi film could be shown to guests following a fire sacrifice ritual for the opening of a new men's sitting place built by a Gujar landholder.

9. Though there are no sexually explicit songs in these collections, many of the songs collected and reported by Sharma and his students are every bit as subversive as the ones I tape-recorded in Pahansu and Hathchoya.

tions to ones that are mechanically reproduced. Yet there are forces of change that may specifically threaten women's ability to give voice to cultural criticism in their sung and spoken expressive traditions. Henry, for example, points out that women's participatory music is imperiled by several recent developments in eastern Uttar Pradesh. Electric amplification of taped music at weddings and other events may sometimes discourage women from singing themselves, and in urban areas, professional singers may be hired to lead the ritual songs (1988: 112, citing Tewari 1977). In the Chhattisgarh region of Central India, many women's traditions are being supplanted by music from All-India Radio and films shown in "video halls" (Flueckiger 1991: 192–96). In Pahansu, loud and raucous bands of male musicians playing Western instruments are invariably hired at weddings nowadays, and their music always seemed to me to grow more insistent as women's singing commenced; women's voices are drowned out entirely on a few of my tapes.

Changing educational expectations may also have a profound impact on the performance of oral traditions. Flueckiger, for example, reports that in Chhattisgarh songs that celebrate female sexuality are viewed by men as "bad songs" (*bura git*). Male village leaders argue that "our educated girls shouldn't be singing these kinds of songs" (Flueckiger 1991: 192–93). As they define the kinds of behavior compatible with literacy, males once again threaten the continuation of female expressive genres and the voicing of women's particular perceptions of gender and kinship.

A recent development in western Uttar Pradesh over the last five to ten years has been the commercial videotaping of wedding events. These tapes are then made available to relatives who attended the marriage. This was just beginning to be fashionable in some of the small towns and villages in the area in 1990, and I was able to see only a few of these wedding tapes. They appeared to be records primarily of the activities presided over by men: the Sanskritic wedding rites of course, but most footage was given over to shots of the important male guests and their socializing, eating, and drinking. I did not see any footage of women's rites or women's singing. There is every indication that videotaping will become more and more a marker of a properly managed wedding in rural Uttar Pradesh. If this happens, will the tapes in fact further deemphasize the significance of women's voices, as the videotaped male presences come more and more to be remembered as "the wedding" while the women's presence and women's words go unrecorded? Will women too view these videotapes and come to see their own absence as somehow natural and inevitable, or will they, as we suspect they might, begin to compose songs that are themselves critical responses to this video devaluation of women's ritual and social roles?

Far more ominous than the mere replacing of women's voices by cassette music or the omission of women's images from wedding tapes is the blatant exploitation of women's songs for the titillation of male audiences. As we have seen in these chapters, women's songs frequently use erotic imagery to challenge male-authored characterizations of female nature and female sexuality. Cassette producers in northern India have recently begun to record and market renditions of what they term *masala* ("spicy") songs, women's erotic folk songs ordinarily sung in courtyards from which males have been barred. The market for cassette tapes in general is overwhelmingly male in India, and Peter Manuel draws attention to the way in which these particular songs are marketed: "The male orientation of such cassettes is particularly evident in their covers, which generally depict a scantily clad seductively posed woman, archetypically offering herself to the male gaze. Such covers naturally suggest a certain interpretation to listeners" (1993: 175). I have not seen these tapes in Pahansu or Hathchoya, and so I cannot yet comment on their possible impact on women's expressive traditions. But as women's songs of protest are transformed into pornography by the Indian recording industry we see yet another way that female voices are manipulated and exploited by powerful males. And therefore we may question Appadurai's argument that electronic recordings of "folk music" merely extend the plasticity and diversity of indigenous traditions (1991: 473). In this case, at least, what is at issue is less the abstract notion of "authenticity" than the invention of novel means by which women's speech is drawn into the orbit of male control.

Thus the vexed issue of "authenticity" itself may involve considerations of gender, if in fact it is specifically female voices that tend to be silenced, transformed, marginalized, or exploited by professionalization, by electronic media, or by the definitions of the proper uses of literacy posed by powerful males. These developments that may compromise the resistance exhibited in women's expressive genres are of some significance, since in India, as elsewhere, the performance of song and story provides, as we have tried to demonstrate, a privileged arena for women's subversive speech. But for every attempt to silence women's songs, there have also been attempts, like those of the *sāthins* in Rajasthan, to heighten the power of their resistance and to bring them into increasingly politicized and public arenas.

We do not know the answers to these questions about the future of women's spoken and sung resistance, about the future of women's distinctive expressive genres. We have witnessed, though, the complexity and the power of these words, and some of the instances in which such words have flowed into the lived worlds of women in Uttar Pradesh and Rajasthan. Though women's discourse may both sustain and undermine hegemonic gender representations, and though women speak from diverse kinship, class, and caste positionings, we believe that women's oral traditions will continue to speak creatively and provocatively to the changing circumstances of women's lives and to the steps being taken by Indian feminists, both rural and urban, to ensure that their voices will be heard.

A critical task in social science and humanities disciplines over the last fifteen to twenty years has been to formulate an understanding of cultural difference while at the same time avoiding the pitfalls of essentializing those cultural differences and of reproducing the tacit assumption that cultures are timelessly fixed or singly voiced and homogeneous. One possible step in the resolution of this issue of representation is to recognize, first, that tradition and resistance are seldom antithetical, that each culture harbors within itself critiques of its most authoritative pronouncements; and second, that while such critiques frequently take the form of such ostensibly "traditional" forms of speech as proverbs, songs, and folktales, they enter at the same time into the realm of the political, as they are deployed in the construction and reconstruction of identities and social worlds in which relations of power are deeply implicated.

Appendix

Rajasthani and Hindi Song Texts

CHAPTER 2

1.
keśyā, āgariyā ko ghāghariyo mu lāy, berī,
syālūṛo mu lāy ra sāngāner ko;
berī, syālūṛā me dīkha sāro ḍīl ra,
ghūngaṭ me dīkha ra gorā gālaṛā.
khājā khājā sagaḷoī ḍīl ra
gālaṛā mat khāje ra parṇyūṅ mārasī

2.
choda chha to ḍūṅgaraṛā le chāl, beri
choda chha to ḍūṅgaraṛā le chāl re
uḍā syū dīkha ra Dallī Agaro

3.
dārī ra dārī ra ṭīmalṭī bāḷī syūṅ lūṅchī bhī ūṅchī hāṅ
chaṛh chhātī mūṅchyā par mūṅtyo
hāṅ ka hāṅ ra
chaṛh chhātī mūṅchyā par mūṅtyo
hāṅ ka hāṅ ra
dhur mālāṅ jādī yo kaī kīdho
hāṅ ka hāṅ ra
andhārī ḍarpūṅ ra dādā
hāṅ ka hāṅ ra
ham na jagātī to tum na muṅtātā
hāṅ k hāṅ ra
tum na jagātā to ham na muṅtātā
hāṅ ka hāṅ ra
dārī ra Ain-bāī bhī khoṭī

4.
haraḷ bharaḷ thāṅrāṅ syālūṛo kare chha
haraḷ bharaḷ thārā syālūṛo
to laḷak lalake thāro ḍīl
lalake thāro ḍīl lalake
dhīrī nāch ye dhīrī nāch ra majejaṇ
thāro ḍholo narkhe, thāro parṇyū narkhe

dhīrī nāch re
haraḷ bharaḷ thārī bālūṛī kare chha
haraḷ bharaḷ thārā chuṛalo kare chha
to laḷak laḷak thāro ḍīl
laḷake thāro ḍīl laḷake
dhīrī nāch ye dhīrī nāch ra majejaṇ
thāro ḍholo narkhe, thāro parṇyū narkhe
. . . .
dhīrī nāch ye dhīrī nach ye majejaṇ
thane goro mānḍe thane goro dekhe
dhīrī nāch re

5.
māro māro re rang bhariyo ḍapaṭo
māro māro re rang bhariyo ḍapaṭo
āyī re Rām Kaśanjī vālī legī re
hāṅ āyī re Gopījī vālī legī re
oṛhyo cho ra bachāyo mālāṅ jādī jī
oṛhyo cho bachāyo mālāṅ jādī kī re
ḍapaṭā re dāj lagāyo re
hāṅ dapaṭā re dāj lagāyo re
dhobaṇ hor dhupāyo mālāṅ jādī kī re
dhobaṇ hor dhupāyo mālāṅ jī re
sarvar jār sukāyo re
hāṅ sarvar jār sukāyo re
ab to ḍapaṭo sameṭ mālāṅ jādī kī re
ab to ḍapaṭo sameṭ mālāṅ jādī kī re
lakh āve lakh jāve re
hāṅ lakh āve lakh jāve re

māro māro re rang bhariyo ḍapaṭo
māro māro re rang bhariyo ḍapaṭo
āyī re Chāṛāṅ kī loṛyāṅ le gī re
. . . .

6.
banā Jaipur jājyo jī
Jaipur syūṅ lājyo dhanakpurī
banā Jaipur jājyo jī
Jaipur syūṅ lājyo dhanakpurī

banī oṛh batāvo ye kasīk lāgai dhanakpurī
banī oṛh batāvo ye kasīk lāūṅ dhanakpurī

banā hariyā hariyā pallā jī
bachāṅ to moryā morṛī maṇḍyā

banā hariyā hariyā pallā jī
bachāṅ to moryā morṛī maṇḍyā

banī oṛh batādyo ye kasīk lāgai dhanakpurī
banī oṛh batādyo ye kasīk lāgai dhanakpurī

banā kasī budh oṛhūṅ jī
śaram loṛyā bīr kī āve

banī mail padhāro ye
uḍh jāyar poḍh jāsyāṅ
banī mail padhāro ye
uḍh jāyar poḍh jāsyāṅ

banā nīnd koni āvai jī
bhūkhā to martā kāḷjyo kaṭe
banā nīnd nahī āvai jī
bhūkhā to martā kāljyo kaṭe

banī lāḍūṛā tulā lāūṅ
ye āpāṅ to donī jīm lesyāṅ
banī lāḍūṛā tulā lāūṅ
ye āpāṅ to donyūṅ jīm lesyāṅ

banā lāḍūṛā na bhāvai jī
oḷyūṅ to loṛyā bīr kī āvai

banā koṭe jājyojī
koṭā syūṅ lājyo dhakapurī
banā koṭe jājyo jī
koṭā syūṅ lyājyo dhanakpurī

banī rathaṛo jupādyūṅ
le jāvo na loṛyā bīr ke ye

banā rath me na baiṭhūṅ jī
oḷyūṅ to thākā jīv kī āvai
banā rath me baiṭhū jī
olyū to thākā jīv kī āvai

7.
sīro jīmtā chamcho to moya chakhāvo sā
  chamcho to moya chakhāvo sā
māṅḍal raḷakyā jāy sā māṅḍaḷ raḷakyā jāy
gelā rājan bāvalā sīrā kā lāgyā dām sā
  chamchā kā lāgya dām sā

māṇḍaḷ raḷakyā jāy
the to lālo jāyyo, jarā so moy batāvo sā
  jarā so moy batāvo sā
māṅḍal raḷakyā jāy sā māṅḍaḷ raḷakyā jāy
ḍholā rājan bāvaḷā lālā rā lāgai dām sā
  baiṭā rā lāgyā dām sā
māṇḍaḷ raḷakyā jāy
gelā rājan bāvaḷā mai dorī pīṛ sā
  gelā rājan bāvaḷā mai dorī pīṛ sā
māṅḍaḷ raḷakyā jāy sā māṅḍaḷ raḷakyā jāy
the to ḍhole phoḍhtā pagāṅtye moy suvāṇo sā
  pagāṅtye moy suvāṇo sā
māṇḍaḷ raḷakyā jāy
gelā rājan bāvaḷā agalāṅ ma lālo sūto chha
  bagalā ma pyārī āpkī
sarāṇai churalo lākh ko
  pagātyāṅ pāyal bājai sā
māṇḍaḷ raḷakyā jāy

8.
mākā susarājī kah chha jī
bahū na bhāve maṭar phaḷī,
mākā susarājī kah chha jī
bahū na bhāve maṭar phaḷī,
māke koī mat lyājyo jī
lyāvaḷo māko ghar ko dhaṇī,
māke koī mat kyājyo jī
lyāvaḷo māko ghar ko dhaṇī
va to atarī sī suṇte jī
kamar ma doī lāt kī dharī
va to atarī sī suṇtē jī
kamar man vāke lāt kī dharī
vākā bāī sā bolyā jī khasīk lāgī maṭar phaḷī,
vākā bāī sā bolyā jī khasīk lāgī maṭar phaḷī,
va to lāḍ-laṛāyā jī jebā ma lyāyā maṭar phaḷī
va to lāḍ laḍāyā jī thelyā ma lyāyā maṭar phaḷī
(ends in laughter)

9.
chāndī kī to rel baṇālyo sonā ko anjan jī, banā
bāḷū ret ma rel chalāve
the bābū men anjan jī, banā
rang mel ma rel calāsyāṅ
the bābū meṅ anjan jī, banā

10.
banā thākā alvar kā pankhā kī ḍāṅḍī sonā kī lagvāy
banā thākā ḍholyā ka adhbīch uḍelo alvar ko pankho

11.
āḍe gele ākaṛo re
jīkā pīḷā pān
Rām Kaśan jī ka choro hogyo lapaṛā sā kān
mārī bharī charī ūtāro jī chhoṭā sā bhartār
chhoṭo chhoṭo kāṅī kare re
dekh marad kī choṭ
no mīnāṅ ma lālo khalādyūṅ
beṭhī mojyo māṇ

12.
baṛ par beṭho bagalo bolyo
baṛ par beṭho bagalo bolyo
suṇ bagalā rī bātāṅ re
hāṅ suṇ bagalā rī bātāṅ re
bārā baras Rām Kaśanjī ke regī
bārā baras Rām Kaśanjī ke regī
ṭhalaṛak ṭhālaṛ regī re
hāṅ ṭhalaṛak ṭhālaṛ regī re
ek rāt Bhūrā jī ke regī
ek rāt Rāmjī ka regī
jhaṭpaṭ lālo legī re
hān jhaṭpaṭ lālo legī re
bhalī karī re mārā dudyālā biyāī
bhalī karī re mārā rūpālā biyāī
bānjhaṛyā ro nāṅv kaḍāyo re
hān banjhaṛyā ro jalam sudhāryo re

13.
ghoṭo māro rāng rangīlo paṛyo gavāṛā bīch
āī re Rām Kaśan jī kī lūṅṭī ḷegī ṭāgāṅ bīch
ghoṭā khāṅ ra giyo chho re
alabelaṛī kī lār
ghoṭo ghoṭo kāī kare re ghoṭo devar jeṭ
ghoṭo ghoṭo kāī kare re ghoṭo devar jeṭ
jeṭ bacyāro kāī kare
Bhūrā jī ko regyo peṭ

14.
kāḷī laraṛī ūn banā
lāḍā kī māyaṛ pūn banā

15.
lāṛā kī māyaṛ sāṅṭo māṅgyo
le lagaṛā kī phāṛ re
yo to sāṅṭo mīṭho lāgyo orūṅ bāsyāṅ bāṛ ra
bhosyā maṅ desyūṅ kāṛ ra,
bhosyā maṅ desyūṅ kāṛ ra.

16.
keśyā thāro lagaḍo phīpalī ko pheṛ
berī thāro lagaḍo phīpalī ko pheṛ
bhagataṅ ko bhosyo ra bīghā chyār

keśyā ḍhol nagāṅrā bāgaṅ ḍhaṇḍ kī pāḷ
berī ḍhol nagāṅrā bāgaṅ ḍhaṇḍ kī pāḷ ra
alagoṅchā bāgaṅ ra bāḷū ret ma

keśyā bhosaṛī na chaṇā rukhālī mel
berī bhosaṛī na chaṇā rukhālī mel
lagaḍo to āvaṅ ra būṭā pāṛto

bhosaṛī par khelaṅ kālo nāg
beri bhosaṛī par khelaṅ kāḷo nāg re
nephā par khelaṅ ra bhūryo bāndaro

bhosaṛī ka bāndo ghughar māl
berī bhosaṛī ka bāndho ghughar māl re
berī lagaḍā ka bāndho ra phūṭo ṭokaro

bhosyo rat ko bāsī ra
taṛakan sīro puṛī karsī
lāgaṛo rāt ko bāsī ra
taṛakaṅ sīro puṛī karsī

17.
keśyā khelaṅ chha to hoḷī phelī khel
berī khelaṅ chha to hoḷī phelī khel ra
phachaṅ to paṛaṅ ra karṛo thāṅvaṛo

18.
berī khel chha to Lādū Nāth jī vālī na khel
berī khel chha to Rāmlāl jī vāli na khel ra
orāṅ kā lāge ra rapiyā ḍoḍsaṅ

19.
ye lugāyā kā ghar par
sūkhaṅ līlī bhājī re,

yā sūkhaṅ līlī bhājī re
sārī lugāyāṅ yūṅ khevaṅ
mūṅ lāmbe lagaṛ rājī re
muṅ lāmbe lagaṛ rājī re

CHAPTER 3

1.
kaṅkar ūpar kaṅkarī.
merī maiyyā re jāī.
āī kā rakhiyo mān re hāṅ.
maiṅ terī āī pāhunī.
merī maiyyā re jāī.
terī bhī āge dhivaṛī.
merī maiyyā re jāī.
bāg bagīche bech ke.
merī maiyyā re jāī.
to mere maṅḍho o pe āiye re hāṅ.
bāg bagīche nā bikai.
merī maiyyā re jāī.
bāgoṅ kī śobhā jāvai re hāṅ.
tāl talave bech ke.
merī maiyyā re jāī.
to mere maṅḍho o pe āiye re hāṅ.
tāl talave nā bikai.
merī maiyyā re jāī.
tāloṅ kī śobhā jāvai re hāṅ.
kuve re kuviye bech ke.
merī maiyyā re jāī.
to mere maṅḍho o pe āiye re hāṅ.
kuve kuviye nā bikai.
merī maiyyā re jāī.
kuvoṅ kī śobhā jāvai re hāṅ.
saṛak saṛako bech ke.
merī maiyyā re jāī.
to mere maṅḍho o pe āiye re hāṅ.
saṛak saṛako nā bikai.
merī maiyyā re jāī.
sarakoṅ kī śobhā jāvai re hāṅ.
laiṅḍhe kī bhurī bech ke.
merī maiyyā re jāī.
to mere maṅḍho o pe āiye re hāṅ.
laiṅḍhe kī bhurī nā bikai.
merī maiyyā re jāī.
laiṅḍhe kī śobhā jāvai re hāṅ.

thāno kī ghoṛī bech ke.
merī maiyyā re jāī.
to mere maṅḍho o pe āiye re hāṅ.
thāno kī ghoṛī nā bikai.
merī maiyyā re jāī.
thāno kī śobhā jāvai re hāṅ.
bhābho kā haṅslā bech ke.
merī maiyyā re jāī.
to mere maṅḍho o pe āiye re hāṅ.
bhābho kā haṅslā nā bikai.
merī maiyyā re jāī.
haṅslā bahū ke bāp kā.
merī maiyyā re jāī.
mahal aṭariyā bech ke.
merī maiyyā re jāī.
to mere maṅḍho o pe āiye re hāṅ.
mahal aṭariyā nā bikai.
merī maiyyā re jāī.
mahalo kī śobhā jāvai re hāṅ.
thārī bhābho rūsnī manātā to lā dayī vār re hāṅ.
kaṅkar ūpar kaṅkarī.
merī maiyyā re jāī.
thāre bhatīje rūṇjūṇe sajato to lā dayī vār re hāṅ.
sochā re bānchī kyā karo.
gīṇ mīṇ gīṇ mīṇ kyā karo.
barasoṅ kā mūsal dhār re hāṅ.
kyā thārā gaḍḍā dūr rahā.
kyā thārā bail kachail re hāṅ.
rāmpāl ke baṛe bhātiye.
kāntā bahan ke bhātiye re hāṅ.

2.
bhāt nautan ko chalī lalī.
lalī ke sir pai guṛ kī ḍalī.
jo rī lalī tujhe kapṛa re chāhiye.
bajājī kā baḍ jā lalī.
lalī ke sir pai guṛ kī ḍalī.
jo rī lalī tujhe sonā rī chāhiye.
sunāroṅ kā baḍ jā lalī.
lalī ke sir pai guṛ kī ḍalī.
jo ri lalī tujhe bartan chāhiye.
ṭhaṭheroṅ kā baḍ jā lalī.
lalī ke sir pai guṛ kī ḍalī.

3.
gore gore gāl hai ghūṅgharāle bāl hai.
tārakasi kā jhablā pahane kaise suṅdar lāl hai.

bhaiyyā thānedār hai bhābhī dildār hai.
māṅg le rī naṇadī āj kī bahār hai.
ṭīkā nahīṅ dūṅgī naṇadī māthe kā siṅgār hai.
biṅdī nahīṅ duṅgī naṇadī bahan kā karār hai.
kuṇdal nahīṅ dūṅgī naṇadī kānoṅ kā siṅgār hai.
magar nahīṅ dūṅgī naṇadī bahan kā karār hai.

4.
bābal kā ghar chhoṛ lāḍlī ho gaī āj parāyī re.
jin galiyoṅ meṅ bachpan bītā ho gaī āj parāyī re.
bābā rovai dādī rovai rovai sab parivār re.
chhoṭā sā merā bhaiyyā rovai chhoṛ chalī māṅ jāī re.

5.
mat karnā man ko udās.
ammā phir se milūṅgī.
dādas ko apnī maiṅ dādī kahūṅgī.
tāyas ko apnī maiṅ tāī kahūṅgī.
dādī nā āyegī yād, ammā phir se milūṅgī.
taī nā āyegī yād, ammā phir se milūṅgī.

6.
lākh maiṅne chāhā maiṅ dāī ko bulāūṅgī.
mujhe kyā khabar thī ki ḍākṭar dauṛī āyegī.
de do neg dilā do neg dene kī bahār hai.
lākh maiṅne chāhā maiṅ ammā ko bulāūṅgī.
mujhe kyā khabar thī ki sāsū dauṛī āyegī.
de do neg dilā do neg dene kī bahaī hai.
lākh maiṅne chāhā maiṅ dādī ko bulāūṅgī.
mujhe kyā khabar thī ki dādas dauṛī āyegī.
de do neg dilā do neg dene kī bahār hai.
lākh maiṅne chāhā maiṅ bahan ko bulāūṅgī.
mūjhe kyā khabar thī ki nanad dauṛī āyegī.
de do neg dilā do neg dene kī bahār hai.
lākh maiṅne chāhā maiṅ baṛī bhābhī ko bulāūṅgī.
mujhe kyā khabar thī ki jiṭhānī dauṛī āyegī.
de do neg dilā do neg dene kī bahār hai.
lākh maiṅne chāhā maiṅ chhoṭī bhābhī ko bulāūṅgī.
mujhe kyā khabar thī ki durānī dauṛī āyegī.
de do neg dilā do neg dene kī bahār hai.
lākh maiṅne chāhā maiṅ buā ko bulāūṅgī.
mujhe kyā khabar thī ki phuphas dauṛī āyegī.
de do neg dilā do neg dene kī bahār hai.

7.
sir pai to mere baṅṭā ṭokaṇī.
jhūmar pai ajab bahār.

tāvalī bulāiye rī māṅ,
joṛ rahī do hāth.
sās ke ghar jī nā lāgai,
aur pardesī sāth.
tāvalī bulāiye rī māṅ,
joṛ rahī do hāth.
mere sāth kī khelaiṅ guṛiyā,
maiṅ chal dī sasurāl.
tāvalī bulāiye rī māṅ,
joṛ rahī do hāth.

8.
pīlī merī biṅdī pīlā merā ṭīkkā mere sir pai pīlā kheś.
bīrā mujhe le chaliye.
burā burā susar kā deś.
bīrā mujhe le chaliye.
merā koī nahīṅ hai is deś.
bīrā mujhe le chaliye.
maiṅ to khaṛī urāūṅ kāle kāk.
bīrā mujhe le chaliye.

CHAPTER 4

1.
nā paharūṅ rī sāsū nā paharūṅ rājā ke binā biṅdī ṭīkkā nā paharūṅ rī.
ve āvai haiṅ bahū ve āvai haiṅ, lanḍhaurevāle rājā thāre ve āvai haiṅ.
nā āvai rī sāsū nā āvai rī mare hue duniyā meṅ nā āvai rī.
nā mārai bahū na mārai jahar bhare bol mere nā mārai.
ta khoī rī sāsū ta khoī rī lanḍhaurevālī rājgaḍḍī ta khoī rī.

2.
kamare aṅdar maiṅ khaṛī sitārā banke.
ā jā more bālamā bahānā bharke.
tattā sā pānī sābun kī ṭikiyā nahāyā nahīṅ jātā akelā karke.
ā jā more bālamā bahānā bharke.
tattī sī pūrī halavā aur sabjī khāyā nahīṅ jātā akelā karke.
ā jā more bālamā bahānā bharke.
chāṅdan ke chāṅdnī meṅ chausaṭh bichhāyā soyā nahīṅ jātā akelā karke.
ā jā more bālamā bahānā bharke.

3.
banā bulāvai banī nā āvai.
ā jā merī pyārī rī aṭariyā sūnī paṛī.
maiṅ kaise āūṅ re bābā jī khaṛe haiṅ.
lambā sā ghūṅghaṭ kāṛh ke pāyal utār ke.
chalī āo banṛī jī aṭariyā sūnī paṛī.

4.
kaise āūṅ maiṅ kaise āūṅ tumhāre pās.
bane terī dādī baṛī chakchāl.
hamse laṛkai palang se aṛkai
bichhā laī khāṭ.
gorī merī hāthoṅ se le lo talvār.
ghumātī āo chalātī āo hamāre pās.
ḍholak bājai maṅjīre bājai, bājaiṅ sārī rāt.

5.
maiṅ to terī gailo chālu ho ho naṇadī ke bīrā.
tere hī jāne pai terī ammā kām batāvai.
maiṅ to kyonā hāth lagāūṅ ho ho naṇadī ke bīrā.

maiṅ to terī gailo chālu ho ho naṇadī ke bīrā.
tere hī jāne pai terī bhābhī kām batāvai.
sāre hī kuṅbe ke bartan mere se maṅjvātī hai.
maiṅ to kyonā hāth lagāūṅ ho ho naṇadī ke bīrā.
maiṅ to terī gailo chālu ho ho naṇadī ke bīrā.
tere hī jāne pai terī bahan kām batāvai.
sāre hī kuṅbe ke kapṛe mere se dhulātī hai.
maiṅ to kyonā hāth lagāūṅ ho ho naṇadī ke bīrā.

maiṅ to terī gailo chālu ho ho naṇadī ke bīrā.
tere hī jāne pai terā bhaiyyā kām batāvai.

6.
he rī maiṅ to laṛnā nā jānu merī sās.
chāhe taṛkai nyārī kar deṅ.
chāhe sāre hī kamre le leṅ mere rājā kā kamrā mujhe de deṅ.

he rī maiṅ to laṛnā nā jānu merī sās.
chāhe taṛkai nyārī kar deṅ.
chāhe sārā hī gahaṇā le leṅ mere rājā kī aṅguṭhī mujhe de deṅ.

he rī maiṅ to laṛnā nā jānu merī sās.
chāhe taṛkai nyārī kar deṅ.
chāhe sāre ḍāṅgar le leṅ mere rājā kā kaṭrā mujhe de deṅ.

he rī maiṅ to laṛnā na jānu merī sās.
chāhe taṛkai nyārī kar den.
chāhe sāre kapṛe le leṅ mere rājā kā rūmāl mujhe de deṅ.

he rī maiṅ to laṛnā nā jānu merī sās.
chāhe taṛkai nyārī kar deṅ.
chāhe sāre bartan le leṅ mere rājā kā gilās mujhe de deṅ.

7.
baṅtā bhī ṭhāyā maiṅne ṭhāī ṭokaṇī.
bharaṇ chalī jal nīr kueṅ pai bhīṛ sī hoy rahī.
bārah baras pichai rājā ghar āye.
dehalī pai baiṭhī merī sās.
ammā bhī dīkhai bahan bhī dīkhaī.
vahī nā dīkhai byāhī nār.
pahalī kaṭārī jab mārī ghumāyakai,
lagi gaṭṭe kī oṭ.
dūjī kaṭārī jab mārī ghumāyakai,
lagī ārī ke bīch.
tījī kaṭārī jab mārī ghumāyakai,
ṭukṛe banāke sāṛhe chār.
pahale to rī ammā hāth dhulāiye,
pher dhulāiye talvār.
kyā to rī beṭā tanai hīraṇ māre,
kyā māre khargoś.
nā to rī ammā hamne hīraṇ māre,
nā māre khargoś.
māṅ bahanoṅ kī koī nā suniyo,
ghar ka ho jā nāś.

8.
jal kī machhaliyā sāsū bikne ko āi jī.
sab to rī levai sāsū, jal kī machhaliya jī.
hamko bhī le do sāsū, jal kī machhaliyā jī.
sab din detī sāsū halavā pūrī jī.
rājā kī āvai sunkai jaharoṅ kā pyālā jī.
jaharoṅ kā pyālā pīkai nīṅd ghir āī jī.
kahāṅ paṛ sovai sāsū jagah batā do jī.
ūṅchī aṭārī bahū lāl kivāṛī jī.
vahīṅ paṛ sovo bahū sej thārī jī.
bārah baras pīch'he piyā ghar āye jī.
sab to rī dīkhai ammā ek nā dīkhai jī.
māṅ bhī dīkhai mhārī bahan bhī dīkhai,
ek nā dīkhai ammā sajanoṅ kī beṭī jī.
ūṅchī aṭārī beṭā lāl kivāṛī jī,
vahīṅ paṛ so gaī beṭā, sajanoṅ kī beṭī jī.
ek hāṅk mārī ammā, do hāṅk mārī jī,
tab bhī nā bolī ammā, sajanoṅ kī beṭī jī.
bāgoṅ meṅ jāiyo beṭā, phūl chhaṛī lāiyo jī,
mār jagāiyo beṭā, sajanoṅ kī beṭī jī.
ek chhaṛī mārī ammā do chhaṛī mārī jī.
tab bhī nā bolī ammā, sajanoṅ kī beṭī jī.
tār dupaṭṭā rājā, dekkhan lag gaye jī.

marī ya paṛī hai ammā, sajanoṅ kī beṭī jī.
bāgoṅ meṅ jāiyo beṭā, chandan kaṭāiyo jī.
phūṅk jalāiyo beṭā, sajanoṅ ki beṭī jī.
phūṅk seṅk jab ghar ko āye jī,
dehalī pai baiṭhe rājā, rudan machāvai jī.
kahe ko rovai beta, rudan machāvai jī.
apne beṭā ko maiṅ to chār byāh dūṅ jī.
do gorī do sāṅvalī jī,
apne beṭā ko maiṅ to chār byāh dūṅ jī.
chāroṅ ko ammā merī, kueṅ meṅ ḍālo jī.
ek nā rakhi ammā, sajanoṅ ki beṭī jī.
tān dupaṭṭā rājā paṛkai to soye ji.
supne meṅ āiyo gorī, hāl batāiyo jī.
hor din detī rājā, halavā pūrī jī.
thārī āvai sunkai jaharoṅ ke pyāle jī.
jaharoṅ ke pyāle pikai nīṅd ghir āi jī.
kahāṅ paṛ sovai sāsū jagah batāiyo jī.
ūṅchī aṭārī re rājā, lāl kivāṛī jī.
koṭhe pai chaṛhkai rājā, dījo duhāī jī,
gharvā ujāṛā yāro, māṅ bahan ne jī.

9.
merī sās baṛī chakchāl.
rām maiṅ piyā kī pyārī.
maiṅ chākki pai baiṭhī maiṅne moṭā moṭā pīsā.
usne dhar ūṅglī pasāyā.
rām maiṅ piyā kī pyārī.
jab ūṅglī pasāyā usne beṭā bhī sikhāyā.
jab beṭā bhī sikhāyā vo godī kaṭīlī lāyā.
usne dhīre dhīre mārī.
jab dhīre dhīre mārī maiṅ charh kamare pai soī.
rām maiṅ piyā kī pyārī.
jab kamare pai soī vo ser laḍḍū lāyā.
rām maiṅ piyā kī pyārī.
jab ser laḍḍū lāyā maiṅne ulṭe hī bagāye.
rām maiṅ piyā kī pyārī.
jab ulṭe hi bagāye vo ginke lāyā maiṅne ḍeṛh laḍḍū khāyā.
rām maiṅ piyā kī pyārī.
jab ḍeṛh laḍḍū khāyā mujhe pyās bhī lag gayī.
rām maiṅ piyā kī pyārī.
jab pyās bhī lag gayī vo to bhar ke loṭā lāyā.
rām maiṅ piyā kī pyārī.
jab bhar ke loṭā lāyā, maiṅne ḍeṛh ghūṅṭ pī.
rām maiṅ piyā kī pyārī.
jab ḍeṛh ghūṅṭ pī mujhe jāḍā bhī chaṛhāyā.
rām maiṅ piyā kī pyārī.

jab jāḍā bhī chāṛhāyā, vo lāl rajāī lāyā.
rām maiṅ piyā kī pyārī.
jab lāl rajāī lāyā, mujhe garmī bhī chaṛhāyī.
rām maiṅ piyā kī pyārī.
jab garmī bhī chaṛhāyī vo lāl bījanā lāyā.
rām maiṅ piyā kī pyārī.
jab lāl bījanā lāyā, maiṅne dhīre dhīre jholī.
rām maiṅ piyā kī pyārī.

10.
biṅdī mat paharo gorī ṭīkkā mat paharo.
nācho mat gorī najar lag jayegī.
do janoṅ kī joṛī akelā kar jayegī.
chāṅdne se ghar meṅ aṅdherā kar jayegī.

11.
kidhar kī ghaṭā ūmagī jī,
e jī koī kidhar barsan hār.
indar rājā bāgoṅ men jhuk rahe jī.
pūrab kī ghaṭā ūmagī jī,
e ji koī pachchham barsan hār.
indar rājā bāgoṅ meṅ jhuk rahe jī.
ek achambhā sāsū maiṅ sunā jī.
e jī koī thāre beṭā kā dūjā byāh.
indar rājā bāgoṅ meṅ jhuk rahe jī.
kyā ya to sāsū ham haiṅ ochchhe gharoṅ kī,
e jī koī kyā ham lāi thoṛī dāt.
indar rājā bāgoṅ meṅ jhuk rahe jī.
nā to bahū tum ochchhe gharoṅ kī,
e ji koī nā tum lāi thoṛī dāt.
indar rājā bāgoṅ meṅ jhuk rahe jī.
tum to bahū mhārī sāṅvalī jī,
e jī koī beṭā ko gorī dhan kā chāv.
indar raja bāgoṅ meṅ jhuk rahe jī.
susar ko puchhan bahanoṅ maiṅ chalī jī.
e jī koī thāre beṭā kā dūjā byāh.
indar rājā bāgoṅ meṅ jhuk rahe jī.
kyā ya to susar ham haiṅ ochchhe gharoṅ kī,
e jī koī kyā ham lāi thoṛī dāt.
indar rājā bāgoṅ meṅ jhuk rahe jī.
nā to bahū tum ochchhe gharoṅ kī,
e jī koī nā tum lāi thoṛī dāt.
indar rājā bāgoṅ meṅ jhuk rahe jī.
tum to bahū mhāri sāṅvalī jī,
e jī koī beṭā ko gorī dhan kā chāv.
indar rājā bāgoṅ meṅ jhuk rahe jī.

naṅadī ko puchhan bahanoṅ maiṅ chalī jī.
e jī koī thāre bīrā kā dūjā byāh.
indar rājā bāgoṅ meṅ jhuk rahe jī.
kyā ya to naṇadī ham ochchhe gharoṅ kī,
e jī koī kyā ham lāi thoṛī dāt.
indar rājā bāgoṅ meṅ jhuk rahe jī.
nā to bhābhī tum ochchhe gharoṅ kī,
e jī koī nā tum lāi thoṛī dāt.
indar rājā bāgoṅ meṅ jhuk rahe jī.
tum to bhābhī merī sāṅvalī jī,
e jī koī bīrā ko gorī dhan kā chāv.
indar rājā bāgoṅ meṅ jhuk rahe jī.
rājā ko puchhan bahanoṅ maiṅ chalī jī.
e jī koī thārā to kahiye dūjā byāh.
indar rājā bāgoṅ meṅ jhuk rahe jī.
kyā ya to ham rājā ochchhe gharoṅ kī,
e jī koī kyā ham lāi thoṛī dāt.
indar rājā bāgoṅ meṅ jhuk rahe jī.
nā tum gorī ochchhe gharoṅ kī,
e jī koī nā tum lāi thoṛī dāt.
indar rājā bāgoṅ meṅ jhuk rahe jī.
tum to gorī merī sāṅvalī jī,
e jī koī ham ko gorī dhan kā chāv.
indar rājā bāgoṅ meṅ jhuk rahe jī.
kaun to rājā thāre ṭehale karaigī,
e jī koī kaun to gāvai maṅgalchār.
indar rājā bāgoṅ meṅ jhuk rahe jī.
māṅ to mhārī gorī ṭehale karaigī,
e jī koī bahaneṅ to gāvai mangalchār.
indar raja bāgoṅ meṅ jhuk rahe jī.
kaun to rājā thārī barāt chaṛhaigā,
e jī koī kaun to kharche borī dām.
indar raja bāgoṅ meṅ jhuk rahe jī.
bhāī to gorī mhārī barāt charhaigā,
e jī koī bābal kharche borī dām.
indar rājā bāgoṅ meṅ jhuk rahe jī.
koṭṭhe to chaṛhke bahanōn dekhtī jī,
e jī koī kitane chaṛhī hai barāt.
indar raja bāgoṅ meṅ jhuk rahe jī.
laṅgaṛe to lūlle bahanoṅ ḍeṛh sau jī,
e jī koī gaṅjoṅ kā oṛ nā peṛ.
indar rājā bāgoṅ meṅ jhuk rahe jī.
saukkan āī bahanoṅ maiṅ sunī jī.
e jī koī dhaṛdhaṛ chaṛhā hai bukhār.
indar rājā bāgoṅ meṅ jhuk rahe jī.
saukkan dekhan bahanoṅ maiṅ chalī jī.

e jī koī khoṭṭā rupaiyā mere hāth.
indar rājā bāgoṅ meṅ jhuk rahe jī.
saukkan nautan bahanoṅ maiṅ chalī jī.
e jī koī bis bharī karī maiṅne khīr.
indar rājā bāgoṅ meṅ jhuk rahe jī.
saukkan marī bahanoṅ maiṅ sunī jī.
e jī koī jāḍḍe se utarā bukhār.
indar rājā bāgoṅ meṅ jhuk rahe jī.
saukkan rovan bahanoṅ maiṅ chalī jī.
e jī koī lambā sā ghūṅghaṭ kāṛh.
indar rājā bāgoṅ meṅ jhuk rahe jī.
man to rovai bahanoṅ dil haṅsai jī,
e jī koī jivaṛā to karai kilaul.
indar rājā bāgoṅ meṅ jhuk rahe jī.

12.
gorī taṛak naukarī jāṅge, āvaige bārah sāl meṅ.
rājā taṛak hī naukarī jāiyo chāhe āiyo aṭhārah sāl meṅ.
un ne jāto hī chiṭṭhī gerī paṅjāban lāvai sāth meṅ.
merā devar roṭī khāvai, devar roṭī bād meṅ khāiyo,
kal baiṅch sunā do tār ne.
bhābhī rājī khuśī mhārā bhāīyyā, paṅjāban lāvai sāth meṅ.
ve bārah sāl meṅ āye paṅjāban lāye sāth meṅ.
ve daṛbaṛ koṭhā chaṛh gaye paṅjāban chaṛh gayī sāth meṅ.
pīchhe se maiṅ bhī chaṛh gayī, dūdh kā belā hāth meṅ.
gorī yansai talai utar jā paṅjāban lāye sāth meṅ.
maiṅ daṛbaṛ nīche āyī mujhe hāth gaṅdāsā ṭhāyā.
mujhe jāto hī rājā māre paṅjāban mārī sāth meṅ.
maiṅ baiṭhī palaṅg pai roī.

Glossary of Hindi and Rajasthani Words

There are regional differences in the pronunciation and meaning of many of the terms that appear in this glossary. In most cases, we have given the term as it is used in the book. If a term appears in a chapter on Uttar Pradesh, it is given in its Hindi form here; if it appears in a chapter on Rajasthan, we give the Rajasthani variant. In most cases, this is noted in the definition. If regional variation is slight, there is no specification of the term's provenance.

Bahū.	Wife, son's wife.
Banā.	A type of wedding song, in both Rajasthan and Uttar Pradesh. The term itself may be translated as "bridegroom-prince" or simply "young bridegroom."
Banī.	A type of wedding song in Uttar Pradesh. The term may be translated as "young bride."
Bhāī.	Brother.
Bhajan.	Devotional hymn. In Ghatiyali, the term is sometimes used almost as a synonym for *bhakti*, referring to meditative devotional practice or the singing of hymns.
Bhakti.	Worshipful love flowing upward, usually to deities. It is often associated with antihierarchical ideas expressed in poetry and song.
Bhāṅg.	An intoxicating liquid hemp preparation.
Bhāt.	In Uttar Pradesh, gifts given by a mother's brother at the wedding of his sister's son or daughter. In Ghatiyali, the term is *maino*.
Bhāt nyautnā.	"Invitation for the giving of *bhāt*"; in Uttar Pradesh, the ritual visit of a woman to her brother's house to announce the wedding of her son or daughter, and her expectation of the gifts that her brother will give in *bhāt*. Songs are usually sung on this occasion by the women of the brother's village.
Bidāī.	"Departure," the term used to describe the ritual at which a new bride leaves for the conjugal home for the first time, just after the wedding. "Songs of the departure," *bidāī gīt*, are sung on this occasion by the women of the bride's village.

Buā. Father's sister.

Chāchī. Father's younger brother's wife.

Chiṭṭhī. "Letter," the term used to refer to the formal letter sent by the bride's family to the groom's to settle the engagement of the pair.

Dādī. Father's mother.

Dādas. Husband's father's mother.

Dahej. Dowry; the gifts given by the bride's family to the groom's upon the marriage and on a number of ritual and life-course events thereafter.

Dān. A religious gift, most often in Pahansu given in a ritual context, with the intention of disbursing evil and inauspiciousness. The giving of *dān* also enhances the "prestige and honor" (*izzat*) of the donor.

Devar. Husband's younger brother, with whom an informal joking relationship is permitted.

Dhiyānī. Married daughter or married sister.

Gālī. Insult or verbal abuse. In both Rajasthan and Uttar Pradesh, the term is used to refer to a kind of insult song, often of a bawdy nature, sung at weddings and other occasions of encounter between relatives by marriage.

Ghūṅghaṭ. In both Rajasthan and Uttar Pradesh, the veiling of the face in the presence of one's husband or his senior male kin, and any senior men in one's conjugal village, to show deference and to exhibit modesty and shame.

Guwāṅḍ. In Uttar Pradesh, a group of neighboring villages, ones that share a boundary with one's own village.

Hak. "Right," often used in Uttar Pradesh with reference to the right to receive gifts at certain specified ritual occasions.

Izzat. Honor, respect, prestige.

Jachchā. A woman who has recently given birth.

Jeṭh. Husband's elder brother, for whom a woman must show deference and respect and in whose presence she veils her face.

Kanyā dān. "Gift of a virgin," the gifting away of a daughter at marriage.

Keśyā. In Rajasthan, bawdy songs sung on and around certain festival occasions.

Khoṛiyā. In Pahansu and Hathchoya, a women's dancing and singing session. Women gather in a courtyard, away from males, and sing dancing songs while one by one they get up to dance in the center of the group.

Kuṅbā. "Lineage," a group of people related through the male line, together with their wives.

Mausī.	Mother's sister.
Mel.	Harmony, concord, intimacy, agreement.
Milāī.	In Uttar Pradesh, a type of informal gift, usually a small amount of cash, given to one's married sisters upon meeting them in their conjugal village or some other place. In Ghatiyali, this gift is called *malni*.
Nāchne kā gīt.	"Dancing song," sung at weddings, births, and festival occasions in Pahansu and Hathchoya.
Nanad.	Husband's sister.
Nāśubh.	Inauspiciousness.
Nautaṅkī.	A form of popular Hindi regional theater.
Oṛhnī.	"Wrap," an essential item of clothing for married and adult women, used in both Rajasthan and Uttar Pradesh to cover the head and face. See *ghūṇghaṭ*.
Pāhunī.	Literally "female guest," a term often used to refer to outmarried women returning to visit their natal place.
Pāoṅ dabānā.	"Massaging the feet," an act of deference performed by married women for their husband's senior female kin. In Rajasthan, this act is called *pāv lāgno*.
Pāp.	Sin or evil.
Parāyā/ī.	Alien, foreign, other. The feminine form *parāyī* is often used to describe a daughter's or sister's relation to her natal kin after her marriage.
Parosā.	In Pahansu, a food packet distributed to kinsmen and neighbors at a feast or ritual occasion. In Ghatiyali, this gift is called *kanso* or *lavano*.
Pativratā.	Wife who is submissive and faithful to her husband, the "ideal wife" in many male expressive genres and in much ordinary talk.
Pherā.	"Circling" the sacrificial fire, the central and most important wedding rite.
Pīhar.	The natal village or natal place of a married woman.
Pītas.	In Uttar Pradesh, husband's father's younger brother's wife.
Purohit.	A Brahman priest serving a particular family in the performance of its domestic rituals, often as part of an hereditary relationship.
Rājā.	Literally "king," a term often used to refer to the husband in women's songs, where it has been translated as "husband-lord."
Rāvalā.	In Rajasthan, the Rajput neighborhood in a village.
Riśtā.	"Relationship," a term generally used in connection with a relative by marriage. Women are often said to share a *riśtā* with their natal kin after their marriage, but not a "bodily connection" (*śarīr kā sambaṅdh*).
Salvār-kamīz.	Baggy pants with drawstring waist and quilted ankle

	piece, and long loose shirt, worn in Pahansu and Hathchoya by most women but in Ghatiyali only by young girls and Muslims.
Sāṅg.	A form of popular theater in western Uttar Pradesh, employing poetry, song, and dance. It is performed primarily by traveling troupes of male actors, and in Pahansu and Hathchoya the audience is composed almost entirely of males.
Śaram.	Modesty, shyness, "shame," qualities often deemed essential for a proper wife and daughter-in-law.
Sās.	Spouse's mother, but used most frequently by women for husband's mother.
Sāsū.	Same as *sās*.
Sasurāl.	Spouse's natal place, but used most frequently by women for their conjugal village/home.
Sāthin.	Literally "female companion," the term is used for volunteer workers in a program in Rajasthan that provides information and assistance to village women in their fight against oppression.
Satī.	Literally "virtuous woman." A woman who casts herself on the flames of her husband's funeral pyre.
Suhāg.	Literally "good fortune" (from Sanskrit *saubhāgya*), but used exclusively to denote the good fortune of a married woman whose husband is alive.
Tāī.	Father's elder brother's wife.
Tāyas.	Husband's father's elder brother's wife.
Vādā.	Gifts of cloth and other items carried by women as they travel between their natal home and conjugal home.

Bibliography

Abu-Lughod, Lila. 1986. *Veiled Sentiments: Honor and Poetry in a Bedouin Society*. Berkeley: University of California Press.

———. 1990. The Romance of Resistance: Tracing Transformations of Power through Bedouin Women. *American Ethnologist* 17(1): 41–55.

Alcoff, Linda. 1988. Cultural Feminism versus Post-Structuralism: The Identity Crisis in Feminist Theory. *Signs* 13(3): 405–36.

Amore, Roy C., and Larry D. Shinn. 1981. *Lustful Maidens and Ascetic Kings*. New York: Oxford University Press.

Appadurai, Arjun. 1986. Is Homo Hierarchicus? *American Ethnologist* 13(4): 745–61.

———. 1988. Putting Hierarchy in Its Place. *Cultural Anthropology* 3(1): 36–49.

———. 1991. Afterword. In *Gender, Genre, and Power in South Asian Expressive Traditions*, edited by Arjun Appadurai, Frank J. Korom, and Margaret A. Mills, 467–76. Philadelphia: University of Pennsylvania Press.

Archer, William G. 1985. *Songs for the Bride: Wedding Rites of Rural India*. New York: Columbia University Press.

Ardener, Edwin. 1975. Belief and the Problem of Women. In *Perceiving Women*, edited by Shirley Ardener, 1–17. New York: John Wiley and Sons.

Arnold, David. 1984. Gramsci and Peasant Subalternity in India. *Journal of Peasant Studies* 11(4): 155–77.

Babb, Lawrence A. 1970. Marriage and Malevolence: The Uses of Sexual Opposition in a Hindu Pantheon. *Ethnology* 9(2): 137–48.

———. 1976. *The Divine Hierarchy*. New York: Columbia University Press.

———. 1982. Glancing: Visual Interaction in Hinduism. *Journal of Anthropological Research*: 387–401.

Banerjee, Sumanta. 1989. Marginalization of Women's Popular Culture in Nineteenth Century Bengal. In *Recasting Women: Essays in Colonial History*, edited by Kumkum Sangari and Sudesh Vaid, 127–79. New Delhi: Kali for Women.

Bardhan, Kalpana, ed. and trans. 1990. *Of Women, Outcastes, Peasants, and Rebels*. Berkeley: University of California Press.

Basso, Ellen B. 1985. *A Musical View of the Universe*. Philadelphia: University of Pennsylvania Press.

Bauman, Richard. 1977. *Verbal Art as Performance.* Prospect Heights, Ill.: Waveland Press.

———. 1986. *Story, Performance, and Event: Contextual Studies of Oral Narrative.* Cambridge: Cambridge University Press.

Baweja, Harinder. 1992. The Second Sex Awakens. *India Today,* October 31, 45–47.

Beidelman, T. O. 1986. *Moral Imagination in Kaguru Modes of Thought.* Bloomington: Indiana University Press.

Bennett, Lynn. 1983. *Dangerous Wives and Sacred Sisters: Social and Symbolic Roles of High-Caste Women in Nepal.* New York: Columbia University Press.

Blackburn, Stuart, and A. K. Ramanujan. 1986. Introduction. In *Another Harmony: New Essays on the Folklore of India.* Berkeley: University of California Press.

Blanchet, Therese. 1984. *Women, Pollution, and Marginality: Meanings and Rituals of Birth in Rural Bangladesh.* Dhaka: University Press.

Bloch, Maurice. 1987. Symbols, Song, Dance, and Features of Articulation: Is Religion an Extreme Form of Traditional Authority? Chap. 2 in *Ritual, History, and Power.* London: Athlone Press.

Bourdieu, Pierre. 1977. *Outline of a Theory of Practice.* Cambridge: Cambridge University Press.

Briggs, Charles. 1985. The Pragmatics of Proverb Performance in New Mexican Speech. *American Anthropologist* 87(4): 793–810.

———. 1986. *Learning How to Ask: A Sociolinguistic Appraisal of the Role of the Interview in Social Science Research.* Cambridge: Cambridge University Press.

———. 1992. "Since I am a Woman, I Will Chastise My Relatives": Gender, Reported Speech, and the (Re)production of Social Relations in Warao Ritual Wailing. *American Ethnologist* 19(2): 337–61.

Bryce, Winifred. 1964. *Women's Folk-Songs of Rajputana.* Delhi: Publications Division, Ministry of Information and Broadcasting, Government of India.

Burke, Kenneth. 1969. *A Grammar of Motives.* Berkeley: University of California Press.

———. 1973. *The Philosophy of Literary Form.* Berkeley: University of California Press.

Bynum, Caroline Walker. 1987. *Holy Feast and Holy Fast: The Religious Significance of Food to Medieval Women.* Berkeley: University of California Press.

Carstairs, G. Morris. 1975. Village Women of Rajasthan. In *Indian Women,* edited by Devaki Jain, 229–36. Delhi: Publications Division, Ministry of Information and Broadcasting, Government of India.

Chakravarti, Uma. 1991. Review of *The Perfect Wife,* by I. Julia Leslie. *Contributions to Indian Sociology* 25(1): 184–85.

Chatterjee, Partha. 1989. Colonialism, Nationalism, and Colonialized Women: The Contest in India. *American Ethnologist* 16: 622–33.

Chatterji, Roma. 1986. The Voyage of the Hero: The Self and the Other in One Narrative Tradition of Purulia. In *The Word and the World: Fantasy, Symbol, and Record,* edited by Veena Das, 95–114. New Delhi: Sage Publications.

Clifford, James. 1988. *The Predicament of Culture: Twentieth-Century Ethnography, Literature, and Art.* Cambridge, Mass.: Harvard University Press.

Coburn, Thomas B. 1982. Consort of None, Sakti of All: The Vision of the Devi-Mahatmya. In *The Divine Consort: Radha and the Goddesses of India,* edited by J. S. Hawley and D. M. Wulff, 153–65. Berkeley: Graduate Theological Union.

Cohn, Bernard S. 1968. Notes on the History of the Study of Indian Society and Culture. In *Structure and Change in Indian Society,* edited by M. Singer and B. S. Cohn, 3–28. Chicago: Aldine.

———. 1984. The Census, Social Structure, and Objectification in South Asia. *Folk* 26: 25–49.

———. 1985. The Command of Language and the Language of Command. In *Subaltern Studies IV: Writings on South Asian History and Society,* edited by Ranajit Guha, 276–329. Delhi: Oxford University Press.

Crooke, William. 1910. Religious Songs from Northern India. *The Indian Antiquary* 39: 268–87, 321–50.

———. 1911. Songs of the Mutiny. *The Indian Antiquary* 40: 123–24, 165–69.

Cunningham, Alexander. 1882. *Report of a Tour in the Punjab in 1878–79.* Archaeological Survey of India, vol. 14. Calcutta: Office of the Superintendent of Government Printing.

Daniel, Sheryl B. 1980. Marriage in Tamil Culture: The Problem of Conflicting "Models." In *The Powers of Tamil Women,* edited by Susan S. Wadley, 61–92. Syracuse, N.Y.: Maxwell School of Citizenship and Public Affairs.

———. 1983. The Tool Box Approach of the Tamil to the Issues of Moral Responsibility and Human Destiny. In *Karma: An Anthropological Inquiry,* edited by C. F. Keyes and E. V. Daniel, 27–62. Berkeley: University of California Press.

Das, Veena. 1976a. Indian Women: Work, Power, and Status. In *Indian Women from Purdah to Modernity,* edited by B. R. Nanda. 129–45. Delhi: Vikas.

———. 1976b. Masks and Faces: An Essay on Punjabi Kinship. *Contributions to Indian Sociology* 10: 1–30.

———. 1982. Kama in the Scheme of Purusarthas: The Story of Rama. In *Way of Life: King, Householder, Renouncer,* edited by T. N. Madan, 183–203. Delhi: Vikas.

———. 1986. The Work of Mourning: Death in a Punjabi Family. In *The Cultural Transition,* edited by Merry I. White and Susan Pollak, 179–210. Boston and London: Routledge and Kegan Paul.

———. 1988. Femininity and the Orientation to the Body. In *Socialisation, Education, and Women: Explorations in Gender Identity,* edited by K. Chanana, 193–207. New Delhi: Orient Longman.

———. 1989a. Subaltern as Perspective. In *Subaltern Studies VI: Writings on South Asian History and Society,* edited by Ranajit Guha, 310–24. Delhi: Oxford University Press.

———. 1989b. Voices of Children. *Daedalus* 118(4): 263–94.

———. 1990a. Introduction. In *Communities, Riots, and Survivors,* edited by Veena Das, 1–36. Delhi: Oxford University Press.

———. 1990b. Our Work to Cry, Your Work to Listen. In *Communities, Riots, and Survivors,* edited by Veena Das, 345–98. Delhi: Oxford University Press.

Davis, Natalie Zemon. 1975. Women on Top. In *Society and Culture in Early Modern France,* 124–51. Stanford: Stanford University Press.

de Certeau, Michel. 1984. *The Practice of Everyday Life.* Berkeley: University of California Press.

de Lauretis, Teresa. 1984. *Alice Doesn't.* Bloomington: Indiana University Press.

———, ed. 1986. *Feminist Studies/Critical Studies.* Bloomington: Indiana University Press.

Derne, Steve. 1988. Images of the Fierce Goddess: Psychoanalysis and Religious Symbols—A Response to Kondos. *Contributions to Indian Sociology* 22(1): 89–93.

Dhruvarajan, Vanaja. 1989. *Hindu Women and the Power of Ideology.* Granby, Mass.: Bergin and Garvey.

Dimock, Edward C., Jr. 1982. A Theology of the Repulsive: The Myth of the Goddess Sitala. In *The Divine Consort: Radha and the Goddesses of India,* edited by J. S. Hawley and D. M. Wulff, 184–203. Berkeley: Graduate Theological Union.

Doniger, Wendy, trans. [*See also* O'Flaherty, Wendy Doniger]. 1991. *The Laws of Manu.* London and New York: Penguin.

Dube, Leela. 1988. On the Construction of Gender: Hindu Girls in Patrilineal India. *Economic and Political Weekly* 23(18): 11–19.

Dumont, Louis. 1957. *Hierarchy and Marriage Alliance in South Indian Kinship.* Occasional Papers of the Royal Anthropological Institute of Great Britain and Ireland, no. 12. London.

———. 1966. Marriage in India: The Present State of the Question. *Contributions to Indian Sociology* 9: 90–114.

———. 1975. Terminology and Prestations Revisited. *Contributions to Indian Sociology,* n.s. 9(2): 197–215.

———. 1980. *Homo Hierarchicus.* Chicago: University of Chicago Press.

———. 1986. *Affinity as a Value.* Chicago: University of Chicago Press.

Eck, Diana L. 1981. *Darsan: Seeing the Divine Image in India.* Chambersburg Pa.: Anima Books.

Eglar, Zekiye, 1960. *A Punjabi Village in Pakistan.* New York: Columbia University Press.

Egnor, Margaret Trawick. 1978. The Sacred Spell and Other Conceptions of Life in Tamil Culture. Ph.D. diss., Department of Anthropology, University of Chicago.

———. 1986. Internal Iconicity in Paraiyar "Crying Songs." In *Another Harmony: New Essays on the Folklore of India*, edited by Stuart Blackburn and A. K. Ramanujan, 294–344. Berkeley: University of California Press.

Entwistle, Alan W. 1984. Sāñjhī—Images for a Twilight Goddess. *Visible Religion* 3: 43–79.

Erdman, Joan L. 1985. *Patrons and Performers in Rajasthan*. Delhi: Chanakya.

Erndl, Kathleen M. 1989. Rapist or Bodyguard, Demon or Devotee? Images of Bhairo in the Mythology and Cult of Vaiṣṇo Devi. In *Criminal Gods and Demon Devotees*, edited by Alf Hiltebeitel, 239–50. Albany: State University of New York Press.

———. 1993. *Victory to the Mother: The Hindu Goddess of Northwest India in Myth, Ritual, and Symbol*. New York: Oxford University Press.

Fernandez, James. 1986. *Persuasions and Performances: The Play of Tropes in Culture*. Bloomington: Indiana University Press.

Flueckiger, Joyce Burkhalter. 1989. Caste and Regional Variants in an Oral Epic Tradition. In *Oral Epics in India*, edited by Stuart H. Blackburn et al., 33–54. Berkeley: University of California Press.

———. 1991. Genre and Community in the Folklore System of Chhattisgarh. In *Gender, Genre, and Power in South Asian Expressive Traditions*, edited by Arjun Appadurai, Frank J. Korom, and Margaret A. Mills, 181–200. Philadelpia: University of Pennsylvania Press.

Friedrich, Paul. 1978. *The Meaning of Aphrodite*. Chicago: University of Chicago Press.

Fruzzetti, Lina M. 1982. *The Gift of a Virgin: Women, Marriage, and Ritual in a Bengali Society*. New Brunswick, N.J.: Rutgers University Press.

Gal, Susan. 1991. Between Speech and Silence: The Problematics of Research on Language and Gender. In *Gender at the Crossroads of Knowledge: Feminist Anthropology in the Postmodern Era*, edited by Micaela di Leonardo, 175–203. Berkeley: University of California Press.

Geertz, Clifford. 1968. *Islam Observed*. New Haven: Yale University Press.

Gluckman, Max. 1963. Rituals of Rebellion in South East Africa. In *Order and Rebellion in Tribal Africa*. New York: Free Press.

Gokhale-Turner, Jayashree. 1981. *Bhakti* or *Vidroha*: Continuity and Change in Dalit Sahitya. In *Tradition and Modernity in Bhakti Movements*, edited by Jayant Lele, 29–42. Leiden: E. J. Brill.

Gold, Ann Grodzins. 1982. *Village Families in Story and Song: An Approach through Women's Oral Tradition in Rajasthan*. Indiakit Series, Outreach Educational Project, South Asia Language and Area Center, University of Chicago.

———. 1988a. *Fruitful Journeys: The Ways of Rajasthani Pilgrims*. Berkeley: University of California Press.

———. 1988b. Spirit Possession Perceived and Performed in Rural Rajasthan. *Contributions to Indian Sociology* 22(1): 35–63.

———. 1991. Gender and Illusion in a Rajasthani Yogic Tradition. In *Gender, Genre, and Power in South Asian Expressive Traditions*, edited by Arjun Appadurai, Frank J. Korom, and Margaret A. Mills, 102–35. Philadelphia: University of Pennsylvania Press.

———. 1992. *A Carnival of Parting*. Berkeley: University of California Press.

———. N.d. Mother Ten's Stories. In *Readings in Indian Religions*, edited by Donald S. Lopez, Jr. Princeton: Princeton University Press. Forthcoming.

Goody, Jack. 1990. *The Oriental, the Ancient, and the Primitive*. Cambridge: Cambridge University Press.

Gossen, Gary H. 1973. Chamula Tzotzil Proverbs. In *Meaning in Mayan Languages*, edited by M. S. Edmonson, 205–33. The Hague: Mouton.

Gough, Kathleen. 1956. Brahman Kinship in a Tamil Village. *American Anthropologist* 58: 826–53.

Grierson, George. 1884. Some Bihārī Folk-Songs. *Journal of the Royal Asiatic Society*: 196–246.

———. 1886. Some Bhoj'purī Folk-Songs. *Journal of the Royal Asiatic Society*: 207–67.

Grima, Benedicte. 1991. The Role of Suffering in Women's Performance of *Paxto*. In *Gender, Genre, and Power in South Asian Expressive Traditions*, edited by Arjun Appadurai, Frank J. Korom, and Margaret A. Mills, 81–101. Philadelphia: University of Pennsylvania Press.

Guha, Ranajit. 1983. *Elementary Aspects of Peasant Insurgency in Colonial India*. Delhi: Oxford University Press.

———. 1987. Chandra's Death. In *Subaltern Studies V: Writings on South Asian History and Society*, edited by Ranajit Guha, 135–65. Delhi: Oxford University Press.

———. 1989. Dominance Without Hegemony and Its Historiography. In *Subaltern Studies VI: Writings on South Asian History and Society*, edited by Ranajit Guha, 210–309. Delhi: Oxford University Press.

Gujar, Bhoju Ram, and Ann Grodzins Gold. 1992. From the Research Assistant's Point of View. *Anthropology and Humanism Quarterly* 17(3/4): 72–84.

Hanks, William F. 1989. Text and Textuality. *Annual Review of Anthropology* 18: 95–127.

Hansen, Kathryn. 1988. The Virangana in North Indian History, Myth, and Popular Culture. *Economic and Political Weekly* 23 (18): 25–33.

———. 1992. *Grounds for Play: The Nautanki Theatre of Northern India*. Berkeley: University of California Press.

Harrison, Regina. 1989. *Signs, Songs, and Memory in the Andes: Translating Quechua Language and Culture*. Austin: University of Texas Press.

Henry, Edward O. 1975. North Indian Wedding Songs. *Journal of South Asian Literature* 11(1–2): 61–94.

———. 1988. *Chant the Names of God: Musical Culture in Bhojpuri-speaking India*. San Diego: San Diego State University Press.
Herrell, Richard. 1992. The Symbolic Strategies of Chicago's Gay and Lesbian Pride Day Parade: In *Gay Culture in America: Essays From the Field*, edited by Gilbert Herdt, 225–52. Boston: Beacon Press.
Hershman, Paul. 1977. Virgin and Mother. In *Symbols and Sentiments*, edited by Ioan Lewis, 269–92. London: Academic Press.
Herzfeld, Michael. 1991. Silence, Submission, and Subversion: Toward a Poetics of Womanhood. In *Contested Identities*, edited by Peter Loizos and Evthymios Papataxiarchis, 79–97. Princeton: Princeton University Press.
Hiltebeitel, Alf. 1988. *The Cult of Draupadi*. Vol. 1, *Mythologies: From Gingee to Kuruksetra*. Chicago: University of Chicago Press.
Holmberg, David. 1989. *Order in Paradox: Myth, Ritual, and Exchange among Nepal's Tamang*. Ithaca, N.Y.: Cornell University Press.
Holmström, Lakshmi, ed. 1991. *The Inner Courtyard: Stories by Indian Women*. London: Virago Press.
Inden, Ronald. 1986a. Orientalist Constructions of India. *Modern Asian Studies* 20(3): 401–46.
———. 1986b. Tradition against Itself. *American Ethnologist* 8(4): 762–75.
———. 1990. *Imagining India*. Cambridge, Mass.: Basil Blackwell.
Inden, Ronald, and Ralph Nicholas. 1977. *Kinship in Bengali Culture*. Chicago: University of Chicago Press.
Jackson, Michael. 1982. *Allegories of the Wilderness: Ethics and Ambiguity in Kuranko Narratives*. Bloomington: Indiana University Press.
Jacobson, Doranne. 1975. Songs of Social Distance. *Journal of South Asian Literature* 11(1–2): 45–60.
———. 1977a. Flexibility in North Indian Kinship and Residence. In *The New Wind: Changing Identities in South Asia*, edited by Kenneth David, 263–83. The Hague: Mouton.
———. 1977b. The Women of North and Central India: Goddesses and Wives. In *Women in India: Two Perspectives*, 17–111. New Delhi: Manohar.
———. 1978. The Chaste Wife: Cultural Norm and Individual Experience. In *American Studies in the Anthropology of India*, edited by Sylvia Vatuk, 95–138. New Delhi: Manohar.
———. 1982. Purdah and the Hindu Family in Central India. In *Separate Worlds: Studies of Purdah in South Asia*, edited by H. Papanek and G. Minault, 81–109. Delhi: Chanakya.
Jardine, Alice A. 1985. *Gynesis: Configurations of Woman and Modernity*. Ithaca, N.Y.: Cornell University Press.
Jayakar, Pupul. N.d. *The Earthen Drum: An Introduction to the Ritual Arts of India*. New Delhi: National Museum.
Jayawardana, Kumari. 1986. *Feminism and Nationalism in the Third World*. London: Zed Books.
Jeffery, Patricia, Roger Jeffery, and Andrew Lyon. 1989. *Labour Pains and*

Labour Power: Women and Childbearing in India. London: Zed Books.
Kakar, Sudhir. 1978. *The Inner World*. Delhi: Oxford University Press.
———. 1986. Erotic Fantasy: The Secret Passion of Radha and Krishna. In *The Word and the World: Fantasy, Symbol, and Record*, edited by Veena Das, 75–94. New Delhi: Sage Publications.
———. 1990. *Intimate Relations*. Chicago: University of Chicago Press.
Kamleshwar. 1966. Rājā nirbaṅsiyā. In *Rājā nirbaṅsiyā*. 2d ed. Varanasi: Bharatiya Jnanapitha Prakashan.
Karp, Ivan. 1988. Laughter at Marriage: Subversion in Performance. *Journal of Folklore Research* 25 (1–2): 35–52.
Karve, Irawati. 1965. *Kinship Organization in India*. 2d ed. Bombay: Asia Publishing House.
Katrak, Ketu H. 1992. Indian Nationalism, Gandhian Satyagraha, and Representations of Female Sexuality. In *Nationalisms and Sexualities*, edited by Andrew Parker, Mary Russo, Doris Sommer, and Patricia Yaeger, 395–406. New York and London: Routledge.
Keesing, Roger M. 1985. Kwaio Women Speak: The Micropolitics of Autobiography in a Solomon Island Society. *American Anthropologist* 87(1): 27–39.
Kelly, John. 1988. From Holi to Diwali on Fiji: An Essay on Ritual and History. *Man* 23: 40–55.
Khare, R. S. 1982. From *Kanya* to *Mata*: Aspects of the Cultural Language of Kinship in Northern India. In *Concepts of Person: Kinship, Caste, and Marriage in India*, edited by Akos Ostor, Lina Fruzzetti, and Steve Barnett, 143–71. Cambridge, Mass.: Harvard University Press.
Kinsley, David. 1981. Devotion as an Alternative to Marriage in the Lives of Some Hindu Women Devotees. In *Tradition and Modernity in Bhakti Movements*, edited by Jayant Lele, 83–93. Leiden: E. J. Brill.
———. 1987. *Hindu Goddesses: Visions of the Divine Feminine in the Hindu Religious Tradition*. Delhi: Motilal Banarsidass.
Kishwar, Madhu. 1985. Gandhi on Women. *Economic and Political Weekly* 20(4): 1691–1702.
Kolenda, Pauline. 1967. Regional Differences in Indian Family Structure. In *Regions and Regionalism in South Asian Studies*, edited by Robert Crane, 147–225. Durham: Duke University Program in Comparative Studies on Southern Asia Monograph Series, no. 5.
———. 1968. Region, Caste, and Family Structure: A Comparative Study of the Indian "Joint" Family. In *Structure and Change in Indian Society*, edited by M. Singer and B. S. Cohn, 339–96. Chicago: Aldine.
———. 1982. Pox and the Terror of Childlessness: Images and Ideas of the Smallpox Goddess in a North Indian Village. In *Mother Worship: Theme and Variations*, edited by J. J. Preston, 227–50. Chapel Hill: University of North Carolina Press.
———. 1984. Woman as Tribute, Woman as Flower: Images of "Woman" in Weddings in North and South India. *American Ethnologist* 11: 98–117.

———. 1990. Untouchable Chuhras through Their Humor: "Equalizing" Marital Kin through Teasing, Pretence, and Farce. In *Divine Passions: The Social Construction of Emotion in India,* edited by Owen M. Lynch, 116–53. Berkeley: University of California Press.

Kondos, Vivienne. 1986. Images of the Fierce Goddess and Portrayals of Hindu Women. *Contributions to Indian Sociology* 20(2): 173–97.

Kumar, Nita. 1991. Widows, Education, and Social Change in Twentieth Century Banaras. *Economic and Political Weekly* 26(17): 19–25.

Lederman, Rena. 1980. Who Speaks Here? Formality and the Politics of Gender in Mendi, Highland Papua New Guinea. *Journal of the Polynesian Society* 89(4): 477–98.

Leslie, I. Julia. 1989. *The Perfect Wife: The Orthodox Hindu Woman According to the* Stridharmapaddhati *of Tryambakayajvan*. Delhi: Oxford University Press.

Levi-Strauss, Claude. 1969. *The Elementary Structures of Kinship*. Boston: Beacon Press.

Limon, Jose E. 1981. The Folk Performance of "Chicano" and the Cultural Limits of Political Ideology. In *"And Other Neighborly Names": Social Process and Cultural Image in Texas Folklore,* edited by Richard Bauman and Roger D. Abrahams, 197–225. Austin: University of Texas Press.

Luard, Charles Eckford. N.d. Home Life, Nursery Songs, etc.; Bhopal, Dhar, etc. Luard MSS. Collection. India Office Library, London.

Lutgendorf, Philip. 1991. *The Life of a Text: Performing the* Ramcaritmanas *of Tulsidas*. Berkeley: University of California Press.

McGilvray, Dennis B. 1982. Sexual Power and Fertility in Sri Lanka: Batticaloa Tamils and Moors. In *Ethnography of Fertility and Birth,* edited by Carol P. MacCormack, 25–73. London: Academic Press.

Madan, T. N. 1962. Is the Brahmanic *gotra* a Grouping of Kin? *Southwestern Journal of Anthropology* 18: 59–77.

Mani, Lata. 1985. The Production of an Official Discourse on *Sati* in Early Nineteenth-Century Bengal. In *Europe and Its Others,* edited by Francis Barker, et al., 89–127. Colchester: University of Essex.

———. 1989. Contentious Traditions: The Debate on *Sati* in Colonial India. In *Recasting Women: Essays in Colonial History,* edited by Kumkum Sangari and Sudesh Vaid, 88–126. New Delhi: Kali for Women.

Manuel, Peter. 1993. *Cassette Culture: Popular Music and Technology in North India*. Chicago: University of Chicago Press.

March, Katherine. 1984. Weaving, Writing, and Gender. *Man* 18(4): 729–44.

Marglin, Frédérique Apffel. 1982. Kings and Wives: The Separation of Status and Royal Power. In *Way of Life: King, Householder, Renouncer,* edited by T. N. Madan, 155–81. Delhi: Vikas.

———. 1985a. Female Sexuality in the Hindu World. In *Immaculate and Powerful: The Female in Sacred Image and Social Reality,* edited by C. W. Atkinson, C. H. Buchanan, and M. R. Miles, 39–59. Boston: Beacon Press.

———. 1985b. *Wives of the God-King*. Delhi: Oxford University Press.

Marriott, McKim. 1966. The Feast of Love. In *Krishna: Myths, Rites, and Attitudes*, edited by Milton B. Singer, 200–212. Chicago: University of Chicago Press.

Mayer, Adrian. 1960. *Caste and Kinship in Central India*. Berkeley: University of California Press.

Meeker, Michael, Kathleen Barlow, and David Lipset. 1986. Culture, Exchange, and Gender: Lessons from the Murik. *Cultural Anthropology* 1(1): 6–73.

Mehta, Rama. 1981. *Inside the Haveli*. New Delhi: Arnold-Heinemann.

Mies, Maria. 1982. *The Lace Makers of Narsapur: Indian Housewives Produce for the World Market*. London: Zed Books.

Mohanty, Chandra. 1984. Under Western Eyes: Feminist Scholarship and Colonial Discourses. *Boundary 2* 12(3): 333–58.

Murthy U. R. Anantha. 1976. *Samskara*. Delhi: Oxford University Press.

Nag, Dulali. 1990. Representation of Women in Postcolonial India. Paper presented at the annual meeting of the Association for Asian Studies, Chicago. April.

Nandy, Ashis. 1983. *The Intimate Enemy: Loss and Recovery of Self under Colonialism*. Delhi: Oxford University Press.

———. 1990. *At the Edge of Psychology: Essays in Politics and Culture*. Delhi: Oxford University Press.

Narayan, Kirin. 1986. Birds on a Branch: Girlfriends and Wedding Songs in Kangra. *Ethos* 14(1): 47–75.

Narayana Rao, V. N. 1989. Images of Food, Love, and War in Medieval Telugu Literature. Paper presented at the annual meeting of the Association for Asian Studies, Washington, D. C. April.

———. 1991. A Ramayana of Their Own: Women's Oral Tradition in Telugu. In *Many Ramayanas: The Diversity of a Narrative Tradition in South Asia*, edited by Paula Richman, 114–36. Berkeley: University of California Press.

Nicholas, Ralph W. 1982. The Village Mother in Bengal. In *Mother Worship: Themes and Variations*, edited by J. J. Preston, 92–209. Chapel Hill: University of North Carolina Press.

Nicholas, Ralph W., and Aditi Nath Sarkar. 1976. The Fever Demon and the Census Commissioner: Sitala Mythology in Eighteenth and Nineteenth Century Bengal. In *Bengal: Studies in Literature, Society, and History*, edited by Marvin Davis, 3–33. East Lansing, Mich.: Asian Studies Center Occasional Papers.

Ochs, Eleanor. 1992. Indexing Gender. In *Rethinking Context: Language as an Interactive Phenomenon*, edited by Alessandro Duranti and Charles Goodwin, 335–58. Cambridge: Cambridge University Press.

O'Flaherty, Wendy Doniger. [*See also* Doniger, Wendy]. 1980. *Women, Androgynes, and Other Mythical Beasts*. Chicago: University of Chicago Press.

———. 1981. *The Rig Veda*. Harmondsworth: Penguin Books.

———. 1986. *Sexual Doubles and Sexual Masquerades*. The University Lecture in Religion at Arizona State Univerity. Tempe, Ariz.: Department of Religious Studies, Arizona State University.

O'Hanlon, Rosalind. 1988. Recovering the Subject: Subaltern Studies and Histories of Resistance in Colonial South Asia. *Modern Asian Studies* 22(1): 189–224.

———. 1991. Issues of Widowhood: Gender and Resistance in Colonial Western India. In *Contesting Power: Resistance and Everyday Social Relations in South Asia*, edited by Douglas Haynes and Gyan Prakash, 62–108. Berkeley: University of California Press.

Oldenburg, Veena. 1990. Lifestyle as Resistance. *Feminist Studies* 16(2): 259–88.

Ortner, Sherry. 1984. Theory in Anthropology since the Sixties. *Comparative Studies in Society and History* 26: 126–66.

Papanek, Hanna, and Gail Minault, eds. 1982. *Separate Worlds: Studies of Purdah in South Asia*. Delhi: Chanakya.

Parkin, David. 1980. The Creativity of Abuse. *Man* 15: 45–64.

Parry, Jonathan, 1979. *Caste and Kinship in Kangra*. London: Routledge and Kegan Paul.

Pathak, Zakia, and Rajeswari Sunder Rajan. 1989. Shahbano. *Signs* 14: 558–82.

Peterson, Indira. 1988. The Tie That Binds: Brothers and Sisters in North and South India. *South Asian Social Scientist* 4(1): 25–52.

Pinney, Christopher. 1989. Representations of India: Normalisation and the "Other." *Pacific Viewpoint* 29(2): 144–62.

Prakash, Gyan. 1990. Writing Post-Orientalist Histories of the Third World: Perspectives from Indian Historiography. *Comparative Studies in Society and History* 32(2): 383–408.

———. 1991. Becoming a Bhuinya: Oral Traditions and Contested Domination in Eastern India. In *Contesting Power: Resistance and Everyday Social Relations in South Asia*, edited by Douglas Haynes and Gyan Prakash, 145–74. Berkeley: University of California Press.

Raheja, Gloria Goodwin. 1988a. India: Caste, Kingship, and Dominance Reconsidered. *Annual Review of Anthropology* 17: 497–522.

———. 1988b. *The Poison in the Gift: Ritual, Prestation, and the Dominant Caste in a North Indian Village*. Chicago: University of Chicago Press.

———. 1989. Centrality, Mutuality, and Hierarchy: Shifting Aspects of Intercaste Relationships in North India. *Contributions to Indian Sociology* 23(1): 79–101.

———. 1991. Negotiating Kinship and Gender: Essentializing and Contextualizing Strategies in North Indian Song and Narrative Traditions. Paper presented at conference, Language, Gender, and the Subaltern Voice: Framing Identities in South Asia, April 20–23, University of Minnesota.

———. 1993. Women's Speech Genres, Kinship, and Contradiction. In *Women as Subject*, edited by Nita Kumar. Calcutta: Stree.

———. N.d. "Crying When She's Born and Crying When She Goes Away": Marriage and the Idiom of the Gift in Pahansu Song Performance. In *Hindu Marriage from the Margins*, edited by Lindsey Harlan and Paul Courtwright. New York: Oxford University Press. Forthcoming.

Rajgarhiya, Campadevi. N.d. *Bārah mahīnoṅ kā tyauhār*. Calcutta: Hari Arts Press.

Rakesh, Mohan. 1975. Married Women. In *Hindi Stories*, translated by Usha S. Nilsson. Madison, Wis.: South Asia Language and Area Center.

Ramanujan, A. K., trans. 1973. *Speaking of Siva*. Harmondsworth: Penguin.

———. 1982. On Women Saints. In *The Divine Consort: Radha and the Goddesses of India*, edited by J. S. Hawley and D. M. Wulff, 316–24. Berkeley: Graduate Theological Union.

———. 1986. Two Realms of Kannada Folklore. In *Another Harmony: New Essays on the Folklore of India*, edited by Stuart H. Blackburn and A. K. Ramanujan, 41–75. Berkeley: University of California Press.

———. 1989a. Is There an Indian Way of Thinking? An Informal Essay. *Contributions to Indian Sociology* 23(1): 41–58.

———. 1989b. Where Mirrors Are Windows: Toward an Anthology of Reflections. *History of Religions*. 28(3): 188–216.

———. 1991a. A Flowering Tree: A Woman's Tale. Paper presented at conference, Language, Gender, and the Subaltern Voice: Framing Identities in South Asia, University of Minnesota. April 20–23.

———. 1991b. *Folktales from India*. New York: Pantheon Books.

Rao, Raja. 1967. *Kanthapura*. New York: New Directions.

Reynolds, Holly Baker. 1988. Sisters Protect Brothers: Two Tamil Women's Rituals. Paper presented at conference, Women's Rites, Women's Desires, Harvard University. April.

Robinson, Sandra. 1985. Hindu Paradigms of Women. In *Women, Religion, and Social Change*, edited by Y. Y. Haddad and E. B. Findly, 181–216. Albany: State University of New York Press.

Rosaldo, Renato. 1989. *Culture and Truth: The Remaking of Social Analysis*. Boston: Beacon Press.

Roy, Manisha. 1975. *Bengali Women*. Chicago: University of Chicago Press.

———. 1979. Animus and Indian Women. *Harvest (Journal for Jungian Studies)* 25: 70–79.

Rubin, Gayle. 1975. The Traffic in Women: Notes on the "Political Economy" of Sex. In *Toward an Anthropology of Women*, edited by R. Reiter. New York: Monthly Review Press.

Rushdie, Salman. 1990. *Haroun and the Sea of Stories*. London: Granta Books/Viking.

Said, Edward. 1979. *Orientalism*. New York: Random House.

Samskarta, Nanuram. 1968. *Rājasthānī lok sāhitya*. Borunda: Rupayan Samsthan.

Sax, William. 1991. *Mountain Goddess: Gender and Politics in a Himalayan Pilgrimage*. New York: Oxford University Press.

Scott, James C. 1985. *Weapons of the Weak: Everyday Forms of Peasant Resistance*. New Haven: Yale University Press.

———. 1990. *Domination and the Arts of Resistance: Hidden Transcripts*. New Haven: Yale University Press.

Seitel, Peter. 1977. Saying Haya Sayings: Two Categories of Proverb Use. In *The Social Use of Metaphor: Essays on the Anthropology of Rhetoric*, edited by J. David Sapir and J. Christopher Crocker, 75–99. Philadelphia: University of Pennsylvania Press.

Sen, Ramprasad. 1982. *Grace and Mercy in Her Wild Hair: Selected Poems to the Mother Goddess*, translated by Leonard Nathan and Clinton Seely. Boulder, Colo.: Great Eastern.

Seremetakis, C. Nadia. 1991. *The Last Word: Women, Death, and Divination in Inner Mani*. Chicago: University of Chicago Press.

Sharma, Surendra, ed. 1983. *Lokollās*. Khatauli, Muzaffarnagar: Sri K. K. Jain Degree College.

———, ed. 1984. *Kauravī lok sāhitya*. Khatauli, Muzaffarnagar: Sri K. K. Jain Degree College.

Sharma, Ursula. 1978. Women and Their Affines: The Veil as a Symbol of Separation. *Man* 13: 218–33.

Sherzer, Joel. 1987a. A Discourse-Centered Approach to Culture. *American Anthropologist* 89(2): 295–309.

———. 1987b. A Diversity of Voices: Men's and Women's Speech in Ethnographic Perspective. In *Language, Gender, and Sex in Comparative Perspective*, edited by Susan U. Philips, Susan Steele, and Christine Tanz, 95–120. Cambridge: Cambridge University Press.

Shulman, David Dean. 1986. Battle as Metaphor in Tamil Folk and Classical Traditions. In *Another Harmony: New Essays on the Folklore in India*, edited by Stuart Blackburn and A. K. Ramanujan, 105–30. Berkeley: University of California Press.

Spivak, Gayatri Chakravorty. 1985a. Can the Subaltern Speak? Speculations on Widow Sacrifice. *Wedge* 7/8: 120–30.

———. 1985b. The Rani of Sirmur. In *Europe and Its Others*, edited by Francis Barker et al., 128–51. Colchester: University of Essex.

———. 1985c. Subaltern Studies: Deconstructing Historiography. In *Subaltern Studies IV: Writings on South Asian History and Society*, edited by Ranajit Guha, 330–63. Delhi: Oxford University Press.

———. 1988. *In Other Worlds: Essays in Cultural Politics*. New York and London: Routledge.

———. 1992. Woman in Difference: Mahasweta Devi's "Douloti the Bountiful." In *Nationalisms and Sexualities*, edited by Andrew Parker, Mary Russo, Doris Sommer, and Patricia Yaeger, 96–117. New York and London: Routledge.

Suleri, Sara. 1992. *The Rhetoric of English India*. Chicago: University of Chicago Press.

Tambiah, Stanley J. 1989. *Bridewealth and Dowry* Revisited. *Current Anthropology* 30(4): 413–35.

Temple R. C. 1884–1900. *Legends of the Panjab*. 3 vols. Bombay: Education Society's Press.

Tewari, Laxmi G. 1977. Ceremonial Songs of the Kanyakubja Brahmans. *Essays in Arts and Sciences* 6: 30–52.

———. 1988. Sohar: Childbirth Songs of Joy. *Aisan Folklore Studies* 47(2): 257–76.

Tharu, Susie, and K. Lalita, eds. 1991. *Women Writing in India: 600 B.C. to the Early Twentieth Century*. New York: Feminist Press.

Tiwary K. M. 1968. The Echo-Word Construction in Bhojpuri. *Anthropological Linguistics* 10(4): 32–38.

Trautmann, Thomas. 1981. *Dravidian Kinship*. Berkeley: University of California Press.

Trawick, Margaret. 1988. Spirits and Voices in Tamil Songs. *American Ethnologist* 15: 193–215.

———. 1990. *Notes on Love in a Tamil Family*. Berkeley: University of California Press.

———. 1991. Wandering Lost: A Landless Laborer's Sense of Place and Self. In *Gender, Genre, and Power in South Asian Expressive Traditions*, edited by Arjun Appadurai, Frank J. Korom, and Margaret A. Mills, 224–66. Philadelphia: University of Pennsylvania Press.

Urban, Greg. 1991. *A Discourse-Centered Approach to Culture: Native South American Myths and Rituals*. Austin: University of Texas Press.

Vatuk, Sylvia. 1969. Reference, Address, and Fictive Kinship in Urban North India. *Ethnology* 8(3): 255–72.

———. 1971. Trends in North Indian Urban Kinship: The "Matrilateral Asymmetry" Hypothesis. *Southwestern Journal of Anthropology* 27(3): 287–307.

———. 1975. Gifts and Affines. *Contributions to Indian Sociology* 5: 155–96.

———. 1980. The Aging Woman in India: Self-Perceptions and Changing Roles. In *Women in Contemporary India and South Asia*, edited by Alfred de Souza, 287–309. New Delhi: Manohar.

———. 1982a. Forms of Address in the North Indian Family. In *Concepts of Person: Aspects of Kinship, Caste, and Marriage in India*, edited by Akos Ostor, Lina Fruzzetti, and Steve Barnett, 56–98. Cambridge, Mass.: Harvard University Press.

———. 1982b. Purdah Revisited: A Comparison of Hindu and Muslim Interpretations of the Cultural Meaning of Purdah in South Asia. In *Separate Worlds: Studies of Purdah in South Asia*, edited by H. Papanek and G. Minault, 54–78. Delhi: Chanakya.

———. 1985. South Asian Cultural Conceptions of Sexuality. In *In Her Prime: A New View of Middle-Aged Women*, edited by Judith K. Brown and Virginia Kerns. Granby, Mass.: Bergin and Garvey.

Vatuk, Ved Prakash. 1969. *Thieves in My House: Four Studies in Indian Folklore of Protest and Change*. Varanasi: Viswavidyalaya Prakashan.

Vatuk, Ved Prakash, and Sylvia Vatuk. 1976. The Social Context of Gift Exchange in North India. In *Main Currents in Indian Sociology*, vol. 2, *Family and Social Change in Modern India*, edited by Giriraj Gupta, 207–32. Delhi: Vikas.

———. 1979a. The Anthropology of Sāng—A North Indian Folk Opera. In *Studies in Indian Folk Traditions*, edited by Ved P. Vatuk, 15–37. New Delhi: Manohar.

———. 1979b. The Lustful Stepmother in the Folklore of Northwestern India. In *Studies in Indian Folk Traditions*, edited by Ved P. Vatuk, 190–221. New Delhi: Manohar.

Wadley, Susan S. 1975. *Shakti: Power in the Conceptual Structure of Karimpur Religion*. Chicago: Department of Anthropology, Series in Social, Cultural and Linguistic Anthropology, no. 2.

———. 1977. Women and the Hindu Tradition. In *Women in India: Two Perspectives*, 113–39. New Delhi: Manohar.

———. 1978. Texts in Contexts: Oral Traditions and the Study of Religion in Karimpur. In *American Studies in the Anthropology of India*, edited by Sylvia Vatuk, 309–41. New Delhi: Manohar.

———. 1980a. *Readings in Karimpur Folklore*. Syracuse, N.Y.: Syracuse University College of Arts and Sciences.

———. 1980b. Sitala. *Asian Folklore Studies* 39(1): 33–62.

———, ed. 1980c. *The Powers of Tamil Women*. Syracuse, N.Y.: Maxwell School of Citizenship and Public Affairs.

———. 1983. The Rains of Estrangement: Understanding the Hindu Yearly Cycle. *Contributions to Indian Sociology* 17(1): 51–85.

———. N.d. *Struggling with Destiny, Karimpur Lives 1925–1984*. Berkeley: University of California Press. Forthcoming.

Warren, Kay Barbara, and Susan C. Bourque. 1985. Gender, Power, and Communication: Women's Responses to Political Muting in the Andes. In *Women Living Change*, edited by Susan C. Bourque and Donna Robinson Divine, 225–86. Philadelphia: Temple University Press.

White, Hayden. 1978. *Tropics of Discourse: Essays in Cultural Criticism*. Baltimore: Johns Hopkins University Press.

Willis, Roy. 1981. *Learning to Labor*. New York: Columbia University Press.

Wolf, Margery. 1972. *Women and the Family in Rural Taiwan*. Stanford: Stanford University Press.

———. 1991. Beyond the Patrilineal Self: Constructing Gender in China. Paper presented at conference, Matrilineality and Patrilineality in Comparative and Historical Perspective, May 1, University of Minnesota.

Wulff, Donna M. 1985. Images and Roles of Women in Bengali Vaisnava *padāvalī kīrtan*. In *Women, Religion, and Social Change*, edited by Y. Y. Haddad and E. B. Findly, 217–46. Albany: State University of New York Press.

Yanagisako, Sylvia, and Jane Collier. 1987. Toward a Unified Analysis of Gender and Kinship. In *Gender and Kinship*, edited by Jane Collier and Sylvia Yanagisako, 14–50. Stanford: Stanford University Press.

Yang, Anand. 1989. Whose Sati? Widow Burning in Early Nineteenth Century India. *Journal of Women's History* 1(2): 8–33.

Zelliott, Eleanor. 1981. Chokhamela and Eknath: Two *Bhakti* Modes of Legitimacy for Modern Change. In *Tradition and Modernity in Bhakti Movements*, edited by Jayant Lele, 136–56. Leiden: E. J. Brill.

Index

Compositor:	Asco Trade Typesetting Limited
Text:	10/13 Palatino
Display:	Palatino
Printer:	Maple-Vail Book Manufacturing Group
Binder:	Maple-Vail Book Manufacturing Group